BEHAVIOR SCIENCE BIBLIOGRAPHIES

KOREA

AN ANALYTICAL GUIDE TO BIBLIOGRAPHIES

Hesung Chun Koh, Editor
Joan Steffens, Assistant Editor

HUMAN RELATIONS AREA FILES PRESS
New Haven
1971

REF
Z
3316
.A1
.K64

Development and publication of this bibliography
has been financed in part by Grants GN-492 and
GN-821 from the National Science Foundation.

LIBRARY OF CONGRESS CATALOG CARD NUMBER: 70-125119
ISBN 0-87536-241-9

This book is dedicated to

Social science researchers struggling
with documentary research,

Scholars in Korean studies, and

All those who have contributed to the improvement
of the quality of bibliography

CONTENTS

II. ANALYTICAL INDEXES

III. CITATIONS WITH COMPLETE ANALYSIS AND ANNOTATION

PREFACE

This is the second bibliography to be published as a result of the Korean Social Science Bibliography Computerization Project of the Human Relations Area Files[1], a methodological pilot project which has been supported by National Science Foundation grants GN-492 and GN-821.

In the course of compiling the first bibliography for the project, *Social Science Resources on Korea: A Preliminary Computerized Bibliography* (2 vols. New Haven, Human Relations Area Files, 1968), we were impressed by the large number of bibliographies that exist on Korea. As an initial step toward refining the content of the preliminary bibliography and developing the HRAF Automated Bibliographic System (HABS), the present volume, *Korea: An Analytical Guide to Bibliographies* was produced.

Although two other major guides to bibliographies on Korea have been published, the present volume differs significantly from these previous works in that our bibliography attempts to serve social science researchers and to present the most comprehensive bibliography of bibliographies on Korean studies. Methodologically speaking, this volume puts forth a new intellectual framework and a computerized means for bibliographic control.

The present format is far short of the ideal one, which we hope to make possible in the future by the continued development of computer programs and by the use of photocomposition techniques. In view of the greater flexibility that is possible through the use of a computerized bibliographic method such as HABS, we can readily modify the forms and the

---

1. This project was launched in 1966 as an attempt to promote Korean studies in the Western world. It also served as a pilot project for adapting computerized techniques to the problems of bibliographic control for social science research and for the handling of non-Western language materials. The system of automated bibliographic control developed in the course of the Korea Project (the HRAF Automated Bibliographic System, or HABS) has now been adopted by the Human Relations Area Files in processing its bibliographies.

organization of a bibliography and can revise and up-
date it with a minimum of effort. Different ranges
of information depth are presented in the four sections of this bibliography, and the data elements are
combined and ordered in various ways. It is hoped
the present publication may stimulate the imagination
of the user as to other possible types of output.
We would therefore appreciate reactions and advice
from all who use this bibliography, so that we can
bring about a more comprehensive, accurate, and above
all a more useful bibliography for future users.
    For the theoretical and methodological back-
ground of HABS and its implications for an information system for area studies see:

Koh, Hesung C.
    1966   A social science bibliographic system:
            orientation and framework. *In Behavior
            Science Notes*, I, no. 3: 145-163.

    1967a   A social science bibliographic system: com-
            puter adaptations. *In American Behavioral
            Scientist*, 10, no. 5: 2-5.

    1967b   Social science and Korean studies, resources.
            In Behavior Science Notes, 2, no. I: 31-54.

    1969a   An automated bibliographic system: HABS.
            In Toward an automated comprehensive East
            Asian bibliographic system, Special Con-
            ference Supplement to *Behavior Science
            Notes*, 4, no. I: 70-80.

    1969b   On the analysis and control of data quality
            for comparative research: a computerized
            system. *In Proceedings of the VIIIth Inter-
            national Congress of Anthropological and
            Ethnological Sciences*. Vol. 2: Ethnology.
            Ueno Park, Tokyo, Science Council of Japan:
            28-32.

    1969c   Some potentials for social science research
            on Korea: a computerized bibliographic sys-
            tem. *In Proceedings of the Conference on
            Korea held at Western Michigan University
            April 6-7, 1969:* 206-219.

    1971   Toward an integrated information system for
            Asian studies. *In Newsletter of the Associ-
            ation for Asian Studies*, 16, no. 3: 12-27.

                                Hesung Chun Koh
November 1970   New Haven, Connecticut

INTRODUCTION

This bibliography has been compiled primarily
for scholars who are working on social science research, to aid them in finding bibliographic references to a wide range of topics, both general and
specific, which are related to Korean society and
culture. An effort has also been made to meet the
research needs of those in the field of the humanities.
The editors thus hope that the bibliography will
serve all users who seek references to recorded data
on Korean society and culture.

SCOPE

An attempt has been made to be as comprehensive
as possible and approximately 500 bibliographies are
included here. These are in eight languages and cover
publications issued over a 70-year period, beginning
with 1896 and extending to 1970. This bibliography
contains not only sources of book length but also
journal articles, serials, and dissertations. Bibliographic essays which appear as chapters in books,
bibliographic references, and bibliographic notes are
also included. Various other materials -- such as
catalogs of libraries, private collections, book ex-
hibits, and indexes to journals and newspapers -- all
of which can help a user find additional references
have also been processed in this publication.

COMPILATION

Data Gathering

Initial information on bibliographies was drawn
from 29 published bibliographies and 17 major library
catalogs selected as the result of a systematic exam-
ination of over 80 published bibliographies and nearly 60 library catalogs, as well as the Editor's personal bibliography file. Whenever possible, information drawn from these bibliographies and library cards
was checked against the original documents at the
Library of Congress or at one of three university libraries: Yale, Harvard, and the University of
California (Berkeley).

Standardization of Descriptive Information and Supplementary Research

Each entry was standardized according to the HABS citation style. In addition, romanization of authors and titles when necessary, translation of non-Western language titles, the language and location of documents, and the sources of information were supplied after a considerable amount of research. The McCune-Reischauer system of romanization for Korean sources, the Wade-Giles for Chinese, and the Hepburn for Japanese were used as far as practicable.

Coding

Each information category, such as author, title, periodical or series title, etc., and each element, such as short title, translated title, year of publication, etc., are separately identified by means of a standard numeric code or other type of tag. These codes and the bibliographic data are stored together in machine-readable form. This means that such indexes as author, title, periodical, series title, and publication year can be generated automatically by computer programming, without additional work by the bibliographer.

The form and content of each bibliography are also coded, to permit automatic ordering and organization. The following codes appear on the top line of each entry in Section III of this bibliography as "Leader Area" information: material type, language of title, country of publication, plus general and specific codes for topical, temporal, and area subjects which are coded alphanumerically. These codes allow economical and ready reorganization of bibliographies by computer programming.

Classification and Indexing

The uniqueness of this bibliography lies in its approach to classification and organization, which is one of the key characteristics of the HRAF Automated Bibliographic System (HABS). Not only the topical focus of each bibliography but also its geographical and temporal concerns are separately indexed, resulting in three distinct subject indexes. Each of these three dimensions (topic, area, and time) are in turn classified and indexed by two different approaches, a structured and semistructured classification approach. These are further explained in the Guide to Section II.

Annotation

Both our own annotations and those supplied by others, published or unpublished, have been incorporated in the bibliography, along with the name of the annotator and the year the annotation was done. It is hoped that this approach to annotation may lessen much duplication of effort and promote more systematic accumulation of annotations and proper acknowledgment of earlier efforts by others.

HOW TO USE THE BIBLIOGRAPHY

The bibliography is divided into four main sections, plus an appendix and a list of references. Users are urged to read the guide to each section before attempting to use the bibliography. Sections III (Citations with Complete Analysis and Annotation) and IV (Serial Publications) contain the most complete information on all the entries. However, most users will need various combinations of both Section I (Abbreviated Citations by Major Subjects), and Section II (Analytical Indexes), in order to utilize Section III. Bibliographies of serials are separately handled in Section IV and are included only in the title index.

All alternate names or variations in romanization have been included in the indexes of authors, titles, personal and corporate subjects, and geographical subjects to facilitate ready and complete retrieval, even at the risk of repetition. Because some of these variations are the result of the inherent nature of the library cataloging practices we followed (especially when information on journal articles was incorporated with that of monographs), we have made no effort to standardize these names at this time. Cross-referencing of different names for the same person and consolidation of separate index entries for a single author can be provided through additional computer programming. Handwritten lists of authors and titles in Chinese, Japanese, and Korean characters follow Sections III and IV and the appendix.

Additional Citations

The Appendix includes material that was processed in June 1970, when the main project had already been completed. We were unable to enter complete information on these entries according to our standardization and research procedures, and did not have time to search for the original sources themselves. Therefore, only author, title, and year of publication for monographs and minimal citations for journal articles and other types of materials are presented here. These entries have not yet been incorporated into the various analytical indexes, except for the title index.

References

In addition to the sources listed as References, bibliographic notes and references in the following sources were consulted:

An, Chŏng-bok. Tongsa kangmok [Outline of Korean history]. Seoul, Chōsen Kosho Kankōkai, 1915. 4 v.

Fujitsuka, Rin. Richō no gakujin to Kenryū bunka [Scholars of Yi Dynasty Korea and Ch'ien-lung culture]. *In Chōsen Shina bunka no kenkyū,* I (1929): 283-332.

Henderson, Gregory. Korea: the politics of the vortex. Cambridge, Harvard University Press, 1968. 16, 479 p.

Kim, C. I. Eugene. Aspects of social change in Korea. Ed. by C. I. Eugene Kim and Ch'angboh Chee. Kalamazoo, Korea Research and Publications [c. 1969]. 10, 272 p. charts, tables.

Koh, Hesung Chun. Religion, social structure and economic development in Yi dynasty Korea. [Boston] 1959. 257 p. Dissertation (Sociology) -- Boston University.

Sŏ, Kŏ-jŏng, ed. Tongmunsŏn [Anthology of Korean literature]. [Ed. by] Sŏ Kŏ-jŏng [and others]. Seoul, Chōsen Kosho Kankōkai, 1914. 130 v. in 7.

Potential Use of the System and Capabilities for "Tailor-made Bibliographies"

The various forms and combinations of information components that are presented in the five sections of this bibliography indicate only a portion of the actual programming now available through the use of HABS. For example, a subject index now keyed to identification numbers could be replaced by one including the last names of the authors and the years of publication. Indexes can also be arranged by the time period covered or by the language of the document. Users of this bibliography can visualize the kinds and varieties of additional bibliographies and

indexes that are possible by examining closely the
Guide to Section III, especially the Guide to Information in Complete Citation. Because the categories
listed in this guide and their elements are uniquely
identified in the data base, these items can be used
for sorting either separately or in combination.
Some information elements and/or categories can be
either printed or suppressed or used for printing
only but not for filing. Given adequate funds, each
researcher can obtain from this system a bibliography
that is tailor-made to fit his own individual needs.

ACKNOWLEDGMENTS

One of the chief aims of our Korea Project and
of HABS has been to stimulate the systematic accumulation of descriptive, analytical, and annotative
bibliographic data within a single frame of reference,
and to make maximum use of published and unpublished
bibliographies and library catalog cards, in addition
to extensive library searching and primary data gathering. We are indebted to the compilers and editors
of all the volumes listed as References. We acknowl-
edge our indebtedness especially to the following
publishers, who have given us permission to quote
from their publications: University of California
Press, Berkeley, California (*Korean Studies Guide,*
by B. H. Hazard, Jr., et al., 1954: 4-10, 157); Monumenta Serica Institute (*Japanese studies on Korean
history since World War II,* by Yoshiji Okamoto, *in
Monumenta Serica, 22, pt.* 2 (1963); 470-532); Korea
Branch, Royal Asiatic Society (*Bibliography of
Western literature on Korea from the earliest time
until 1950,* by G. St. G. M. Gompertz, Transactions
of the Korea Branch of the Royal Asiatic Society, 40,
Seoul, Korea, 1963: 255-263); the Catholic University
of America (*Reference Guide to Korean Materials,
1945-1959,* by Key P. Yang, May 1960, as a partial ful-
fillment of his M.S. in Library Science degree); and
the University of Arizona Press, Tucson, Arizona
(*Japan and Korea: a critical bibliography,* by
Bernard S. Silberman, 1962: 255-263).
        Eugene Wu and Sungha Kim of the Harvard-Yenching
Library; Warren Tsuneishi, Edwin Beal, Jr., and
Key P. Yang of the Library of Congress; Elizabeth Huff
of the University of California, Berkeley (now re-
tired); Il Se Chang, of the Central National Library,
Seoul, Korea; Wei-ying Wan, University of Michigan
Library (then of Yale University Library); and Bernice
Field, of Yale University, all generously supported
the project by rendering a variety of consulting
services and, above all, by making their data accessible to the project.
        The present bibliography is only a portion of a
larger project in which other special subject bibliographies have also been prepared. Many staff members contributed toward the publication of this bibliography, and the nature and amount of work done by

individual members of the HRAF Korea Project staff
was widely varied.

STAFF MEMBERS OF THE HRAF KOREA PROJECT

KOH, HESUNG C.
    Director of the project; theoretical and meth-
    odological development, including the classifi-
    cation system; selecting sources, assigning ma-
    jor classification headings; editing and writing.

STEFFENS, JOAN
    Coordinator of project; editing, classification,
    coding; training and supervision of staff;
    editing, proofreading, and assembling final out-
    put for publication; also assisting in refine-
    ment of methodology.

YUN, SANG SOON
    Location search and cataloging of sources in
    Korean, Japanese, and English (including romani-
    zation and translation of titles); some proof-
    reading and correcting; indexing Japanese
    sources.

LEE, MYUNG SOOK
    Cataloging and indexing sources in Korean and
    English.

YOO, YOUNG HYUN
    Library research; supplementing cataloging in-
    formation and library classification; preliminary
    editing and proofreading.

MA, CHENG-RUEY
    Library research; processing sources in Chinese;
    general assistance to project director.

GIBSON, ELLA
    Keypunching and printing by IBM 870 Document
    Writer; proofreading and typing; other assis-
    tance.

CRAWFORD, GEORGE
    Programming of IBM 7090 and 1401.

BEDELL, GEORGE
    Programming of IBM 870 Document Writer and con-
    sulting on printing.

    Margaret Brown also contributed toward pro-
gramming. The calligraphy was by Kazuko Matsuzawa

(Chinese characters and <u>Kana</u>) and Suyong Chun
(<u>Han'gŭl</u>). Susan Bontemps and Edith White assisted
the project in various ways as research assistants.

We are grateful to the following HRAF staff mem-
bers who acted as general consultants and advised on
format, organization, etc.: Frank W. Moore, Frank M.
LeBar, Timothy J. O'Leary, Robert O. Lagacé, George R.
Bedell, and Elizabeth P. Swift. Mrs. Swift, HRAF
Press Editor, and Lorna T. Bissell also helped edit
the introductory materials. The project has been
most fortunate to receive guidance and support from
Frederick Kilgour, Ohio College Library Center, and
David Weisbrod, Yale University Library Development
Department, two experts on library automation and
computerization.

The generous support of the National Science
Foundation, Office of Science Information Service,
and especially the guidance and help provided by
Drs. Gordon Ward and Randall Worthington were invaluable in the preparation of this volume and in the
basic development of the system.

The editors would like to express their sincere
appreciation to Clellan S. Ford, President, and
Frank W. Moore, Executive Director, of HRAF for their
guidance and for their assistance in administrative
and research matters, and to Bertram Frankenberger,
Jr. for financial consultation. We would like to
thank so many scholars, librarians, and other col-
leagues, too numerous to list, who enthusiastically
supported the project and provided moral and intellectual support. The Editor extends her deep appreciation to her husband, Kwang Lim, and to her children, for their generous understanding and support.
Last, but not least, the Editor acknowledges her indebtedness to the staff members of the Project, and
especially to Joan Steffens, for their willing and
able assistance.

SECTION I
ABBREVIATED CITATIONS BY MAJOR SUBJECTS

GUIDE TO SECTION I

This section presents abbreviated bibliographic citations, arranged in order by broad social science concepts. Since the complete information for each citation, with analysis and annotation, is arranged by mutually exclusive identification numbers for each entry in Section III, only the author, title, and English translation of non-Western titles (plus name of the journal, volume number, and pages in the case of journal articles) are indicated here.

Entries were originally classified by 36 major classification headings developed for the HRAF Korea Project (see the topical code in the Guide to Section III). However, 9 of those 36 headings, for which there are not enough data, have been dropped from this section. Three of the original major headings (reference works, general bibliographies, and intercultural relations) are further subdivided and are listed under slightly revised category headings which seem more appropriate to the data classified.

Users who seek further materials related to the topical headings appearing in this section should consult the four topical indexes in Section II and make use of Cross-reference Table A, at the end of this section.

Users of this bibliography who wish to search entries in the nine categories which do not appear in Section I, but which are included in the Major Subject Headings of the HRAF Korea Project, should consult Cross-reference Table B. This table may be used in conjunction with the Topical Indexes of Section II.

REFERENCE MATERIALS

BIBLIOGRAPHIES OF BIBLIOGRAPHIES

Henthorn, William E., comp. A guide to reference
and research materials on Korean history: an
annotated bibliography.   01128

Nunn, Godfrey Raymond, 1918-. East Asia: a
bibliography of bibliographies.   11656

Paek, In. Han'guk sŏji kwan'gye munhŏn mongnok
[A list of books related to Korean bibliography].
In Sŏjihak, 2 (1969): 62-76.   04076

Paek, In. Han'guk sŏji kwan'gye munhŏn mongnok
[A list of books related to Korean bibliography].
In Sŏjihak, 1 (1968): 34-54.   04077

Sŏng, Tae-gyung. Han'guk sŏji ŭi sŏji
[Bibliography of Korean bibliography]. In Kukhoe
Tosŏgwanbo, 3, no. 5-7 (June-Aug. 1966).   04094

Sŏul Taehakkyo. Tosŏgwan. Han'guk sŏji kwan'gye
munhŏn mongnok (An index of Korean
bibliographies). In Sŏul Taehakkyo Tosŏgwanbo, 4
(1966): 27-75.   01062

Yang, Key Paik. Present status of Korean research
tools.   06763

Yunesuko Higashi Ajia Bunka Kenkyū Senta, Tokyo.
Bibliography of bibliographies of East Asian
studies in Japan. Comp. by Centre for East Asian
Cultural Studies.   01021

BIBLIOGRAPHIC ESSAYS

Chōsen geibunshi [Korean literary culture].   11241

Courant, Maurice [Auguste Louis Marie], 1865-1939.
Bibliographie coréenne. The introduction.
Translated by Mrs. W. Massy Royds. In Transactions
of the Korea Branch of the Royal Asiatic Society,
25 (1936): 1-99.   01034

Courant, Maurice [Auguste Louis Marie], 1865-1939.

Chōsen shoshi joron [Introduction to Korean
bibliography]. [Tr. by] Ogura Chikao. In Dokusho,
2, no.3 (1938): 1-31.   01095

Courant, Maurice [Auguste Louis Marie], 1865-1939.
Chosŏn munhwasa sŏsŏl [Introduction to Korean
cultural history]. [Tr. by] Kim Su-gyŏng.   01036

Furuya, Kiyoshi. Tokugawa jidai ni okeru Chōsen no
shoseki [A study of Korean books preserved in
Japan during the Edo period]. In Gakutō (The
Beacon light of learning), 11, no.10-11, (1907);
12, no.6 (1908).   01013

Ikeuchi, Hiroshi.   Chōsen kanhoku no yon chishi
[Four geographical records of the northern part of
Korea]. In Chōsen gakuhō, 1 (1951): 239-244. 00390

Kungnip Chungang Tosŏgwan. P'yŏngyang, Korea.
Sŏjihak pu.   Chosŏn sŏjihak kaegwan
[Introduction to Korean bibliography].   00058

Kuroda, Ryō, 1890-.   Chōsen kyūsho kō [Studies of
old Korean books].   00165

McCune, Shannon Boyd-Bailey. Geographic
publications of Hermann Lautensach on Korea. In
Far Eastern quarterly, 5 (1946): 330-332.   01090

McCune, Shannon Boyd-Bailey.   Recent books on Korea.
In Geographical review, 36 (Apr. 1946): 327-329.
                                                       00110

Mishina, Shōei.   The development of the studies of
Korean history and culture in Japan. By Mishina
Shōei and Murakami Yoshio. In Acta Asiatica:
bulletin of the Institute of Eastern Culture, 9
(1965): 83-110.   00131

Oda, Shōgo.   Chōsen shiseki kaidai kōgi [Lectures
on Korean historical sources]. In Seikyū gakusō,
23 (1936): 145-161.   01022

Suematsu, Yasukazu.   Kōrai bunken shōroku [Notes
on the historical materials for the study of the
Koryŏ kingdom]. In Seikyū gakusō, 6, 8, 12 (1931-
1932).   00177

Suematsu, Yasukazu.   Sambōshū henkan ko [A
critical study of the publication of the Sambong-

jip]. In Chōsen gakuhō, 1 (1951): 55-68.   00393

Tokio, Shunjo, comp. **Chōsen kosho mokuroku** [A
classified catalog of old Korean books].   11440

Trollope, Mark Napier. **Corean books and their
authors.** In Transactions of the Korea Branch of
the Royal Asiatic Society, 21 (1932): 1-58.   00130

Underwood, Horace H. **Occidental literature on
Korea.** In Transactions of the Korea Branch of the
Royal Asiatic Society,20 (1931): 1-15.   03724

LIBRARY CATALOGS

China, Republic

Kuo-li Chung-yang t'u-shu-kuan, ed. **T'ai-wan kung-
ts'ang Kao-li-pen lien-ho mu-lu** [Bibliography of
Chinese literature published in Korea and located
in Taiwan public libraries and research
institutions]. In Tung Tso-pin et al. Chung Han
wen-hua lun-chi.   01123

France.

Courant, Maurice (Auguste Louis Marie), 1865-1939.
Catalogue des livres chinois, coréens, japonais.
                                                  11928

Great Britain.

British Museum. London. [Department of Oriental
Printed Books and Manuscripts]. **Title index to
the descriptive catalog of Chinese manuscripts
from Tunhuang in the British Museum.** By E. D.
ᴜrinsᵗead.   11945

Great Britain. War Office. Library. **Catalog of the
War Office Library.**   01028

Royal Empire Society. London. Library. **Subject
catalog.** V.4. Ed. by Lewin Evans.   00158

Japan.

Catalog of the Asiatic library of Dr. G. E. Morrison
(now a part of the Oriental Library, Tokyo,
Japan).   11936

Hara, Sanshichi, ed.   Imanishi Hakushi shūshū
Chōsen kankei bunken mokuroku (Catalog of the
Korean materials collected by the late Prof. Dr.
R. Imanishi).   00065

Kichōsho maikurofirumu mokuroku [A list of
microfilm copies of valuable books].   11915

Kyōtō Daigaku. Bungakubu Toshoshitsu, ed.   Imanishi
Bunko mokuroku [Catalog of Dr. R. Imanishi's
collection].   00175

Maema, Kyōsaku, 1868-1942, ed.   Kosen sappu
[Annotated bibliography of old Korean books].
                                                     00067

Miki, Sakae.   Yōan-in zoshochū no Chōsen isho
[Korean medical books in the Yōan-in Collection].
In Chōsen gakuhō, 1 (1951): 263-270.   01016

Naikaku Bunko Kanseki bunrui mokuroku [A classified
catalog of Korean books in the National Diet
Library].   11913

Nakamura, Eikō.   Hōsa Bunko Chōsenbon tenkansho
kaisetsu (Explanatory notes on the Korean books
collected in the Hōsa Library, Nagoya). In Chōsen
gakuhō, 13 (1958): 203-220.   00187

National Diet Library. Reference and Bibliography
Division, ed.   Catalog of materials on Korea in
the National Diet Library, 2: Foreign books. 10560

Oho Terauchi Bunkō tosho mokuroku [Catalog of Gen.
M. Terauchi's collection, now preserved in
Yamaguchi Women's Junior College].   00169

Osaka Furitsu Toshokan kanpon mokuroku.   [Catalog
of Korean books in the Osaka Prefectural Library,
March, 1916].   00163

Tōyō Bunko, ed.   Chōsen kankei bunken tenji mokuroku
[Annotated catalog of old rare Japanese and
Western publications concerning Korea preserved in

the Tōyō Bunko].   00171

Tōyō Bunko, ed.   Tōyō Bunko Chōsenbon bunrui
mokuroku, fu, annanbon mokuroku [Classified
catalog of Korean books in the Tōyō Bunko with a
catalog of Annamese books appended].   00170

Tōyōgaku Bunken Sentā Renraku Kyōgikai, ed.
Nihonbun, Chūgokubun, Chōsenbun tō chikuji
kankōbutsu mokuroku   (Union catalog of the
periodicals in Japanese, Chinese, Korean and other
languages preserved in the Tōyō Bunko, Tōyō Bunka
Kenkyūjo, Tokyo Univ. and Jinbun Kagaku Kenkyūjo,
Kyōto Univ.).   00189

Uyehara, Cecil H., comp. Checklist of archives in
the Japanese Ministry of Foreign Affairs, Tōkyō
Japan, 1868-1945. Compiled by Cecil H. Uyehara,
under the direction of Edwin G. Beal, Jr.   00134

Young, John, comp. Checklist of microfilm
reproductions of selected archives of the Japanese
Army, Navy and other government agencies, 1868-
1945.   00116

Korea.

Catalog of the foreign books in the Government-
General Library, Seoul, Korea.   11937

Catalog of the Landis Library. In Transactions of
the Korea Branch of the Royal Asiatic Society, 3
(1904): 41-61.   04182

Chŏn'guk tosŏgwan illam [A nation-wide list of
libraries].   11901

Chŏnsi tosŏ mongnok [A list of books on exhibition-
-Seoul National University].   11906

Han'guk Yŏn'gu Tosŏgwan. Seoul, Korea List of the
Korean Research Center Koreana collection: in
commemoration of sixth anniversary. [Ed. by Chon
Dong].   11787

Kakto ch°aekp°an mongnok [A list of wood-block
printed books in each province].   11903

Keijō Furitsu Toshokan.   Tosho mokuroku [Catalog

of Keijō Furitsu Toshokan as of July 31, 1933].
00068

Keijō Teikoku Daigaku. Fuzoku Toshokan, ed. Chōsen
kochizu tenkan mokuroku [Exhibition catalog of
old maps of Korea]. 00182

Keijō Teikoku Daigaku. Fuzoku Toshokan, comp. Keijō
Teikoku Daigaku Fuzoku Toshokan, Wakan shomei
mokuroku [Keijo Imperial University Library title
catalog of Japanese and Chinese books]. 00181

Kim, Kŭn-su. Chosŏn tosŏ mongnok [A list of
Korean books]. 11899

Ko-tosŏ chŏnsihoe ch°ulp°um tosŏ haesŏl [An
annotated bibliography of books put on exhibition
by the Old Book Exhibition Association]. 11907

Korea (Government-General of Chōsen, 1910-1945), ed.
Chōsen Sōtokufu ko tosho mokuroku [General
catalog of old books in the Library of Government-
General of Korea]. 00107

Korea (Government-General of Chōsen, 1910-1945), ed.
Chōsen Sōtokufu tosho mokuroku [Classified
catalog of the collections of the Government-
General of Chōsen]. 00192

Korea (Government-General of Chōsen, 1910-1945).
Chōsen tosho kaidai [Annotated bibliography of
Korean books]. 00022

Kosŏ chŏnsi mongnok [A list of old books on
exhibition--Sungmyŏng Women's University]. 11900

Kukka Chaegŏn Ch°oego Hoeŭi Tosŏgwan. Changsŏ
mongnok--Tongyangsŏ, Sŏyangsŏ pullyu mongnok 4294
nyŏn siwŏl siboil hyŏnjae- (Classified catalog
of books in the National Assembly Library of
Korea). 00075

Kungnip Chungang Tosŏgwan. Seoul, Korea, ed.
Han'guk sŏmok, 1945-1962 (Korean national
bibliography, 1945-1962). 00073

Kungnip Tosŏgwan. Changsŏ pullyu mongnok--Haebang
ijŏn ilsŏbu [Classified catalog of Japanese books
published before 1945 in the National Library]. 00079

Kungnip Tosŏgwan.   Ch'ulp'um tosŏ mongnok (Book
week exhibit). Oct. 20-26, 1959.   09105

Kungnip Tosŏgwan.   Kungnip Tosŏgwan kwijungbon kosŏ
mongnok   [Bibliography of rare books of the
National Library].   10576

Kyujanggak sŏmok [Catalog of the Royal Library,
Kyujanggak].   11962

Murphey, Sunny. Koreana Collection (as of 1 April
1967).   11424

Odaesan sago mongnok [List of manuscripts and books
stored in the Royal Archives at Odaesan].   11949

Riōshoku. Shomuka.   Riōke Zoshokaku kotosho
mokuroku   [Catalog of old books kept at the
Library of Yi Royal House].   00168

Sŏ, Myŏng-ŭng,   1716-1787. Sŏsŏ sŏmok ch'obon
[Draft catalog of manuscripts and printed books of
Korea in the Royal Library].   11950

Sŏ, Myŏng-ŭng,   1716-1787, comp. Kyujang ch'ongmok
4 kwŏn [Catalog of the Chinese collection in the
Royal Library, Kyujanggak].   11948

Sŏul Taehakkyo. Mullikwa Taehak. Tonga Munhwa
Yŏn'guso.   Kyujanggak tosŏ Han'gukpon
ch'ongmongnok (Catalog of Korean books and
manuscripts in the Kyujanggak Collection, Seoul
National University Library).   00106

Sŏul Taehakkyo. Pusok Tosŏgwan   Kyujanggak tosŏ
mongnok--Han'guk   [Catalog of the Kyujanggak
collection of Korean books].   00076

Sŏul Taehakkyo. Tosŏgwan.   Ilsa Karam Mun'go kosŏ
chŏja mongnok   [An author catalog of rare books
of the Ilsa and Garam collections in Seoul
National University Library).   11293

Sŏul Taehakkyo. Tosŏgwan.   Sŏul Taehakkyo kaegyo
isipchunyŏn kinyŏm kwijung tosŏ chŏnsihoe chŏnsi
tosŏ mongnok 1966-nyŏn 10-wŏl 13-18-il   (A
bibliography of rare books, exhibited in
commemoration of the 20th anniversary of Seoul
National University, October 13-18, 1966).   11290

9

Steele, Marion. Subject index to periodical
material on Korea in the Yongsan Special Services
Library.   11425

Teishitsu tosho mokuroku [Catalog of the imperial
libraries].   11242

Tŏksindang sŏmok [Catalog of Tŏksindang books].
                                                      00095

Tongguk Taehakkyo. Seoul, Korea. Koryŏ pulsŏ
chŏn'gwan mongnok [Exhibition catalog of Buddhist
literature of Koryŏ dynasty].   01066

Tongguk Taehakkyo. Seoul, Korea. Koryŏ sagyŏng
chŏn'gŭn mongnok [Exhibition catalog of Koryŏ
Buddhist scriptures in manuscript].   01067

Tongguk Taehakkyo. Seoul, Korea. Tosogwan Kosŏ
mongnok chipsŏng [Catalog of Korean rare books].
                                                      11566

Tongguk Taehakkyo. Seoul, Korea.   Yijo chŏn'gi
kugyŏk pulsŏ chŏn'gwan mongnok [Exhibition
catalog of Buddhist scriptures translated into
Korean during the first half of Yi dynasty]. 01068

Tongguk Taehakkyo. Seoul, Korea. Pulgyo Munhwa
Yŏn'guso. Yijo chŏn'gi pulsŏ chŏn'gwan mongnok
[Exhibition catalog of Buddhist literature
published during the first half of Yi dynasty].
                                                      01069

Trollope, Mark Napier.   Short list of Korean books
[in the Chosen Christian College Library]. In
Transactions of the Korea Branch of the Royal
Asiatic Society, 21 (1932): 59-104.   03066

U.S.A.

Books in the Brooklyn Public Library on the Far
East, China, Japan, Korea, Manchuria, Russia and
Siberia.   11933

Columbia University. Kŭmsu kangsan (Works on
Korea).   00100

Fang, Chao-ying. The Asami Library: a descriptive

catalog. Ed. by Elizabeth Huff.   11898

Gerow, Bert A. Publications in Japanese on Korean
  anthropology: a bibliography of uncataloged
  materials in the Kanaseki Collection, Stanford
  University Library.   00007

Harvard University. Library. Harvard-Yenching
  Library. A classified catalog of Korean books in
  the Harvard-Yenching Institute Library at Harvard
  University.   11452

Harvard University. Library. Harvard-Yenching
  Library. A classified catalog of Korean books in
  the Harvard-Yenching Library Harvard University.
  V.2.   11453

Schroeder, Peter Brett. Korean publications in the
  National Agricultural Library.   00129

Taylor, Louise Marion. Catalog of books on China in
  the Essex Institute, Salem, Mass., U.S.A.   11935

U.S. National Archives. Preliminary inventory of
  the records of the Headquarters, United Nations
  Command (Record Group). Compiled by Paul Taborn
  and Andrew Putignano.   11946

Yang, Key Paik. Reference guide to Korean
  materials, 1945-1959.   00020

U.S.S.R.

Denney, Ruth N., tr. Selections from "The holdings
  in Oriental Studies in the great libraries of the
  Soviet Union. Articles and notes".   11916

Paige, Glenn D. The Korean collection of the
  Division of Oriental Manuscripts, Institute of
  Oriental Studies, Academy of Sciences of the USSR.
  A bibliographical note. In Asiatic research
  bulletin, 1, no.9 (September 1958): 2-3.   04169

Petrova, Ol'ga Petrovna. Opisanie pis'mennykh
  pamiatnikov koreĭskoĭ kultury v.2.   11788

BIBLIOGRAPHIES OF PERIODICALS

Chōsen no zasshi [Korean magazines]. In Japan.
Mombushō. Daigaku Gakujutsukyoku. Gakujutsu
chikuji kankōbutsu mokuroku.   04170

Chōsen-nai hakkō shinbunshi ichiranhyō [A catalog
of newspapers published in Korea].   11914

Korea (Republic) Kongbobu. Kongboguk. Chǒnggi
kanhaengmul silt°ae illam [Directory of Korean
periodicals and newspapers].   11569

Kukhoe Tosǒgwan. Seoul, Korea. Sasǒguk,   ed.
Han'guk sinmun chapchi ch°ongmongnok 1883-1945
[Catalog of Korean newspapers and periodicals,
1883-1945].   11448

Tōhō Gakkai. Tōhōgaku kankei zasshi mokuroku
[Bibliography of Japanese periodicals relating to
Oriental studies].   00172

Tōyōgaku Bunken Sentā Renraku Kyōgikai, ed.
Nihonbun, Chūgokubun, Chōsenbun tō chikuji
kankōbutsu mokuroku (Union catalog of the
periodicals in Japanese, Chinese, Korean and other
languages preserved in the Tōyō Bunko, Tōyō Bunka
Kenkyūjo, Tokyo Univ. and Jinbun Kagaku Kenkyūjo,
Kyōto Univ.).   00189

Yi, Pyǒng-mok. Han'guk ūi taehak chǒnggi
kanhaengmul pu-kodǔng kyoyuk kigwan myonggam
[Bibliography of University periodicals of Korea,
1945-1964, with directory of institutions of
higher education°   11885

INDEXES TO PERIODICAL LITERATURE

Chindan hakpo ch°ong mokch°a [Title index to
articles in Chindan hakpo, v.1-24]. In Chindan
hakpo, 25/27 (1964): 506-512.   01129

Ch°oe, Sun-ja, comp. Han'guk chapchi mongnok,
1896-1945 (Korean magazine index. 1896-1945). By
Soon Ja Choi.   00072

Chǒn, Munam. An index to English periodical

literature published in Korea, 1945-1966.   11423

Chōsen Gakkai. Chōsen gakuhō no daiisshū kara dai
gojisshū made no sōmokuji (Index to Chōsen gakuhō
from no.1 to nc.50). In Chōsen gakuhō, no.50
(1969): 5-77.   04073

Chōsen Sōtokufu Kambō Bunshoka, ed. Sōkan irai no
sō-mokuji benran [Index to articles appearing in
Chōsen since the publication of its first issue].
01130

Elrod, Jefferson McRee. An index to English
language periodical literature published in Korea,
1890-1940.   00006

General index to the first twenty volumes of the
Geographical Journal: 1893-1902.   11939

General index to the second twenty volumes of the
Geographical Journal 1903-1912.   11940

Henthorn, William E. Korean views of America 1954-
1964: an annotated bibliography.   11177

Jinruigaku zasshi sōsakuin [General index to
Jinruigaku zasshi, v.1-50].   00197

Kinchaku Geunro-gya sōmokuji   [General index to the
Kŭlloja, a DPRK journal nos. 16, 17]. In Chōsen
kenkyū geppō, 13 (1963): 36.   00180

Kukhoe Tosŏgwan. Seoul, Korea. Sasŏguk. Kaebyŏkchi
ch°ongmokch°a, 1920-1949 [Comprehensive table of
contents of Kaebyŏk, 1920-1949]. [Ed. by] Taehan
Min'guk Kukhoe Tosŏgwan Sasŏguk.   10269

Layard, R. de B. Transactions of the Asiatic
Society of Jaʳan index. First series, Vols. 1-50.
In Transactions of the Asiatic Society of Japan,
Second ser.5 (1928): 89-114.   04183

Mantetsu chōsa geppō sōmokuroku   [General index to
the Mantetsu chōsa geppō]. In Mantetsu chōsa
geppō, 22, no. 1 (1942): 200-244.   01012

Noble, Harold J. Transactions of Korea Branch of
the Royal Asiatic Society. Index to transactions
1-16. In Transactions of the Korea Branch of the
Royal Asiatic Society, 17 (1927).   04184

Seikyū gakusō ronbun choshabetsu sakuin   [Author
index to the Seikyū gakusō, v.1-30].   01002

'Shokō' shuyō kiji mokuroku [Index to major
articles of the Shokō, no.1-142]. In Shokō, 16,
no. 2-3 (1943).   00198

Steele, Marion. Subject index to periodical
material on Korea in the Yongsan Special Services
Library.   11425

Tōhō gakuhō sōmokuji [General index to the Tōhō
gakuhō, v.1-10].   00178

Underwood, Horace H. Index to titles and authors of
papers published in the Transactions of the Korea
Branch of the R.A.S., volumes 1 to 25. In
Transactions of the Korea Branch of the Royal
Asiatic Society,25 (1936): 109-122.   03723

Yu, Hyŏn-suk. Index to Korea, Japanese and Chinese
acquisitions reported in the Quarterly Journal of
the Library of Congress, 1943-1968.   11560

BIBLIOGRAPHIES OF THESES AND DISSERTATIONS

Chŏng, Ch˝ŏl, ed. Han'guk paksa-rok [Korean
scholars].   10329

Haengjŏnghak sŏksa hagwi nomun chemok   [A list of
the theses in administrative science for the M.A.
degree].   11904

Han'guk Yŏn'guwŏn.   Han'guk Sŏk Paksa hagwi nonmun
mongnok 1945-1960 (List of master's and doctor's
degrees offered in Korea, 1945-1960).   00087

Kukhoe Tosŏgwan.   Miguk esŏ suyŏdoen Han'gugin
paksarok   [List of doctorates received in the
U.S. by Koreans].   11427

Shulman, Frank J. Japan and Korea: an annotated
bibliography of doctoral dissertations in Western
languages, 1877-1969.   11976

Sŏk Paksa hagwi nonmun chemok chip [A catalog of
M.A. theses and doctoral dissertations].   11905

14

Sŏksa hagwi nonmun mongnok, 1956-1966   [A list of
M.A. theses, 1956-1966].   11902

Stucki, Curtis W. American doctoral dissertations
on Asia, 1933-1962, including master's theses at
Cornell University.   00023

Stucki, Curtis W. American doctoral dissertations
on Asia, 1933-1958, including appendix of Master's
theses at Cornell University.   00109

GENERAL BIBLIOGRAPHIES

CHINESE

Kuo-li Chung-yang t'u-shu-kuan, ed. Chung-kuo k°an-
hsing Han-kuo chu-shu mu-lu [Bibliography of
literature on Korea written by Koreans and
published in China]. In Tung Tso-pin et al. Chung
Han wen-hua lun-chi.   01044

Kuo-li Chung-yang t'u-shu-kuan, ed. Chung-kuo kuan-
yü Han-kuo chu-shu mu-lu [Bibliography of Chinese
literature on Korea]. In Tung Tso-pin et al. Chung
Han wen-hua lun-chi.   01139

CZECH

Prague. Národní a universitní knihovna. Lidově
demokratické zeme Asie: Korea, Vietnam, Mongolsko;
[výberový seznam literatury]. [Edited by] M.
Kaftan.   11977

ENGLISH

Allied Forces. Southwest Pacific Area. Annotated
bibliography of the Southwest Pacific and adjacent
areas.   00155

California. University. Institute of East Asiatic
Studies. Korean studies guide. Comp. by B.H.
Hazard, Jr. et al. Ed. by Richard Marcus.   00015

California. University. East Asiatic Studies.
Russian supplement to the Korean studies guide.

15

Comp. by Robert L. Beckus and Michael C. Rogers.
00016

Ehrman, Edith. Preliminary bibliography on East
Asia for undergraduate libraries. By Edith Ehrman
and Ward Morehouse.   11834

Gompertz, E. Supplement to 'A partial bibliography
of occidental literature on Korea' by H. H.
Underwood, 1931. By E. Gompertz and G. Gompertz.
In Transactions of the Korea Branch of the Royal
Asiatic Society, 24 (1935): 21-48.   00118

Honda, Minoru, comp. Post-war Japanese research on
the Far East (excluding Japan). Compiled by Honda
Minoru and E. B. Ceadel. In Asia Major, n.s., 4,
no.1 (1954).   01082

Incunabula exhibit: Korean movable type.   11846

Kokusai Bunka Shinkōkai. K.B.S. bibliographical
register of important works written in Japanese on
Japan and the Far East, published during the year
1932-1937.   00121

Kungnip Chungang Tosŏgwan. [Publication list of
the Central National Library, April 17, 1967].
11445

Kyriak, Theodore E., comp. and ed. North Korea
1957-1961: a bibliography and guide to contents of
a collection of United States Joint Publications
Research Service translations on microfilm. 11590

McCune, Shannon Boyd-Bailey. Bibliography of
Western language materials on Korea. Rev., enl.
ed.   00024

Paige, Glenn D. Korea studies in the Soviet Union.
In Korean Research Center bulletin, 13 (1960): 47-
57.   04168

Paige, Glenn D. A survey of Soviet publications on
Korea, 1950-1956. In Journal of Asian Studies, 17
(Aug. 1958): 579-594.   04167

16

Park, Yung-ja. Korean publications in series: a
subject bibliography.   11558

Quan, L. King. Introduction to Asia; a selective
guide to background reading.   00132

Row, Soon Myong Kim. A checklist of Korean
periodicals, 1945-1966.   11559

Silberman, Bernard S. Japan and Korea: a critical
bibliography.   00008

Surveys and Research Corporation. Washington, D.C.
An interim report to the government of the
Republic of Korea. [By James S. Fitzgerald].
[Korean translation by Lee Jay Cho].   00144

Talbot, Phillips, ed. A select bibliography: Asia,
Africa, Eastern Europe, Latin America.   00142

Teng, Ssu-yü, 1906-, comp. Japanese studies on
Japan and the Far East.   01065

Underwood, Horace H. A partial bibliography of
occidental literature on Korea from early times to
1930. In Transactions of the Korea Branch of the
Royal Asiatic Society, 20 (1931): 17-185 and 1-17.
                                                 00120

U.S. Bureau of the Census. Bibliography of social
science periodicals and monograph series: North
Korea, 1945-1961. By Foreign Manpower Research
Office, Bureau of the Census, under grant from
Office of Science Information Service, National
Science Foundation.   00004

U.S. Bureau of the Census. Bibliography of social
science periodicals and monograph series: Republic
of Korea, 1945-1961. By Foreign Manpower Research
Office, Bureau of the Census, under grant from
Office of Science Information Service, National
Science Foundation.   00005

U.S. Library of Congress. Reference Department.
Korea: a preliminary bibliography. Comp. by Helen
Dudenbostel Jones et al.   01070

U.S. Library of Congress. Reference Department.
Korea: an annotated bibliography of publications
in the Russian language. Compiled by Albert Parry,

John T. Dorosh, and Elizabeth Gardner Dorosh.
00012

U.S. Library of Congress. General Reference and
Bibliography Division. Non-self-governing areas
with special emphasis on mandates and
trusteeships: a selected list of references. Comp.
by Helen F. Conover.
00139

U.S. Library of Congress. Select list of books
(with reference to periodicals) relating to the
Far East. Compiled under the direction of Appleton
Prentiss Clark Griffin, Chief Bibliographer. 11943

Vos, Frits. [Review of] Korean studies guide. In
T´oung-pao, 43, no. 5 (1955): 408-431.
01137

Wenckstern, Friedrich von, comp. A bibliography of
the Japanese empire; being a classified list of
all books, essays and maps in European languages
relating to Dai Nihon (Great Japan) published in
Europe, America and in the East from 1859-1893 A.
D. (6th year of Ansei-26th of Meiji). To which is
added a facsimile-reprint of: Léon Pagès,
Bibliographie japonaise depuis le 15 sciècle [']
jusqu´à 1859.
00157

Wenckstern, Friedrich von, comp. Bibliography of
the Japanese empire; being a classified list of
the literature in European Languages relating to
Dai Nihon (Great Japan) published in Europe,
America and in the East. V.2. Comprising the
literature from 1894 to the middle of 1906 (27-
39th year of Meiji) with additions and corrections
to the first volume and a Supplement to Léon
Pagès' Bibliographie japonaise. Added is a list of
the Swedish literature on Japan, by Miss Valfrid
Palmgren.
11891

FRENCH

Cordier, Henri. Bibliotheca Sinica: dictionnaire
bibliographique des ouvrages relatifs à l'êmpire
chinois. 2.êd., rev., corr., et considérablement
augm.
00156

Cordier, Henri, 1849-1925, comp. Bibliotheca
Japonica: dictionnaire bibliographique de ouvrages
relatifs à l´empire japonais rangés par ordre

chronologique jusqu'à 1870 suivi d'un appendice
renfermant la liste alphabétique des principaux
ouvrages parus de 1870 à 1912.   01045

Courant, Maurice [Auguste Louis Marie], 1865-1939.
Bibliographie coréenne: tableau littéraire de la
Corée, contenant la nomenclature des ouvrages
publiés dans ce pays jusqu'en 1890 ainsi que la
description et l'analyse détaillées des principaux
d'entre ces ouvrages.   01032

Courant, Maurice [Auguste Louis Marie], 1865-1939.
Bibliographie coréenne. Supplement (jusqu'en
1899).   01033

GERMAN

Kim, Youn Soo. Sozialwissenschaftliche
bibliographie über Korea [Social science
bibliography on Korea].   01122

Nachod, Oskar. Bibliographie von Japan, 1906-1926;
[containing a detailed listing of books and essays
on Japan which have appeared since the publication
of the second volume of Wenckstern "Bibliography
of the Japanese Empire" up to 1926 in European
languages].   00125

Nachod, Oskar. Bibliographie von Japan, 1927-1929,
[with supplements for the years 1906-1926; volume
3 of the collected work, number 9576-13595]. 00140

Nachod, Oskar. Bibliographie von Japan, 1930-1932,
[with supplements for the years 1906-1929; volume
4 of the collected work, number 13596-18398].
[From the unfinished work supplemented and
published by] Hans Praesent.   00141

Nachod, Oskar. Bibliographie von Japan, 1933-1935,
[with supplements for the years 1906-1932; volume
5 of the collected work begun by Oskar Nachod,
number 18399-25376]. [By] Hans Praesent and Wolf
Haenisch.   00145

Nachod, Oskar. Bibliographie von Japan, 1936-1937,
[with supplements for the years 1906-1935; volume
6 of the collected work, number 25377-33621].
[Revised by] Wolf Haenisch [and] Hans Praesent].
                                                  00146

JAPANESE

Chōsen Kagakuin kizō tosho mokuroku [List of books presented by the Academy of Science, DPRK]. In Chōsen kenkyū geppō, 11 (1962): 56-59.　　01008

Chōsen Kagakuin kizō zasshi mokuroku [List of periodicals presented by the Academy of Science, DPRK]. In Chōsen kenkyū geppō, 11 (1962): 40.
01009

Chōsen kankei ōbun bunken mokuroku [Bibliography of Korean studies in European languages]. In Rekishigaku kenkyū, 4 (1935): 130-139.　　01074

Chōsen kankei ōbun tosho kaidai [Annotated bibliography of Korean studies in European languages]. In Ryōsho, 5, 6, 8, 10 (1939-1940).
01075

Chōsen Keizai Kenkyūjo. Chōsen tōkei sōran [An annotated bibliography of statistics and statistical works concerning Korea]. [By] Shikata Hiroshi, et al.　　11572

Chōsen koten mokuroku [A catalog of Korean classics].　　01041

Chōsen Sōtokufu Tosho-kan, ed. Chōsen kosho shōkai [Bibliography of old Korean books].　　11854

Chōsenban koshomoku [A catalog of the old books published in Korea].　　01039

Chosŏn Kosŏ Kanhaenghoe. Seoul, Korea. Chōsen kosho mokuroku [A catalog of old Korean books].
01108

En'ō-sei. Sangoku jidai no tenseki [Classics of Three Kingdom period]. In Bunken hōkoku, 2, no.3 (1936): 16-17.　　04128

Fukuda, Tokuzō, comp. Kankoku kenkyū no bunken [Bibliography cn Korean studies]. In Keiigaku, 110 (1909).　　01078

Furukawa, Kanehide, comp. Chōsen no shoseki [Korean publications]. In Dokusho, 1, no.3 (1937): 2-6.　　01079

20

Furutani, Kiyoshi. Futatabi Tokugawa jidai ni
okeru Chōsen no shoseki ni tsuite [Korean books
of Tokugawa period]. In Gakutō, 12, no. 6 (1908).
04115

Hirose, Bin. Nihon sōsho sakuin [Index to Japanese
collectanea]. 00176

Imamura, Tomoe. Ninjin bunseki kaidai
[Bibliographical literature on ginseng]. In
Chōsen, 213 (1933): 2-34. 04118

Iwasaki, Keishō. Chōsen minzoku gakkai e no tembo
[Prospects of Korean ethnology]. In Dolmen, 2,
no.4 (1933): 112-115. 01132

Kanazawa, Shozaburo, 1872-. Ajia kenkyū ni kansuru
bunken [Books and materials on Asian studies].
01051

Kanazawa, Shozaburō. Chōsen shoseki mokuroku
[Annotated catalog of old Korean books]. 01011

Kanno, Hiroomi. Sorenpō hakkō Chōsen kankei tosho
mokuroku [Bibliography of USSR publications
concerning Korea]. In Chōsen kenkyū geppō, 11
(1962): 51-56. 01010

Kanseki mokuroku kōhon [Provisional catalog of
Korean books]. 11243

Kawachi, Yoshihiro. Bunken shōkai [A review of
publications]. In Chōsen gakuhō, 16 (1960): 167-
188. 00424

Kishi, Yuzuru. Chōsen no tōka kankei shiryō tō
[Data on Korean lamplights]. In Shomotsu Dōkōkai
kaihō, 7 (1940): 4-6. 04119

Kokuritsu Kokkai Toshokan, ed. Chōsen kankei shiryō
mokuroku [A list of data related to Korea].
10570

Korea (Government-General of Chōsen, 1910-1945).
Chōsen ni okeru shuppanbutsu gaiyō [Survey of
publications in Korea]. [Comp. by] Chōsen
Sōtokufu. Keimukyoku. 00164

Korea (Government-General of Chōsen, 1910-1945)
Toshokan. Shinshobu bunrui mokuroku [Classified
catalog of new books].   00053

Kuji, Hanjirō.   Chōsen kenkyū no seika [The result
of Korean study]. In Chōsen gyōsei, 22, no.2
(1942): 19.   04120

Maema, Kyōsaku, comp.   Sensatsu meidai   12 kwŏn
[Annotated bibliography of Korean books].   01058

Morita, Tauson.   Dokutoru Rīsu no Chōsen ni kansuru
Ūshu kinkan shomokuroku [Recently published
Western books cn Korea]. In Gakuto, 7 (1911): 1-8.
                                                01140

Musha, Renzō.   [Chōsen fūzoku-shū] Shosai no tōka
kankei bunken [(Korean customs collection)
published literature on lamp-lights]. In Shomotsu
Dōkōkai kaihō, 9 (1940): 25-26.   04130

Naka, Michiyo.   Taiwan, Chōsen, Manshū shi kenkyū
no shiori   [A guide to the study of Taiwan, Korea,
Manchuria]. In Shigaku zasshi, 11, no.1 (1899):
57-66.   04131

Nitchō Kyōkai.   Chōsen ni kansuru Nihongo-han tosho
mokuroku, 1945-1960 [List of publications on
Korea in Japanese 1945-1960].   00166

Nitchō Kyōkai Ūsakafu Rengōkai,   ed.   Nihon de
shuppan sareta Chōsen ni kansuru tosho mokuroku
[Bibliography cf books on Korea published in
Japan, Aug. 15, 1945-Aug. 15, 1960].   00179

Oda, Shōgo, comp.   Chōsen kosho no ichibetsu [A
brief study of old Korean books]. In Sen-Man
kenkyū, 8, no.8 (1935).   01094

Okuda, Naogi.   Chōsen kokuhō shōkai [Brief
annotations of Korean classical works].   01018

Okudaira, Takehiko.   Chōsen no tenseki [Korean
classics]. In Kinyū Kumiai, 117 (1938).   04121

Okuda,   Takehiko.   Korai-Chō no tenseki ni tsuite
[Books in Koryč dynasty]. In Bunken hōkoku, 2,
no.4 (Apr. 1936): 20-23.   04122

Saikin Chōsen kankei zasshi ronbun mokuroku

[Bibliography of periodical articles concerning
Korea]. In Chōsen kenkyū geppō, 2, 5/6, 8, 11
(1962); 14, 18, 21 (1963).   01007

Sakuragi, Akira.   Chōsen kenkyū no shiori [Korean
studies guide]. In Kokugakuin zasshi, 14, no.1
(1908): 65-73; 14, no.2 (1908): 156-165.   01004

Sakurai, Yoshiyuki.   Meiji shoki no Chōsen kenkyū
[Study on Korea in the early Meiji period]. In
Chōsen kōsei, 2, no.8 (1938).   04134

Sakurai, Yoshiyuki,   comp.   Taishō nenkan Chōsen
kankei bunken kaidai [Annotated bibliography of
source materials on Korea published during Taishō
period]. In Chōsen kōsei, 19 (1940): supplement,
20 (1941).   01099

Sekino, Shinkichi.   Ōbun Chōsen kankei bunken
mokuroku--1940-nen igo kankō shomoku   [Korea:
list of books in European languages, 1940-50]. In
Chōsen gakuhō, 1 (1951): 299-307.   00389

Sen-Man kankei jūyō zasshi kiji mokuroku [Monthly
list of important Japanese articles concerning
Korea and Manchuria]. In Bunken hōkoku, 1, no.1
(1935); 10, no. 11 (1944).   00199

Shima, Gorō.   Chōsenjin taishitsu jinruigaku ni
kansuru bunken mokuroku [Bibliography on Korean
physical anthropology]. In Dolmen, 2, no. 4
(1933): 6-8.   00184

Shimamoto, Hikojirō.   Akiba Takashi Hakushi no
shōgai to gyōseki [Life and works of Dr. Akiba
Takashi]. In Chōsen gakuhō, 9 (Nov. 1955): 303-
322.   06449

Suda, Akiyoshi, 1900-.   Chōsenjin jinruigaku ni
kansuru bunken   [Bibliography on physical
anthropology of the Koreans]. In Jinruigaku
zasshi, 60, no.3 (1949): 123-136.   00183

Tosho sōmokuroku [General catalog of books].   00167

Yūhō Kyōkai. Chōsen Shiryō Kenkyūkai.   Chōsen
kankei bunken shiryō sōmokuroku [Catalog of
reference materials pertaining to Korea]. [Ed. by]
Kondō Ken'ichi.   01026

KOREAN

Chang, Tŏk-sun. Kyujanggak tosŏ chosŏn ŭpchisojae
sŏrhwa pullyu [Classification of folklore printed
in Korean local papers and located at Kyujanggak
Library]. In Tcnga munhwa (Sŏul Tae), 6 (Dec.
1968). 04093

Chŏng, In-bo. Tamwŏn kukhak san'go [Tamwŏn's
essays in Koreanology]. 10334

Chosŏn Minjujuŭi Inmin Konghwaguk Sahoe kwahagwŏn.
Kojŏn Yŏn'guso. P°yŏngyang, Korea. Munhŏn
Yŏn'gusil. Chosŏn kojŏn haeje [Annotated
bibliography of Korean classics]. V.1. [Ed. by] Ha
Yun-do [and] Hwang Pyŏng-hŏn. 00061

Han'guk sŏji munhŏn illam 1941-1942 (Bibliography
on Korean bibliography, 1941-1942). In Sŏji, 1,
no.2 (August 1960): 30-32. 01080

Han'guk sŏji munhŏn illam 1937-1940 (Bibliography
on Korean bibliography, 1937-1940). In Sŏji, 1,
no.1 (Jan. 1960): 42-46. 04074

Han'guk Tosŏgwan Hyŏphoe.
1967 nyŏndo pun sŏnjŏng tosŏ mongnok [Selected
bibliography for the year of 1967]. In Tohyŏp
wŏlbo, 8, no. 6-10 (July/Aug.-Dec., 1967). 04090

Kim, Un-sŏk, ed. Pukhan koejip chŏnsul munhŏn-chip
[Bibliography cn the puppet state of North Korea].
00052

Ko, Hu-sŏk, comp. Han'guk tosŏgwan kwan'gye munhŏn
mongnok, 1921-1961 (Korean library literature).
[Ed. by] Ko Hu-sŏk [and] Hong Sun-yŏng. 00071

Korea (Republic) Kongbobu. Chŏngbu kanhaengmul
mongnok [Bibliography of government publication].
00300

Korea (Republic) Kongbobu. Kongboguk. Chŏnggi
kanhaengmul, sahoe tanch°e, yŏnghwaŏpchi mit
kongyŏnja illamp°yo [Lists of Korean
periodicals, associations, institutions, moving
picture business firms, and theaters]. 00346

Korea (Republic) Mun'gyobu. Chijŏng munhwajae

24

mongnok [List of cultural properties designated by the government]. 01054

Korea (Republic) Mun'gyobu. Kŏm injŏng kyokwayong illamp°yo [A catalog of authorized textbooks]. 10223

Kukhoe Tosŏgwan. Chosŏn ch°ongdokpu Kŭp sosok kwansŏ palgan tosŏ mongnok [A list of books published by the Governemt-General of Chōsen and its related offices]. In Kukhoe Tosŏgwanbo, 4, no. 2 (Feb. 1967); 5, no. 1 (1968). 04100

Kukhoe Tosŏgwan. Haebang chŏn Han'guk kwan'gye munhŏn mongnok: pon'gwan sojangbon [List of literature related to Korea before the liberation of Korea from Japan: publications located at National Assembly Library]. In Kukhoe Tosŏgwanbo, 4, no. 11 (Nov. 1967). 04096

Kukhoe Tosŏgwan. Haebang chŏn kanhaeng Han'guk chapchi mongnok (pongwan sojang) [List of Korean magazine publications before the liberation of Korea from Japan: publications located at the National Assembly Library]. In Kukhoe Tŏsogwanbo, 5, no. 1 (1968). 04097

Kukhoe Tosŏgwan. Han'guk kwan'gye munhŏn mongnok: Mi Stanford Taehakkyo sojang [List of literature related to Korea: literature located at Stanford University, U.S.A.]. In Kukhoe Tosŏgwanbo, 3, no. 9 (Oct. 1966). 04095

Kukhoe Tosŏgwan. Seoul, Korea, ed. Chŏngbu kanhaengmul mongnok (Government publications in Korea, 1948-1965). 11849

Kukhoe Tosŏgwan. Seoul, Korea. Sasŏguk. Ch°amgo Sŏjikwa, ed. Hanmal Han'guk chapchi mokch°a ch°ongnok 1896-1910 (Catalog of contents of Korean periodicals published in the end of Yi dynasty, 1896-1910). 10592

Kungnip Chungang Tosŏgwan. Seoul, Korea, ed. Taehan Min'guk ch°ulp°anmul ch°ong mongnok, 1963-1964 (Korean national bibliography, 1963-1964). 11441

Kungnip Chungang Tosŏgwan. Seoul, Korea, ed. Taehan Min'guk ch°ulp°anmul ch°ong mongnok, 1965 (Korean national bibliography, 1965). 11442

Kungnip Tosŏgwan. Kosŏbu pullyu mongnok
[Classified catalog of old books]. 00080

Kyŏngbuk Taehakkyo. Kyŏngbuk Taehakkyo sŏksa nonmun
palch°wejip (Kyŏngbuk University bulletin:
abstracts of master's theses). 11654

Minjok munhwa kwan'gye munhŏn mongnok
[Bibliography of source materials on Korean
national culture]. In Minjok munhwa yŏn'gu, 1
(1964): 254-336. 01092

Sŏ, Kŏ-jŏng, 1420-1488, ed. Tongguk T°onggam
[Complete mirror of the Eastern Country]. 00091

Sŏ, Yu-gu, 1764-1845. Nup°anko [Study on printed
books]. [Ed. and comp. by Yi Chong-man]. 01027

Sŏk, Chu-myŏng. Chejudo kwan'gye munhŏnjip [A
list of literature on Cheju Island]. By D. M.
Seok. 00001

Sŏul Taehakkyo. Ch°ulp°um tosŏ haesŏl (An
annotated list of rare books exhibited in
commemoration cf the tenth anniversary of Seoul
National University, October 13-17, 1956). 11450

Sŏul Taehakkyo. Pusok Tosŏgwan. Microfilm mongnok
(A list of microfilm records). In Sŏul Taehakkyo
Tosŏgwanbo, 4 (1966): 19-25. 04078

Tokyo Gaikokugo Gakkō. Kankoku Kōyūkai, ed. Hanjŏk
mongnok kobon [A list of Korean manuscripts].
00088

Yi, Chae-ch°ŏl, ed. Han'guk ch°amgo tosŏ haeje,
1910-1958 (Guide to Korean reference books, 1910-
June 1958). Edited by Lee Jai-chul; compiled by
Paik In, Myung Chae-hui and Yun Pyong-tai. 00019

Yi, Hong-jik. Toil han Han°guk ŭi munhŏn [Korean
literature in Japan which was brought from Korea].
In Toksa yŏjŏk (1960): 32-40. 04166

Yi, Hyŏn-jong, ed. Han'guksa yŏn'gu nonmun ch°ong
mongnok, 1900-1966 (Catalog of research treatises
on Korean history 1900-1966). [Ed. by] Yi Hyŏn-
jong [and] Yi Man-su. 11291

Yi, Pyŏng-gi. Han'guk sŏji ŭi yŏn'gu [Study of
Korean bibliography]. In Tongbang hakchi, 3
(1957); 5 (1961). 04087

Yi, Wŏn-sik, comp. Tosŏl kotosŏ kosŏhwa haeje
[Annotated bibliography of old books and paintings
with illustrations]. 01072

Yi, Yong-hŭi, 1917-, ed. Kŭnse Han'guk oegyo munsŏ
ch°ongmok oegukp°yŏn (Catalog of foreign
diplomatic documents relating to Korea, 1845-
1910). Ed. by Lee Yong-Hee. 11292

RUSSIAN

Bibliografiia Koreĭ. In Russia, Ministerstvo
finansov. Opisanie Koreĭ. III. 07114

Kontsevich, L. P. Pervyĭ pamiatnik koreĭskoĭ
pis°mennosti. In Narody Azii i Afriki, 4 (1965):
160-173. 11760

SOCIOCULTURAL PATTERN AND CHANGE

California. University. Institute of East Asiatic
Studies. Korean studies guide. Comp. by B.H.
Hazard, Jr. et al. Ed. by Richard Marcus. 00015

Ch°oe, Chae-sŏk. Sahoehak kwan°gye munhŏn mongnok,
1945-1964 [Bibliography on sociology, 1945-1964].
In Han'guk sahoehak, 1 (Nov. 1964): 115-126. 06761

Ch°oe, Chae-sŏk. Sahoehak kwan°gye munhŏn mongnok,
1964. 9. 21--1965. 12. 31 [Bibliography on
sociology, Sept. 21, 1964-Dec. 31, 1965]. In
Han'guk sahoehak, 2 (Nov. 1966): 180-181. 06762

Chung, Yong-Sun. Publications on Korea in the era
of political revolutions, 1959-1963; a selected
bibliography. Compiled with introduction by Yong-
Sun Chung. 11437

Gerow, Bert A. Publications in Japanese on Korean
anthropology: a bibliography of uncataloged
materials in the Kanaseki Collection, Stanford
University Library. 00007

Gompertz, G. St.G. M. Bibliography of Western
literature on Korea from the earliest time until
1950. 00117

Harvard University. Library. Harvard-Yenching
Library. A classified catalog of Korean books in
the Harvard-Yenching Institute Library at Harvard
University.   11452

Harvard University. Library. Harvard-Yenching
Library. A classified catalog of Korean books in
the Harvard-Yenching Library Harvard University.
V.2.   11453

Human Relations Area Files. HRAF source
bibliography. [Prepared by Joan Steffens and
Timothy J. O'Leary].   11853

Knez, Eugene I. A selected and annotated
bibliography of Korean anthropology. By Eugene I.
Knez and Chang-su Swanson.   01138

Koh, Hesung Chun. Social science resources on
Korea: a preliminary computerized bibliography.
                                                  11852

Koryŏ Taehakkyo. Asea Munje Yŏn'guso. Bibliography
of Korean studies: a bibliographical guide to
Korean publications on Korean studies appearing
from 1945 to 1958. [V.1].   00002

Koryŏ Taehakkyo. Asea Munje Yŏn'guso. Bibliography
of Korean studies: a bibliographical guide to
Korean publications on Korean studies appearing
from 1959 to 1962. [V.2].   00003

Kukhak Yŏn'gu Nonjŏ Ch'ongnam Kanhaenghoe. Kukhak
yŏn'gu nonjŏ ch'ongnam [A general survey of
articles and bcoks on Korean studies].   00010

Lew, Young Ick, comp. Korea on the eve of Japanese
annexation; a classified bibliography for the
study of the late Yi dynasty Korean history in
relation to the Japanese intrusion, 1904-1910.
                                                  10207

Okamoto, Yoshiji.   Japanese studies on Korean
history since World War II. In Monumenta Serica,
22, pt. 2 (1963): 470-532.   06766

Sakurai, Yoshiyuki, ed. Meiji nenkan Chōsen kenkyū
bunken shi [Annotated bibliography of Korean
studies in the Meiji era].   00062

Silberman, Bernard S. Japan and Korea: a critical
  bibliography.   00008

Sŏk, Chu-myŏng. Chejudo kwan'gye munhŏnjip [A
  list of literature on Cheju Island]. By D. M.
  Seok.   00001

Takahashi Tōru Sensei chosaku nempyō (Bibliography
  of Prof. Dr. Tōru Takahashi's writings]. In Chōsen
  gakuhō, 14 (Oct. 1959): 15-22 (1st section). 01134

U.S. Library of Congress. Reference Department.
  Korea: an annotated bibliography of publications
  in Far Eastern languages. Compiled under the
  direction of Edwin G. Beal, Jr., with the
  assistance of Robin L. Winkler.   00011

U.S. Library of Congress. Reference Department.
  Korea: an annotated bibliography of publications
  in Western languages. Compiled by Helen
  Dudenbostel Jones and Robin L. Winkler.   00025

Yang, Key Paik. Reference guide to Korean
  materials, 1945-1959.   00020

Yi, Ki-baek, 1924-. Han'guksa sillon [New
  discussion on Korean history].   11436

ARCHEOLOGY

Chōsen kankei kōkogaku bunken mokuroku
  [Bibliography cf Korean archeology]. In Kōkogaku,
  11 (1940).   01076

Council for Old World Archaeology. Korea: Far East-
  -Area 17. In COWA surveys and bibliographies, 1
  (1959): 7, 26-27; 2 (1961): 14, 43-45; 3 (1964):
  5-6, 25.   01077

Fujita Ryōsaku Sensei chosaku mokuroku [List of
  works of the late Professor Fujita Ryosaku]. In
  Chōsen gakuhō, 20 (1961): 151-178.   01133

Gerow, Bert A. Publications in Japanese on Korean
  anthropology: a bibliography of uncataloged
  materials in the Kanaseki Collection, Stanford
  University Library.   00007

Hara, Sanshichi, ed. Imanishi Hakushi shūshū
Chōsen kankei bunken mokuroku (Catalog of the
Korean materials collected by the late Prof. Dr.
R. Imanishi).   00065

Hewes, Gordon Winaut, 1918-. Archaeology of Korea:
a selected bibliography.   00287

Kim, Chong-uk, comp. Han'guksa kwan'gye yŏn'gu
nonmun mongnok [Bibliography of studies on
Korean history]. In Tongguk sahak, 7 (1963): 126-
168.   01084

Pak, Sŏng-bong, comp. Han'guksa yŏn'gu munhŏn
mongnok [Bibliography on the studies of Korean
history]. In Mulli hakch"ong (Kyŏnghŭi Taehakkyo),
1 (1961): 198-251.   01096

Yi, Hong-jik, 1909-. Han'guk ko-munhwa non'go
(Studies on the ancient culture of Korea). By
Hong-jik Lee.   11726

HISTORY

American Historical Association, comp. Guide to
historical literature. Board of Editors; George
Frederick Howe et al.   01037

Bunken mokuroku: chōsen [Bibliography of source
materials: Korea]. In Rekishigaku nenpō furoku.
                                                           01107

California. University. Institute of East Asiatic
Studies. Korean studies guide. Comp. by B.H.
Hazard, Jr. et al. Ed. by Richard Marcus.   00015

Ch'oe, Sun-ja, comp. Han'guk chapchi mongnok,
1896-1945 (Korean magazine index, 1896-1945). By
Soon Ja Choi.   00072

Chōsen kankei shigaku ronbun mokuroku [List of
magazines and literature on the history of Korea].
In Rekishigaku Kenkyūkai, ed. Chōsen-shi no
shomondai, Rekishigaku kenkyū tokushū-gō.   00063

Chōsen Sōtokufu Chōsenshi Henshū-kai. Chōsen
shiryō tenkan mokuroku [The exhibition lists on
Korean historical data].   11888

Chōsenshi Henshūkai, ed. Chōsen shiryō shūshin
oyobi kaisetsu [Collection of Korean historical
materials and interpretation].   11855

Courant, Maurice [Auguste Louis Marie], 1865-1939.
Bibliographie coréenne: tableau littéraire de la
Corée, contenant la nomenclature des ouvrages
publiés dans ce pays jusqu'en 1890 ainsi que la
description et l'analyse détaillées des principaux
d'entre ces ouvrages.   01032

Courant, Maurice [Auguste Louis Marie], 1865-1939.
Bibliographie coréenne. Supplement (jusqu'en
1899).   01033

Endō, Motoo, 1908-. Kokushi bunken kaisetsu
[Annotated bibliography on history]. [Edited by]
Endō Motoo [and] Shimomura Fujio.   01046

Fang, Chao-ying. The Asami Library: a descriptive
catalog. Ed. by Elizabeth Huff.   11898

Hara, Sanshichi, ed. Imanishi Hakushi shūshū
Chōsen kankei bunken mokuroku (Catalog of the
Korean materials collected by the late Prof. Dr.
R. Imanishi).   00065

Hayashi, Taisuke.   Chōsen no shiseki [Historical
works of Korea]. In Kokugakuin zasshi, 18, no. 5
(1909).   04117

Hayashi, Taisuke.   Chōsen shiseki-kō [Studies on
Korean historical books]. In Shigaku zasshi, 7,
no. 13 (1896).   04116

Henthorn, William E., comp. A guide to reference
and research materials on Korean history: an
annotated bibliography.   01128

Hōbun rekishi-gaku kankei shō-zasshi Tōyō-shi rombun
yomoku [Index of articles and monographs on
Oriental history appearing in Japanese serial
publications and special thesis collections].
                                          01131

Kim, Chong-uk, comp. Han'guksa kwan'gye yŏn'gu
nonmun mongnok [Bibliography of studies on
Korean history]. In Tongguk sahak, 7 (1963): 126-
168.   01084

Kim, G. F. Works of Soviet orientalists on the
history and economics of Korea. By G. F. Kim and
G. D. Tyagai. In Papers presented by the USSR
delegation, XXV International Congress of
Orientalists.   11917

Kim, Yong-dŏk, comp. Kuksa kwan'gye chŏsŏ nonmun
mongnok [Bibliography of books and articles on
Korean history]. In Yŏksa hakpo, 10 (1958): 329-
340.   01114

Korea (Government-General of Chōsen, 1910-1945), ed.
Chōsen Sōtokufu ko tosho mokuroku [General
catalog of old books in the Library of Government-
General of Korea].   00107

Korea (Government-General of Chōsen, 1910-1945).
Chōsen tosho kaidai [Annotated bibliography of
Korean books].   00022

Koryŏ Taehakkyo. Seoul, Korea. Asea Munje Yŏn'guso.
Han'guk kŭnsesa yŏn'gu charyo mongnok--Oegyosa rŭl
chungsimŭro (A list of selected books and
materials on modern and contemporary Korean
history: with special emphasis on those on
diplomatic history published in Korean).   01049

Koryŏ Taehakkyo. Seoul, Korea. Asea Munje Yŏn'guso.
A list of selected books and materials on modern
and contemporary Korean history with special
emphasis on those on diplomatic history
publication in Korea.   00379

Kuji, Hanjirō, comp. Chihō bunka no kiroku: Chōsen
no kyōdoshi chihō shishi [Records of local
culture: local history and geography of Korea]. In
Chōsen kōsei, 20, no.8 (1941).   01088

Maema, Kyōsaku, 1868-1942, ed. Kosen sappu
[Annotated bibliography of old Korean books].
                                                       00067

McCune, Shannon Boyd-Bailey. Bibliography of
Western language materials on Korea. Rev., enl.
ed.   00024

Naitō, Shunpo. Chōsenshi kenkyū (Studies in
history of Korea).   01059

Nakamura, Eikō. Chōsen-shi no henshū to Chōsen
shiryō no shūshū [The compilation of the History
of Korea and the collection of Korean historical
materials]. In Ko bunka no hozon to kenkyū. 06021

Oda, Shōgo. Chōsen shiseki kaidai kōgi [Lectures
on Korean historical sources]. In Seikyū gakusō,
23 (1936): 145-161.   01022

Ogiyama, Hideo. Chōsenshi kankei tosho kaidai
[Annotated bibliography of books on Korean
history]. In Chōsenshi kōza, 8 (1923).   01109

Okamoto, Yoshiji. Japanese studies on Korean
history since World War II. In Monumenta Serica,
22, pt. 2 (1963): 470-532.   06766

Ota, Akira, 1884-. Kan-kan shiseki ni arawaretaru
Nik-Kan kōdaishi shiryō [Korean-Japanese ancient
historical materials which were found in Chinese-
Korean history sources].   11858

Pak, Sŏng-bong. Han'guk kuksa yŏn'gu munhŏn
mongnok, 4 [List of literature on Korean
history]. In Mulli hakch'ong (Kyŏnghŭi Taehakkyo),
4.   04084

Pak, Sŏng-bong. Han'guksa yŏn'gu munhŏn mongnok:
Chŏnhu Ilbon hakkye [Catalog of research
materials on Korean history: postwar Japanese
learned circle]. In Sahak yŏn'gu, 3 (1959): 119-
132; 4 (1959): 143-156.   01097

Sakurai, Yoshiyuki, comp. Chōsen no kyōdoshi,
chihōshi [Chronicles of provinces and local
history of Korea]. In Nippon kosho tōshin, 84
(1937).   01119

Shidehara, Taira. Chōsen shi no sankō shomoku ni
tsuite [On the reference books of Korean
history]. In Tōa no hikari (Ex Oriente lux), 3,
no.11 (1908); 4, no.2 (1909).   01003

Shigakkai, ed. Shigaku bunken mokuroku, 1946-1950
[Catalog of historiographical literature, 1946-
1950].   01006

Shigaku kankei shuyō zasshi rombun mokuroku
[Bibliography of major journal articles on history

and related subjects]. In Shisen, 10 (1958). 01120

Sin, Sŏk-ho, 1904-. Han'guk saryo haesŏlchip
(Annotated bibliography on Korean history). 10582

Sŏ, Kŏ-jŏng, 1420-1488, ed. Tongguk Tʻonggam
[Complete mirror of the Eastern Country]. 00091

Stucki, Curtis W. American doctoral dissertations
on Asia, 1933-1962, including master's theses at
Cornell University. 00023

Takahashi Tōru Sensei chosaku nempyō (Bibliography
of Prof. Dr. Tōru Takahashi's writings]. In Chōsen
gakuhō, 14 (Oct. 1959): 15-22 (1st section). 01134

U.S. Library of Congress. Reference Department.
Korea: an annotated bibliography of publications
in Far Eastern languages. Compiled under the
direction of Edwin G. Beal, Jr., with the
assistance of Robin L. Winkler. 00011

U.S. Library of Congress. Reference Department.
Korea: an annotated bibliography of publications
in the Russian language. Compiled by Albert Parry,
John T. Dorosh, and Elizabeth Gardner Dorosh. 00012

U.S. Library of Congress. Reference Department.
Korea: an annotated bibliography of publications
in Western languages. Compiled by Helen
Dudenbostel Jones and Robin L. Winkler. 00025

Wada, Kiyoshi. Chōsen shiryō [Korean historical
materials]. In Bunbutsu sansei shiryō, 11 (1950).
04123

Yi, Ki-baek, 1924-. Han'guksa sillon [New
discussion on Korean history]. 11436

PHYSICAL SETTING

Cammaerts, Emile, comp. La Corée: bibliographie. In
Bulletin de la Societé Royal Belge de Géographie,
Brussels, 28 (1904): 80-81. 01110

General index to the first twenty volumes of the
Geographical Journal: 1893-1902. 11939

General index to the second twenty volumes of the
Geographical Journal 1903-1912.   11940

Ikeuchi, Hiroshi. Chōsen kanhoku no yon chishi
[Four geographical records of the northern part of
Korea]. In Chōsen gakuhō, 1 (1951): 239-244. 00390

Keijō Teikoku Daigaku. Fuzoku Toshokan, ed. Chōsen
kochizu tenkan mokuroku [Exhibition catalog of
old maps of Korea].   00182

Kim, Yang-sŏn. Han'guk ko-jido yŏn'gu [A study of
old Korean maps]. In Sungdae, 10 (1965).   04083

Korea (Government-General of Chōsen, 1910-1945)
Rinji Tochi Chōsakyoku. Chōsen chishi shiryō
[Materials on Korean geography].   01042

Kuji, Hanjirō, comp. Chihō bunka no kiroku: Chōsen
no kyōdoshi chihō shishi [Records of local
culture: local history and geography of Korea]. In
Chōsen kōsei, 20, no.8 (1941).   01088

Lautensach, Hermann, comp. Korea (1926-1936) mit
Nachträgen aus älterer Zeit [Korea (1926-1936)
with addenda from earlier times]. In
Geographisches Jahrbuch, 53, no.1 (1938): 255-274.
                                                   01089

McCune, Shannon Boyd-Bailey, 1913-. Climate of
Korea: a selected bibliography. March 1, 1941.
                                                   00124

McCune, Shannon Boyd-Bailey. Geographic
publications of Hermann Lautensach on Korea. In
Far Eastern quarterly, 5 (1946): 330-332.   01090

McCune, Shannon Boyd-Bailey. Geomorphology of
Korea: a selected bibliography. November 1, 1941.
                                                   00123

McCune, Shannon Boyd-Bailey, comp. Old Korean
geographical works: a bibliography.   01117

Miura, Hirayuki.   Chōsen saikō no chiri-sho ni
tsuite [Korean geographical books]. In Chōsen
kenkyū shiryō, 59 (1935).   04136

Nagoshi, Nakajirō.   Chōsen chishi shiryō ni tsuite

[As to source materials on Korean geography]. In
Rekishi to chiri, 4 (1920).   01093

Toyota, Shirō.   Chōsen no chizu ni tsuite
[Concerning maps of Korea]. In Chōsen kenkyū
shiryō (1935).   01125

Yi, Kyŏm-no.   Chosŏn kojido mongnok   [A list of old
Korean maps]. In Kukhoe Tosŏgwanbo, 3, no. 6-8
(July-Sept. 1966).   04098

POPULATION

Sakurai, Yoshiyuki,   comp.   Chōsen jinkō rōdō kankei
bunken shiryo   [Source materials on Korean
population and labor problems]. In Chōsen rōdō, 3,
no.1 (1943).   01100

LANGUAGE

Kameda, Jirō.   Meiji jidai Nis-Sen ryogo hikaku ron
rombun hyo   [List of comparative treatises on
Japanese and Korean linguistics that appeared
during the Meiji period]. In Seikyū gakusō, 6
(1931): 148-156.   01135

Kim, Kŭn-su.   Kugŏ kungmunhak kosŏ chimnok
[Bibliography on old literature of Korean language
and literature].   01053

Kukhak Yŏn'gu Nonjŏ Ch'ongnam Kanhaenghoe.   Kukhak
yŏn'gu nonjŏ ch'ongnam   [A general survey of
articles and books on Korean studies].   00010

Lee, Soon Hi, 1926-.   Korea: a selected bibliography
in Western languages, 1950-1958.   00050

Ogura, Shimpei.   U-beijin no Chōsengo kenkyū no
shiryō to natta wakanjo   [Japanese and Chinese
materials used by Western scholars for the study
of Korean language]. In Minzoku, 3, no. 1 (1927):
75-86.   01019

Sakurai, Yoshiyuki.   Hōseko Shigekatsu no Chōsen
gogaku sho ni tsuite, fu Chōsen gogaku shomoku
[The writings of Shigekatsu Hōseko on Korean

language; with an appendix, bibliography of Korean
language studies]. In Chōsen gakuhō, 9 (1956):
455-466.   01005

Yu, T'aeg-il, comp.   Yŏngnam munhŏnnog (Kyŏngnam-
p'yŏn) [Bibliography of source materials on
Kyŏngnam Province]. In Kugŏ kungmunhak, 28 (1965):
127-202.   01104

RELIGION AND PHILOSOPHY

Ch'oe, Sun-ja, comp. Han'guk chapchi mongnok,
1896-1945 (Korean magazine index, 1896-1945). By
Soon Ja Choi.   00072

Chōsen kankei shigaku ronbun mokuroku [List of
magazines and literature on the history of Korea].
In Rekishigaku Kenkyūkai, ed. Chōsen-shi no
shomondai, Rekishigaku kenkyū tokushū-gō.   00063

Courant, Maurice [Auguste Louis Marie], 1865-1939.
Bibliographie coréenne: tableau littéraire de la
Corée, contenant la nomenclature des ouvrages
publiés dans ce pays jusqu'en 1890 ainsi que la
description et l'analyse détaillées des principaux
d'entre ces ouvrages.   01032

Courant, Maurice [Auguste Louis Marie], 1865-1939.
Bibliographie coréenne. Supplement (jusqu'en
1899).   01033

Fujii, Sōju.   Chōsen Bukkyō tenseki tenran mokuroku
[Exhibition catalog of the Korean Buddhist
scriptures]. In Zenshu, 41, no. 7 (1934): 24.
                                                      01014

Gompertz, E.   Supplement to 'A partial bibliography
of occidental literature on Korea' by H. H.
Underwood, 1931. By E. Gompertz and G. Gompertz.
In Transactions of the Korea Branch of the Royal
Asiatic Society, 24 (1935): 21-48.   00118

Hanayama, Shinshō, comp. Bibliography on Buddhism.
                                                      01048

Imanishi, Ryū, comp. Chōsen Bukkyō kankei shoseki
kaidai [An annotated bibliography of Korean
Buddhism]. In Bukkyō shigaku, 1, no.1 (1911): 31-

39; 1, no.2 (1911): 121-125; 1, no.3 (1911): 197-202. 01083

Keijo Tenshu-kokyokai, ed. Chōsen Tenshukyō shiryō tenran mokuroku [Catalog of books and documents on the history of Catholicism in Korea]. 01015

Kim, Wŏn-yong, comp. Yugan''gi pulsŏ mongnok ch''ogo (First list of dated early Korean Buddhistic books). In Sōji, 2, no.1 (Oct. 1961): 15-43. 01085

Korea (Government-General of Chōsen, 1910-1945), ed. Chōsen Sōtokufu ko tosho mokuroku [General catalog of old books in the Library of Government-General of Korea]. 00107

Korea (Government-General of Chōsen, 1910-1945). Chōsen tosho kaidai [Annotated bibliography of Korean books]. 00022

Kuroda, Ryō, 1890-. Chōsen kyūsho kō [Studies of old Korean books]. 00165

Kusuda, Onosaburō. Chōsen Tenshukyō shi ni kansuru omonaru sankō shoseki oyobi rombun [Leading reference books and theses on Korean Catholic church history]. 11856

Kusuda, Onosaburō. Chōsen Tenshukyō shi ni kansuru omonaru sankō chosho oyobi rombun [Leading reference books and theses on Korean Catholic church history]. 11857

March, Arthur Charles, 1880-. A Buddhist bibliography. 01116

Nihon Minzokugaku Kyokai, ed. Minzokugaku kankei zasshi ronbun sōmokuroku, 1925-1959 [Bibliography of Japanese articles in ethnology, 1925-1959]. 11447

Seo, Kyung-bo. A study of Korean Zen Buddhism approached through the Chodangjip. 11860

Streit, P. Robert, 1875-1930. Bibliotheca missionum. [Continued by] P. Johannes Dindinger. 01064

Tokio, Shunjo, comp. Chōsen kosho mokuroku [A classified catalog of old Korean books]. 11440

Tŏksindang sŏmok [Catalog of Tŏksindang books].
00095

Tongguk Taehakkyo. Seoul, Korea. Koryŏ pulsŏ
chŏn'gwan mongnok [Exhibition catalog of Buddhist
literature of Koryŏ dynasty]. 01066

Tongguk Taehakkyo. Seoul, Korea. Koryŏ sagyŏng
chŏn'gŭn mongnok [Exhibition catalog of Koryŏ
Buddhist scriptures in manuscript]. 01067

Tongguk Taehakkyo. Seoul, Korea. Yijo chŏn'gi
kugyŏk pulsŏ chŏn'gwan mongnok [Exhibition
catalog of Buddhist scriptures translated into
Korean during the first half of Yi dynasty]. 01068

Tongguk Taehakkyo. Seoul, Korea. Pulgyo Munhwa
Yŏn'guso. Yijo chŏn'gi pulsŏ chŏn'gwan mongnok
[Exhibition catalog of Buddhist literature
published during the first half of Yi dynasty].
01069

Underwood, Horace H. A partial bibliography of
occidental literature on Korea from early times to
1930. In Transactions of the Korea Branch of the
Royal Asiatic Society, 20 (1931): 17-185 and 1-17.
00120

Yoshino, Sakuzō. Tendōkyō kenkyū shiryō [Source
materials for the study of Ch'ŏndo kyo]. In Kokka
Gakkai zasshi, 33, no.5, 7-10 (1919): 34, no. 1
(1920). 00194

LAW

Asō, Takekame. Richō no hōten [Yijo code]. In
Chōsen, 145 (1927): 81-86. 04127

Ch'oe, Sun-ja, comp. Han'guk chapchi mongnok,
1896-1945 (Korean magazine index, 1896-1945). By
Soon Ja Choi. 00072

Pak, Tong-sŏ. Bibliography of Korean public
administration, September 1945-April 1966. By
Dong-suh Bark and Jai-poong Yoon. 10206

Pak, Tong-sŏ. Han'guk haengjŏng munhŏnjip, 1945-

1966 (Bibliography of Korean public
administration, 1945-1966). [Ed. by] Bark Dong-suh
and Yoon Jai-poong.   11451

Suematsu, Yasukazu.   Sambōshū henkan ko [A
critical study of the publication of the Sambong-
jip]. In Chōsen gakuhō, 1 (1951): 55-68.   00393

Tokio, Shunjo, comp.   Chōsen kosho mokuroku [A
classified catalog of old Korean books].   11440

INTERNATIONAL AND INTERCULTURAL RELATIONS

GENERAL

Blanchard, Carroll Henry, Jr.   Korean War
bibliography and maps of Korea.   11573

Chŏn, Hae-jong.   Han'guk kŭnse taeoe kwan'gye
munhŏn piyo (Manual of Korean foreign relations,
1876-1910). By Chun Hae-jong.   10204

Courant, Maurice [Auguste Louis Marie], 1865-1939.
Bibliographie coréenne: tableau littéraire de la
Corée, contenant la nomenclature des ouvrages
publiés dans ce pays jusqu'en 1890 ainsi que la
description et l'analyse détaillées des principaux
d'entre ces ouvrages.   01032

Courant, Maurice [Auguste Louis Marie], 1865-1939.
Bibliographie coréenne. Supplement (jusqu'en
1899).   01033

Han'guk Yŏn'guwŏn.   Han'guk Sŏk Paksa hagwi nonmun
mongnok 1945-1960 (List of master's and doctor's
degrees offered in Korea, 1945-1960).   00087

Hokusen Manshū Karafuto oyobi Chishima ni okeru
hōjin no hogo oyobi hikiage ni kansuru kōshō
kankei bunken   [Source materials on Japan's
negotiations for the protection and repatriation
of its residents in North Korea, Manchuria and
Sakhalin].   01050

Kerner, Robert Joseph. Northeastern Asia, a
selected bibliography; contributions to the
bibliography of the relations of China, Russia,
and Japan, with special reference to Korea,

Manchuria, Mongolia, and eastern Siberia, in
Oriental and European languages.   00108

Lee, Soon Hi, 1926- . Korea: a selected bibliography
in Western languages, 1950-1958.   00050

McCune, Shannon Boyd-Bailey. Bibliography of
Western language materials on Korea. Rev., enl.
ed.   00024

Okamoto, Yoshiji. Japanese studies on Korean
history since World War II. In Monumenta Serica,
22, pt. 2 (1963): 470-532.   06766

Shulman, Frank J. Japan and Korea: an annotated
bibliography of doctoral dissertations in Western
languages, 1877-1969.   11976

Silberman, Bernard S. Japan and Korea: a critical
bibliography.   00008

Stucki, Curtis W. American doctoral dissertations
on Asia, 1933-1962, including master's theses at
Cornell University.   00023

Yi, Ki-baek, 1924- . Han'guksa sillon [New
discussion on Korean history].   11436

Yi, Yong-hŭi, 1917-, ed. Kŭnse Han'guk oegyo munsŏ
ch°ongmok oegukp°yŏn (Catalog of foreign
diplomatic documents relating to Korea, 1845-
1910). Ed. by Lee Yong-Hee.   11292

RELATIONS WITH SPECIFIC NATIONS

Korea-China

Honda, Minoru. A survey of Japanese contributions
to Manchurian studies. By Honda Minoru and E. B.
Ceadel, comps. In Asia minor, n.s., 5, no.1
(1955): 59-105.   01081

Ito, Hirobumi. Chōsen kosho shiryō [Old source
materials related to negotiations with Korea].
                                          00054

Allied Forces. Southwest Pacific Area. Annotated
bibliography of the Southwest Pacific and adjacent
areas. 00155

Endō, Motoo, 1908-. Kokushi bunken kaisetsu
[Annotated bibliography on history]. [Edited by]
Endō Motoo [and] Shimomura Fujio. 01046

Ito, Hirobumi. Chōsen kosho shiryō [Old source
materials related to negotiations with Korea].
00054

Koryŏ Taehakkyo. Seoul, Korea. Asea Munje Yŏn'guso.
Han'guk kŭnsesa yŏn'gu charyo mongnok--Oegyosa rŭl
chungsimŭro (A list of selected books and
materials on modern and contemporary Korean
history: with special emphasis on those on
diplomatic history published in Korean). 01049

Kukhoe Tosŏgwan. Chosŏn ch°ongdokpu Kŭp sosok
kwansŏ palgan tosŏ mongnok [A list of books
published by the Governemt-General of Chōsen and
its related offices]. In Kukhoe Tosŏgwanbo, 4, no.
2 (Feb. 1967); 5, no. 1 (1968). 04100

Lew, Young Ick, comp. Korea on the eve of Japanese
annexation; a classified bibliography for the
study of the late Yi dynasty Korean history in
relation to the Japanese intrusion, 1904-1910.
10207

Morita, Tauson. Dokutoru Rīsu no Chōsen ni kansuru
Ōshu kinkan shomokuroku [Recently published
Western books cn Korea]. In Gakuto, 7 (1911): 1-8.
01140

Morita, Yoshio. Nipponjin no Chōsen hikiage ni
kansuru bunken shiryō (Bibliography concerning
the Japanese repatriation from Korea). In Chōsen
gakuhō, 13 (Oct. 1958): 221-258. 01023

Nahm, Andrew C., comp. Japanese penetration of
Korea, 1894-1910: a checklist of Japanese archives
in the Hoover Institution. Compiled by Andrew C.
Nahm under the direction of Peter A. Berton. 00128

Naitō, Shunpo. Chōsenshi kenkyū (Studies in
history of Korea). 01059

U.S. Library of Congress. General Reference and
Bibliography Division. Biographical sources for
foreign countries. IV. The Japanese Empire. Comp.
by Nelson R. Burr.   00133

Uyehara, Cecil H., comp. Checklist of archives in
the Japanese Ministry of Foreign Affairs, Tōkyō
Japan, 1868-1945. Compiled by Cecil H. Uyehara,
under the direction of Edwin G. Beal, Jr.   00134

Young, John, comp. Checklist of microfilm
reproductions of selected archives of the Japanese
Army, Navy and other government agencies, 1868-
1945.   00116

Korea-Manchuria

Honda, Minoru. A survey of Japanese contributions
to Manchurian studies. By Honda Minoru and E. B.
Ceadel, comps. In Asia minor, n.s., 5, no.1
(1955): 59-105.   01081

Korea-Russia/U.S.S.R.

Uyehara, Cecil H., comp. Checklist of archives in
the Japanese Ministry of Foreign Affairs, Tōkyō
Japan, 1868-1945. Compiled by Cecil H. Uyehara,
under the direction of Edwin G. Beal, Jr.   00134

Korea-U.S.A.

O'Quinlivan, Michael. An annotated bibliography of
the United States Marines in the Korean war. 00115

U.S. Dept. of State. Division of Publications.
Korea, published material, July 2, 1944 to July 3,
1950.   00143

KOREAN WAR

Blanchard, Carroll Henry, Jr. Korean War
bibliography and maps of Korea.   11573

Chōsen kankei shigaku ronbun mokuroku [List of

magazines and literature on the history of Korea].
In Rekishigaku Kenkyūkai, ed. Chōsen-shi no
shomondai, Rekishigaku kenkyū tokushū-gō. 00063

Great Britain. Imperial War Museum. Library. The
war in Korea, 1950-1953: a list of selected
references.   11795

Han'guk pan'gong yŏnmaeng. Yugio kwan'gye munhŏn
kaeryak [Summaries of literature related to the
Korean War]. In Chayu kongnon 1, no.3 (June).
                                               04082

Koryŏ Taehakkyo. Seoul, Korea. Asea Munje Yŏn'guso.
Han'guk kŭnsesa yŏn'gu charyo mongnok--Oegyosa rŭl
chungsimŭro   (A list of selected books and
materials on modern and contemporary Korean
history: with special emphasis on those on
diplomatic history published in Korean).   01049

Lee, Chong-sik. Korea and the Korean War. In Thomas
T. Hammond, ed. Soviet foreign relations and world
communism: a selected, annotated bibliography.
                                               11761

O'Quinlivan, Michael. An annotated bibliography of
the United States Marines in the Korean war. 00115

So, Chin-chŏl.   Tongnansa kwan'gye charyo haeje.
[Annotated materials related to the Korean War].
In Kongsanjuŭi munje yon'gu, 3 (Nov.).   04085

POLITY

Chungang Inmin Wiwŏnhoe chemunhŏn   [Documents of
the Central People's Committee].   01043

Haengjŏnghak sŏksa hagwi nomun chemok [A list of
the theses in administrative science for the M.A.
degree].   11904

Kongsanjuŭi munje yŏn'gu munhŏn mongnok
[Bibliography of studies on Communism]. In
Kongsanjuŭi munje yŏn'gu, 1, no.1 (1964): 253-255.
                                               01086

Koryŏ Taehakkyo. Seoul, Korea. Asea Munje Yŏn'guso.
Han'guk kŭnsesa yŏn'gu charyo mongnok--Oegyosa rŭl

chungsimŭro   (A list of selected books and
materials on modern and contemporary Korean
history: with special emphasis on those on
diplomatic history published in Korean).   01049

Kukhoe Tosŏgwan.   Chŏngch°i kwan'gye munhŏn mongnok
[A list of books related to political science]. In
Kukhoe Tosŏgwanbo, 4 (1967).   04111

Lee, Soon Hi, 1926-.   Korea: a selected bibliography
in Western languages, 1950-1958.   00050

Moscow. Gosudarstvennaia biblioteka SSSR. im. V. I.
Lenina.   Za edinuiu nezavisi muiu
demokraticheskuiu Koreiu. Kratkiĭ rekomendatel'nyĭ
ukazatel' literatury. [By] N. I. Glagolevskiĭ
[and] L. P. Chernysheva. [Edited by] S. V.
Kazakov.   11978

Nahm, Andrew C., comp.   Japanese penetration of
Korea, 1894-1910: a checklist of Japanese archives
in the Hoover Institution. Compiled by Andrew C.
Nahm under the direction of Peter A. Berton.   00128

Okamoto, Yoshiji.   Japanese studies on Korean
history since World War II. In Monumenta Serica,
22, pt. 2 (1963): 470-532.   06766

Pak, Tong-sŏ.   Bibliography of Korean public
administration, September 1945-April 1966. By
Dong-suh Bark and Jai-poong Yoon.   10206

Pak, Tong-sŏ.   Han'guk haengjŏng munhŏnjip, 1945-
1966   (Bibliography of Korean public
administration, 1945-1966). [Ed. by] Bark Dong-suh
and Yoon Jai-poong.   11451

A selected bibliography of materials on Korean
public administration. In Koh, Byung Chul, ed.
Aspects of administrative development in South
Korea.   07057

Silberman, Bernard S.   Japan and Korea: a critical
bibliography.   00008

Stucki, Curtis W.   American doctoral dissertations
on Asia, 1933-1962, including master's theses at
Cornell University.   00023

Tewksbury, Donald G., comp. and ed.   Source

materials on Korean politics and ideologies. 11832

Tokio, Shunjo, comp. Chōsen kosho mokuroku [A classified catalog of old Korean books]. 11440

U.S. Dept. of State. Division of Publications. Korea, published material, July 2, 1944 to July 3, 1950. 00143

U.S. Library of Congress. Reference Department. Korea: an annotated bibliography of publications in Far Eastern languages. Compiled under the direction of Edwin G. Beal, Jr., with the assistance of Robin L. Winkler. 00011

U.S. Library of Congress. Reference Department. Korea: an annotated bibliography of publications in Western languages. Compiled by Helen Dudenbostel Jones and Robin L. Winkler. 00025

Uyehara, Cecil H., comp. Checklist of archives in the Japanese Ministry of Foreign Affairs, Tōkyō Japan, 1868-1945. Compiled by Cecil H. Uyehara, under the direction of Edwin G. Beal, Jr. 00134

Yang, Key P. Source materials on Korean political developments. In C. I. Eugene Kim, ed. A pattern of political development: Korea. 01126

Yi, Ki-baek, 1924-. Han'guksa sillon [New discussion on Korean history]. 11436

Yi, Mun-yŏng, comp. Han'guk kyŏngje haengjŏng yŏn'gu rŭl wihan charyo ko (Bibliography on public administration for the Korean economy). In Pŏmnyul haengjŏng nonjip, 5 (1963): 225-289. 01127

Yūhō Kyōkai. Chōsen Shiryō Kenkyūkai. Chōsen kankei bunken shiryō sōmokuroku [Catalog of reference materials pertaining to Korea]. [Ed. by] Kondō Ken'ichi. 01026

MILITARY

Bibliographical note: Korean books on tactics. In Asiatic research bulletin, 8, no. 7 (Oct. 1965): 20-25; 8, no. 8 (Nov. 1966): 15-21. 04066

ECONOMY

Chōsen hokuhanbu no nōgyō mondai ni kansuru bunken mokuroku [Bibliography on agricultural problems of North Korea]. In Chōsen kenkyū geppō, 21 (1963): 39-43.　　　　　　　　　　　00186

Chōsen Keizai Kenkyūjo.　Chōsen tōkei sōran　[An annotated bibliography of statistics and statistical works concerning Korea]. [By] Shikata Hiroshi, et al.　　　　　　　　　　　11572

Han, U-gŭn, 1915-.　Han'guk kyŏngje kwan'gye munhŏn chipsŏng (Annotated bibliography of Korean economic history, 1570-1910). By Han Woo-keun.
　　　　　　　　　　　10205

Han'guk chiryu munhŏn illam 1905-1938 (Bibliography cf Korean paper, 1905-1938). In Sŏji, 2, no.1 (Oct. 1961): 48-50.　　04075

Kim, G. F.　Works of Soviet orientalists on the history and economics of Korea. By G. F. Kim and G. D. Tyagai. In Papers presented by the USSR delegation, XXV International Congress of Orientalists.　　　　　　　　　　　11917

Lee, Soon Hi, 1926-.　Korea: a selected bibliography in Western languages, 1950-1958.　　00050

Nahm, Andrew C., comp.　Japanese penetration of Korea, 1894-1910: a checklist of Japanese archives in the Hoover Institution. Compiled by Andrew C. Nahm under the direction of Peter A. Berton. 00128

Nishiyoshi, Reinsensai.　Kankoku heisei kankei bunken rokushu　[Six kinds of literature on Korean monetary system]. In Kahei, 224 (1937).
　　　　　　　　　　　04132

Okamoto, Yoshiji.　Japanese studies on Korean history since World War II. In Monumenta Serica, 22, pt. 2 (1963): 470-532.　　　　06766

Sakurai, Yoshiyuki, comp.　Chōsen jinkō rōdō kankei bunken shiryo　[Source materials on Korean population and labor problems]. In Chōsen rōdō, 3, no.1 (1943).　　　　　　　　　　　01100

Schroeder, Peter Brett. Korean publications in the
National Agricultural Library. 00129

Silberman, Bernard S. Japan and Korea: a critical
bibliography. 00008

Stucki, Curtis W. American doctoral dissertations
on Asia, 1933-1962, including master's theses at
Cornell University. 00023

Surveys and Research Corporation. Washington, D.C.
An interim report to the government of the
Republic of Korea. [By James S. Fitzgerald].
[Korean translation by Lee Jay Cho]. 00144

U.S. Dept. of State. Division of Publications.
Korea, published material, July 2, 1944 to July 3,
1950. 00143

U.S. Library of Congress. Division of Bibliography.
The Japanese empire: industries and
transportation, a selected list of references.
Compiled by Florence S. Hellman, chief
bibliographer. 00138

U.S. Library of Congress. Reference Department.
Korea: an annotated bibliography of publications
in Far Eastern languages. Compiled under the
direction of Edwin G. Beal, Jr., with the
assistance of Robin L. Winkler. 00011

U.S. Library of Congress. Reference Department.
Korea: an annotated bibliography of publications
in the Russian language. Compiled by Albert Parry,
John T. Dorosh, and Elizabeth Gardner Dorosh.
00012

U.S. Library of Congress. Reference Department.
Korea: an annotated bibliography of publications
in Western languages. Compiled by Helen
Dudenbostel Jones and Robin L. Winkler. 00025

Yi, Ki-baek, 1924-. Han'guksa sillon [New
discussion on Korean history]. 11436

Yi, Mun-yŏng, ccmp. Han'guk kyŏngje haengjŏng
yŏn'gu rŭl wihan charyo ko (Bibliography on
public administration for the Korean economy). In
Pŏmnyul haengjŏng nonjip, 5 (1963): 225-289. 01127

Yŏnse Taehakkyo. Sanggyŏng Taehak. Sanŏp Kyŏngyŏng
Yŏn'guso. Sanŏp kyŏngje munhŏn mongnok (1945-
1960) (The bibliography in business and
economics, 1945-1960). By Industrial Research
Center, College of Business Administration, Yonsei
University.   00070

Yoo, Young Hyun. A selected bibliography of
materials on Korean economy. In Joseph Sang-hoon
Chung, ed. Korea: patterns of economic
development.   11446

EDUCATION

Courant, Maurice [Auguste Louis Marie], 1865-1939.
Bibliographie coréenne: tableau littéraire de la
Corée, contenant la nomenclature des ouvrages
publiés dans ce pays jusqu'en 1890 ainsi que la
description et l'analyse détaillées des principaux
d'entre ces ouvrages.   01032

Courant, Maurice [Auguste Louis Marie], 1865-1939.
Bibliographie coréenne. Supplement (jusqu'en
1899).   01033

Eells, Walter Crosby, comp. The literature of
Japanese education, 1945-1954.   11443

Korea (Republic) Mun'gyobu. Kŏm injŏng kyokwayong
illamp°yo [A catalog of authorized textbooks].
                                                        10223

Kyoyuk charyo mongnok [Bibliography of educational
materials].   01057

Sekino, Shinkichi. Chōsen kindai toshokan shiryo
[Sources on modern Korean library history]. In
Shomotsu Dōkōkai kaihō, 18 (1943): 14.   04135

Stucki, Curtis W. American doctoral dissertations
on Asia, 1933-1962, including master's theses at
Cornell University.   00023

Yi, Pyŏng-mok. Han'guk ŭi taehak chŏnggi
kanhaengmul pu-kodŭng kyoyuk kigwan myonggam
[Bibliography of University periodicals of Korea,
1945-1964, with directory of institutions of
higher education].   11885

FAMILY AND KINSHIP

Ch'oe, Chae-sŏk. Han'guk kajok kwan'ge munhŏn
mongnok 1900-1965 [Bibliography on Korean family
relations 1900-1965]. In Han'guk kajok yŏn'gu.
07055

WELFARE

Chōsen iyaku shiryō [Source materials on Korean
medicine]. In Chōsen, 143 (1927): 8-18.   01073

Miki, Sakae   Chōsen iseki ko [A study of old
medical books cf Korea].   01020

Miki, Sakae.   Chōsen isho shi [Bibliography of
Korean books on medicine].   01024

Miki, Sakae.   Yōan-in zoshochū no Chōsen isho
[Korean medical books in the Yōan-in Collection].
In Chōsen gakuhō, 1 (1951): 263-270.   01016

Miki, Sakae, comp.   Chōsen igakushi oyobi
shippeishi no kankō ni tsuite [Publications on
the history of Korean medicine and diseases]. In
Chōsen gakuhō, 10 (1956).   01141

ARTISTIC AND INTELLECTUAL EXPRESSION

VISUAL ARTS

California. University. Institute of East Asiatic
Studies. Korean studies guide. Comp. by B.H.
Hazard, Jr. et al. Ed. by Richard Marcus.

Korea (Republic) Kongbobu. Kongboguk.   Chŏnggi
kanhaengmul, sahoe tanch'e, yŏnghwaŏpchi mit
kongyŏnja illamp'yo [Lists of Korean
periodicals, associations, institutions, moving
picture business firms, and theaters].   00346

Korea (Republic) Mun'gyobu.   Chijŏng munhwajae
mongnok [List of cultural properties designated
by the government].   01054

Koyama, Fujio, comp. Chōsen tōji bunken mokuroku
[Bibliography cf source materials on Korean
pottery]. In Tōki kōza, 13 (1936): 1-24.   01115

Oda, Shōgo.   Chōsen tōjiki ni kansuru jakkan no
bunken ni tsuite [On the books and materials on
Korean ceramics]. In Seikyū gakusō, 3 (1931): 98-
112; 4 (1931): 110-114.   01017

Oda, Shōgo, 1871-, comp. Chōsen tōjishi bunken kō
[Bibliography cn the history of Korean pottery].
                                                   01060

Yi, Hong-jik, 1909-. Han'guk ko-munhwa non'go
(Studies on the ancient culture of Korea). By
Hong-jik Lee.   11726

Yi, Wŏn-sik, comp. Tosŏl kotosŏ kosŏhwa haeje
[Annotated bibliography of old books and paintings
with illustrations].   01072

PERFORMING ARTS

Bibliography of Asiatic musics; tenth installment.
V. Central East Asia: A. General, B. Japan, C.
Korea. Compiled by Richard A. Waterman, William
Lichtenwanger, Virginia Hitchcock Hermann, Horace
I. Poleman, and Cecil Hobbs. In Music Library
Association notes, 2d ser., 7, no.2 (1950): 265-
279.   01105

California. University. Institute of East Asiatic
Studies. Korean studies guide. Comp. by B.H.
Hazard, Jr. et al. Ed. by Richard Marcus.   00015

RECREATION

An, Ch'un-gŭn.   Han'guk pakpo (changgi) sŏjigo
[Bibliography cn Korean chess-changgi]. In Tosŏ,
11.   04086

LITERATURE

Asami, Rintarō.   Chōsen no geibun-shi [Korean art
and literature].   11859

Chang, Ki-gŭn. Han'guk munjip ŭi haeje [Annotated bibliography of Korean anthology]. In Asea hakpo, 3 (May). 04092

Chŏng, In-bo. Tamwŏn kukhak san'go [Tamwŏn's essays in Koreanology]. 10334

Courant, Maurice [Auguste Louis Marie], 1865-1939. Bibliographie coréenne: tableau littéraire de la Corée, contenant la nomenclature des ouvrages publiés dans ce pays jusqu'en 1890 ainsi que la description et l'analyse détaillées des principaux d'entre ces ouvrages. 01032

Courant, Maurice [Auguste Louis Marie], 1865-1939. Bibliographie coréenne. Supplement (jusqu'en 1899). 01033

Kim, Kŭn-su. Kugŏ kungmunhak kosŏ chimnok [Bibliography on old literature of Korean language and literature]. 01053

Kim, Kŭn-su, comp. Han'guk hyŏndaeshi ch"ongnam [Bibliography of modern poetry of Korea]. 01052

Korea (Government-General of Chōsen, 1910-1945), ed. Chōsen Sōtokufu ko tosho mokuroku [General catalog of old books in the Library of Government-General of Korea]. 00107

Kukhak Yŏn'gu Nonjŏ Ch"ongnam Kanhaenghoe. Kukhak yŏn'gu nonjŏ ch"ongnam [A general survey of articles and books on Korean studies]. 00010

Kungnip Chungang Tosŏgwan. P"yŏngyang, Korea. Sŏjihak pu. Chosŏn sŏjihak kaegwan [Introduction to Korean bibliography]. 00058

Lee, Soon Hi, 1926-. Korea: a selected bibliography in Western languages, 1950-1958. 00050

Maema, Kyōsaku, 1868-1942, ed. Kosen sappu [Annotated bibliography of old Korean books]. 00067

Omura, Masuo. Chūgoku yaku Chōsen bungaku sakuhin no mokuroku [A list of Korean literary works translated into Chinese]. In Chōsen kenkyū geppō, 23 (1963): 60-65. 00185

Sŏul Taehakkyo. Pusok Tosŏgwan   Kyujanggak tosŏ
mongnok--Han'guk   [Catalog of the Kyujanggak
collection of Korean books].   00076

Sŏul Taehakkyo. Pusok Tosŏgwan.   Sŏul Taehakkyo
kaegyo sipchunyŏn Kinyŏm Ko Tosŏ Chŏnsihoe
ch°ulp°um tosŏ haesŏl Tan'gi 4289 nyŏn 10 wŏl 13-
17-il   (An annotated list of rare books
exhibited in commemoration of 10th anniversary of
Seoul National University, Oct. 13-17, 1956).
                                                    00069

Sŏul Taehakkyo. Tosŏgwan.   Koryŏ munjip mongnok   (A
catalog of literary works in the Goryeo [Koryŏ]
dynasty). In Sŏul Taehakkyo Tosŏgwanbo, 4 (1966):
77-87.   01121

Tada, Masatomo,   comp.   Chōsen bungaku oboegaki   [A
note on Korean literature]. In Chōsen no toshokan,
4 (1932): 1-9.   01101

Tokio, Shunjo,   comp.   Chōsen kosho mokuroku   [A
classified catalog of old Korean books].   11440

Watanabe, Akira.   Shiragi jidai no bungei shiryŏ
[Data on Silla period literature]. In Chōsen ihō,
(Nov. 1919).   04124

Yi, Chae-uk.   Chōsen no shōsetsu   [Korean fiction].
In Bunken hōkoku, 5, no.5 (1939): 26.   04125

Yi, Pyŏng-gi.   Chosŏn munhak myŏngjŏ haeje
[Annotations on the masterpieces in Korean
literature]. In Munjang, 2, no.8 (1940): 215-231.
                                                    01103

Yi, Sŏng-ŭi,   ed.   Na-Ryŏ yemunji--Silla, Paekche,
Koguryŏ   [A bibliography of literature and arts of
the Three Kingdoms and Koryŏ]. [Ed. by] Yi Sŏng-ŭi
[and] Kim Yak-sil.   10754

Yŏnse Taehakkyo. Kugŏ Kukmunhakhoe.   Han'guk kojŏn
munhak yŏn'gu munhŏn haeje   [Annotated
bibliography of research on Korean classical
literature]. In Inmun kwahak, 5 (1960): 163-199.
                                                    01112

Yu, T°aeg-il,   comp.   Yŏngnam munhŏnnog (Kyŏngnam-
p°yŏn)   [Bibliography of source materials on
Kyŏngnam Province]. In Kugŏ kungmunhak, 28 (1965):
127-202.   01104

CROSS-REFERENCE TABLES

A. "See Also" References

This table gives further references for major subject headings appearing in Section I. These references are to four of the Indexes in Section II. In this table, the major subject headings appear in the first column. The corresponding terms in the Index, called "Major Subjects with Subdivisions", are shown in parentheses when different from the concepts of Section I.

Major Subject Headings	OCM Categories and Headings	L.C. Subject Headings	Key Words, General	Key Words, Specific
ARCHEOLOGY	172.00 Archeology 172.03 Evidence from Epigraphy 172.05 Description of Archeological Sites or Artifacts 764.15 Funerary Mounds, Monuments and Memorials	Antiquities--Catalogs Monuments--Preservation--Catalogs	Archeology Dolmen Inscriptions Monuments Tombs	
BIBLIOGRAPHIES OF PERIODICALS (Bibliography--Periodicals)		Catalogs--Periodicals Catalogs, Periodical Newspapers--Bib. Periodicals--Bib. Periodicals--Bibliography --Union Lists Periodicals--Oriental Studies Union Lists of Periodicals	Periodicals	
BIBLIOGRAPHY OF BIBLIOGRAPHIES (Bibliography--Bibliographies)			Bibliographies	

Subject Headings	OCM Categories and Headings	L.C. Subject Headings	Key Words, General	Key Words, Specific
BIBLIOGRAPHY OF THESES AND DISSERTATIONS (Bibliography--Dissertations)		Dissertations, Academic--Abstracts		
ECONOMY	226.00 Fishing 227.00 Fishing Gear 228.00 Marine Industry 230.00 Animal Husbandry 240.00 Agriculture 241.00 Tillage 243.00 Cereal Agriculture 251.00 Preservation and Storage of Food 252.00 Food Preparation 260.00 Food Consumption 262.00 Diet 270.00 Drink, Drugs, and Indulgence 278.00 Pharmaceuticals 288.00 Textile Industries 289.00 Paper Industry 290.00 Clothing 291.00 Normal Garb 311.00 Land Use 312.00 Water Supply 313.00 Lumbering 314.00 Forest Products 316.00 Mining and Quarrying 317.00 Special Deposits 323.00 Ceramic Industries 340.00 Structures 354.00 Heating and Lighting Equipment	Agriculture--Bib. Agriculture--Economic Aspects Business--Bib. Economic Conditions--Bib. Economic Conditions--Indexes Economics--Bib. Industrial Management--Bib. Industry--Bib. Korea (D.P.R.K.)--Economic Conditions--Bib. Labor and Laboring Classes--Bib.	Agriculture Business Business Policy Butchers Cement Commerce Economic Conditions Economic Geography Economic History Economic Policy Economy Farmers Glass Industrial Psychology Industrial Sociology Industry Lamp-lights Markets Occupational Sociology Paper Peddlers Technology Trade Tribute	Ondol Pobusang

55

Subject Headings	OCM Categories and Headings	L.C. Subject Headings	Key Words, General	Key Words, Specific
	370.00 Energy and Power			
	373.00 Light			
	377.00 Electric Power			
	378.00 Atomic Energy			
	386.00 Paint and Dye Manufacture			
	390.00 Capital Goods Industries			
	420.00 Property			
	423.00 Real Property			
	426.00 Borrowing and Lending			
	427.00 Renting and Leasing			
	428.00 Inheritance			
	430.00 Exchange			
	433.00 Production and Supply			
	436.00 Medium of Exchange			
	436.05 Coinage and Mints			
	439.00 Foreign Trade			
	440.00 Marketing			
	443.00 Retail Marketing			
	450.00 Finance			
	451.00 Accounting			
	453.00 Banking			
	455.00 Speculation			
	456.00 Insurance			
	457.00 Foreign Exchange			
	457.02 Foreign Exchange--Role of Invisible Factors			
	460.00 Labor			
	463.00 Occupational Specialization			
	464.00 Labor Supply and Development			
	466.00 Labor Relations			
	470.00 Business and Industrial Organization			
	472.00 Individual Enterprise			

Subject Headings	OCM Categories and Headings	L.C. Subject Headings	Key Words, General	Key Words, Specific
	474.00 Cooperative Organization 485.01 Travel Services-- Accommodations 489.00 Transportation 511.00 Standard of Living 651.00 Taxation and Public Income 652.00 Public Finance 655.00 Government Enterprise			
EDUCATION	217.00 Archives (e.g. Libraries) 870.00 Education 871.00 Educational System 873.10 Liberal Arts Education-- Degrees	Libraries Textbooks--Catalogs	Dental Education Education	Japanese Education
FAMILY AND KINSHIP	173.02 Dynastic Lists and Genealogies 428.00 Inheritance 580.00 Marriage 582.00 Regulation of Marriage 583.00 Mode of Marriage 585.00 Nuptials 586.00 Termination of Marriage 587.00 Secondary Marriage 590.00 Family 592.00 Household 593.00 Family Relations 597.00 Adoption 600.00 Kinship 601.00 Kinship Terminology 613.00 Lineage		Children Clans Family Genealogy Genealogy, Royal Kinship Marriage Patriarchy Surnames Women	

Subject Headings	OCM Categories and Headings	L.C. Subject Headings	Key Words, General	Key Words, Specific
GENERAL BIBLIOGRAPHIES (Bibliography)	110.00 Bibliography 113.02 Annotated Bibliographies	Bibliographical Exhibitions--Bib. Bibliography Bibliography--Addresses, Essays, Lectures Catalog, Publisher Catalogs Catalogs, Book Catalogs, Rare Book Catalogs, Subject Government Publications--Bib. Incunabula--Bib. Japan--Archives--Catalogs Official Publications--Bib. Rare Books--Bib. U.S.--Government Publications--Korea	Chinese Classics Rare Books	
HISTORY	170.00 History and Culture Change 173.00 Traditional History 173.02 Dynastic Lists and Genealogies 174.00 Historical Reconstruction 175.00 Recorded History 175.01 Written Sources and their Evaluation	History--Bib. History--Periodicals--Indexes History--Sources--Bib. Local History--Bib.	Calender Chronology Dynastic Lists Historiography History	
INDEX TO PERIODICAL LITERATURE (Bibliography--Index)		Periodicals--Indexes		

Subject Headings	OCM Categories and Headings	L.C. Subject Headings	Key Words, General	Key Words, Specific
INTERNATIONAL AND INTERCULTURAL RELATIONS (Intercultural Relations)	177.00 Acculturation and Culture Contact 439.00 Foreign Trade 457.00 Foreign Exchange 648.00 International Relations	Documents, Diplomatic--Bib. Japanese in Korea--Bib.	Diplomatic History Intercultural Relations Intercultural Relations--Korea-China Korea-France Korea-Great Britain Korea-Russia/U.S.S.R. Korea-U.S.A. Tribute	Ajia-shugi Asianism Assasination of the Queen Japanese Colonialism Japanese Imperialism Japanese in Korea Japanese Legation (Seoul) Japanese Military in Korea Japanese Ministry of Foreign Affairs Japanese Nationalism Japanese Occupation Japanese Residency-General in Korea Khitan Liao Overseas Koreans U.S. Marines
KOREAN WAR	720.00 War	U.S. Marine Corps--History--Sources--Bib.		Korean War U.S. Marines
LANGUAGE	190.00 Language 212.00 Writing 213.00 Printing	Language--Periodicals--Indexes	Alphabet Calligraphy Inscriptions Language Linguistics Printing Culture	Han'gŭl Hanmun Hunmin Chŏngŭm

Subject Headings	OCM Categories and Headings	L.C. Subject Headings	Key Words, General	Key Words, Specific
LAW	642.00 Constitution 670.00 Law 671.00 Legal Norms 671.05 Law Codes 692.00 Judicial Authority		Criminal Sociology Law Social Pathology Sociology of Law	
LIBRARY CATALOGS (Bibliography--Catalogs)		Bibliographical Exhibitions Bibliography--Collections Catalogs--Book Exhibitions Catalogs, Classified Catalogs, College Catalogs, Private Library Catalogs, University Library Exhibitions--Bib. Exhibitions--Catalogs Libraries--Catalog--Subject Libraries, Private--Bib. Libraries, University and College--Catalogs Library Catalogs--Bib. Royal Library of YI Dynasty		(See Analytical Index: Personal and Corporate Subjects Index, under name of library or collection)
LITERATURE (Literature, Literature--Poetry)	538.00 Literature 539.00 Literary Texts	Literature (Chinese)--Bib. Literature--Periodicals--Indexes Poetry, Modern--Bib.	Chinese Classics Classics Diaries Literature Literature--Poetry Poetry	Hyangga

Subject Headings	OCM Categories and Headings	L.C. Subject Headings	Key Words, General	Key Words, Specific
MILITARY	700.00 Armed Forces 702.00 Recruitment and Training 710.00 Military Technology		Military National Defense	Japanese Army Japanese Military in Korea Japanese Navy
PERFORMING ARTS (Performing Arts, Performing Arts --Music)	530.00 Fine Arts 533.00 Music 534.00 Musical Instruments 536.00 Drama 537.00 Oratory 546.00 Motion Picture Industry	Motion Picture Industry-- Directories Theaters--Directories	Arts Music	
PHYSICAL SETTING (Physical setting --Geography, including Settlement Pattern and Communication Network)	102.00 Maps 130.00 Geography 131.00 Location 132.00 Climate 133.00 Topography and Geology 134.00 Soil 135.00 Mineral Resources 136.00 Fauna 137.00 Flora 360.00 Settlements 361.00 Settlement Patterns 362.00 Housing 367.00 Parks 368.01 Fire Protection Services 480.00 Travel and Transportation 485.01 Travel Services-- Accommodations 491.00 Highways 496.00 Railways 503.00 Waterways Improvements 504.00 Port Facilities	Climatology--Bib. Exhibitions--Maps--Bib. Forests and Forestry--Bib. Geography--Bib. Geology--Bib. Geomorphology--Bib. Maps--Exhibitions--Bib. Weather--Bib.	Ecology Economic Geography Gazetteers Geography Geomorphology Ginseng Land Maps Salt Tobacco	(See Analytical Index: Geographical Subjects Index)

Subject Headings	OCM Categories and Headings	L.C. Subject Headings	Key Words, General	Key Words, Specific

POLITY	630.00 Territorial Organization
	631.00 Territorial Hierarchy
	640.00 State
	642.00 Constitution
	643.00 Chief Executive
	644.00 Executive Household
	645.00 Cabinet
	646.00 Parliament
	647.00 Administrative Agencies
	647.04 Civil Service
	650.00 Government Activities
	651.00 Taxation and Public
	    Income
	652.00 Public Finance
	654.00 Research and Development
	655.00 Government Enterprise
	656.00 Government Regulation
	659.00 Miscellaneous Government
	    Activities
	660.00 Political Behavior
	665.00 Political Parties
	666.00 Elections
	668.00 Political Movements
	669.00 Revolution
		Administrative and
		    Political Divisions
		North Korea--Politics
		    and Government
		Political Development--
		    Collected Works
		Political Development--
		    Indexes
		Politics and Government--
		    Bib.
			Administration
			Administration, Local
			Communism
			Government
			Government Administra-
			    tion
			Government, Local
			National Defense
			Political Development
			Political Ideology
			Polity
			Public Administration
			Social Policy
				Assassination of
				    the Queen
				Chosen Sotokufu
				Democratic People's
				    Republic of Korea
				Government-General
				    of Korea
				Harbin Incident
				Imo Kullan
				Independence
				    Movement
				Japanese Colonialism
				Japanese Imperialism
				Japanese Occupation
				Kabo Kyŏngjang
				Kapsin Chŏngbyŏn
				Kwagŏ
				Myŏn
				Tokanfu
				Tonghak Revolt
				Tongnip Hyŏphoe
				Tongnip Movement
				Unification
				Yejo

Subject Headings	OCM Categories and Headings	L.C. Subject Headings	Key Words, General	Key Words, Specific
POPULATION	140.00 Human Biology 141.00 Anthropometry 142.00 Descriptive Somatology 144.00 Racial Affinities 160.00 Demography 161.00 Population 162.00 Composition of Population 163.00 Birth Statistics 166.00 Internal Migration 167.00 Immigration and Emigration 167.02 Extent and Destination of Emigration	Somatology--Bib.	Biology Physical Anthropology Population	Overseas Koreans
RECREATION	523.00 Hobbies 524.00 Games 524.04 Games of Calculation 526.00 Athletic Sports 527.00 Rest Days and Holidays 547.00 Night Clubs and Cabarets		Bullfight Kites Recreation	Changgi Ch'uldarigi
REFERENCE MATERIALS			Dictionaries Reference Works	
RELIGION AND PHILOSOPHY	346.00 Religious and Educational Structures 764.00 Funeral 764.04 Funeral--Preservative Techniques 764.05 Determination of Time, Place, and Mode of Burial 764.15 Funerary Mounds, Monuments and Memorials 765.00 Mourning 769.04 Maintaining Relations with the Long Dead	Exhibitions--Catholic Literature Religion--Bib.	Buddhism Christianity Christianity-- Methodists Christianity-- Protestants Christianity--Roman Catholicism Communism Confucianism Divination Dolmen	Ajia-shugi Asianism Chodangjip Chogye Ch'ŏndo kyo Kut Mudang Sirhak Taejanggyŏng Tonghak Tonghak Revolt Zen

Subject Headings	OCM Categories and Headings	L.C. Subject Headings	Key Words, General	Key Words, Specific
	769.05 Ancestor Worship 770.00 Religious Beliefs 771.00 General Character of Religion 773.00 Mythology 775.00 Eschatology 776.00 Spirits and Gods 777.00 Luck and Chance 779.00 Theological Systems 779.04 Sacred Books 780.00 Religious Practices 787.00 Revelation and Divination 792.00 Holy Men 794.00 Congregations 795.00 Sects 797.00 Missions 798.00 Religious Intolerance 812.00 Philosophy		Jesuit Missions Philosophers Philosophy Religion Rites Shamanism Shamans Sutras Taoism Tombs Values	
SOCIOCULTURAL PATTERN AND CHANGE (Sociocultural Pattern, Sociocultural Change)	105.00 Cultural Summary 170.00 History and Culture Change 171.00 Distributional Evidence 177.00 Acculturation and Culture Contact 178.00 Socio-Cultural Trends 180.00 Total Culture 369.00 Urban and Rural Life	Social Conditions--Bib. Social Sciences--Bib.	Ethnography Ethnology Social Change Social Conditions Society Sociocultural Change Travelers' Accounts	Rural Sociology Social Pathology Social Policy Urban Sociology

Subject Headings	OCM Categories and Headings	L.C. Subject Headings	Key Words, General	Key Words, Specific
VISUAL ARTS (Visual Arts, Visual Arts-- Ceramics, Visual Arts--Painting, Visual Arts-- Pottery)	341.00 Architecture 530.00 Fine Arts 531.00 Decorative Art 532.00 Representative Art	Antiquities--Catalogs Art Treasures--Catalogs Catalogs--Cultural Properties Monuments--Preservation-- Catalogs Pottery--History--Bib.	Arts Calligraphy Handicrafts Inscriptions Monuments	
WELFARE (Welfare--Disease, Welfare-- Medicine)	278.00 Pharmaceuticals 302.00 Toilet 302.01 Shaving and Depilation 734.00 Invalidism 736.01 Dependency--Incidence 740.00 Health and Welfare 743.00 Hospitals and Clinics 744.00 Public Health and Sanitation 747.00 Private Welfare Agencies 750.00 Sickness 751.00 Preventive Medicine 756.00 Psychotherapists 757.00 Medical Therapy 758.00 Medical Care		Blood Bank Disease Health Medicine Tuberculosis Welfare	

B. "See" References

This table is a guide to the retrieval of references to major categories which do not appear in Section I of this bibliography, but which are additional categories of the HRAF Korea Project's major subject classification. These major subject headings appear in the first column and are: communications, community studies, conflict, ethnoscience, general works, life cycle, material culture, psychocultural data, social groupings, social stratification, and values. References are to four of the indexes in Section II.

Major Subject Headings	OCM Categories and Headings	L.C. Subject Headings	Key Words, General	Key Words, Specific
COMMUNICATIONS	200.00 Communication 204.00 Press 204.01 Newspapers and Magazines 205.00 Postal System 207.00 Radio and Television 208.00 Public Opinion 213.00 Printing 214.00 Publishing 217.00 Archives 484.00 Travel 489.00 Transportation 546.00 Motion Picture Industry	Censorship of the Press Newspapers--Bib.	Communications Printing Culture	
COMMUNITY STUDIES	620.00 Community 621.00 Community Structure 624.00 Local Officials 625.00 Police		Community Development Community Life Community Studies	Myŏn

Subject Headings	OCM Categories and Headings	L.C. Subject Headings	Key Words, General	Key Words, Specific
CONFLICT	578.00 Ingroup Antagonisms 579.00 Brawls, Riots and Banditry 669.00 Revolution 720.00 War 722.00 Wartime Adjustments 723.00 Strategy 723.05 Propaganda and Psychological Warfare 725.00 Tactics 726.00 Warfare 727.05 Treatment of Captives and Prisoners 728.00 Peacemaking		Conflict Germ Warfare	April Revolution Harbin Incident Hideyoshi's Invasions Imo Kullan Independence Movement Kabo Kyŏngjang Kapsin Chŏngbyŏn Korean War Tonghak Tonghak Revolt
ETHNOSCIENCE	803.00 Mathematics 804.00 Weights and Measures 805.00 Ordering of Time 810.00 Exact Knowledge 813.00 Scientific Method 814.00 Humanistic Studies 814.01 Historiography 814.05 Research in Literature and the Fine Arts 815.00 Pure Science 816.00 Applied Science 820.00 Ideas about Nature and Man 821.00 Ethnometeorology 823.00 Ethnogeography 824.00 Ethnobotany 825.00 Ethnozoology 829.00 Ethnosociology	Anthropology--Bib. Anthropology--Indexes Korean Studies in China--Bib. Korean Studies in Japan--Bib. Korean Studies in Soviet Union--Bib. Korean Studies in U.S.S.R.--Bib. Oriental Studies--Periodicals Oriental Studies--U.S.--Bib. Periodicals--Oriental Studies Social Sciences--Bib.	Anthropology Archeology Arts Asian Studies Astronomy Biology Calendar Criminal Sociology Ecology Education Ethnography Ethnology Ethnoscience Geography Geomorphology History/Historiography Industrial Psychology Industrial Sociology Korean Studies Linguistics Literature	Sirhak

Subject Headings	OCM Categories and Headings	L.C. Subject Headings	Key Words, General	Key Words, Specific
			Occupational Sociology	
			Philosophers	
			Philosophy	
			Physical Anthropology	
			Political Science	
			Rural Sociology	
			Science	
			Social Pathology	
			Social Policy	
			Social Psychology	
			Social Sciences	
			Sociology	
			Sociology of Knowledge	
			Sociology of Law	
			Statistics	
			Systematic Knowledge	
			Urban Sociology	
GENERAL WORKS (see also General Bibliographies)		Folklore--Bib. Folklore--Periodicals--Indexes Social Conditions--Bib.	Classics Diaries Ethnography Ethnology Folklore Gazetteers Social Conditions Society Travelers' Accounts	

Subject Headings	OCM Categories and Headings	L.C. Subject Headings	Key Words, General	Key Words, Specific
LIFE CYCLE	159.00 Life History Materials 159.04 Biographical Materials 159.06 Results of Tests Designed to Measure Acquired Behavior or Personality 840.00 Reproduction 842.00 Conception 844.00 Childbirth	Bio-bibliography	Biography	(See Analytical Indexes: Author Index and Personal and Corporate Subjects Index)
MATERIAL CULTURE	(See categories in Economy)		Bamboo Cement Costumes Glass Handicrafts Lamp-lights Material Culture Paper	
PSYCHOCULTURAL DATA	150.00 Behavior Processes and Personality 181.04 National Character 186.00 Ethnocentrism		Industrial Psychology Social Psychology	
SOCIAL GROUPINGS (Including Social Relations)	463.00 Occupational Specialization 571.00 Social Relationships and Groups 575.00 Sodalities 576.00 Etiquette 577.00 Ethics 578.00 Ingroup Antagonisms 736.01 Dependency--Incidence 738.00 Delinquency	Associations, Institutions, etc.--Directories Societies--Directories	Etiquette Institutions Peddlers Social Groupings	Kye Pobusang

Subject Headings	OCM Categories and Headings	L.C. Subject Headings	Key Words, General	Key Words, Specific
SOCIAL STRATIFICATION	551.00 Personal Names 552.00 Names of Animals and Things 554.06 Symbolic Tokens of Achievement of Prestige 560.00 Social Stratification 561.00 Age Stratification 562.00 Sex Status 563.00 Ethnic Stratification 563.01 Alien and Immigrant Subgroups 564.00 Castes 565.00 Classes 567.00 Slavery		Farmers Peddlers Shamans Slavery Social Stratification Surnames	Haliyang Paekchŏng Mŏsŭm Mudang Yangban
VALUES	181.00 Ethos 183.00 Norms 185.00 Cultural Goals 576.00 Etiquette 577.00 Ethics		Etiquette Political Ideology Values	

SECTION II
ANALYTICAL INDEXES

GUIDE TO SECTION II

One of the major advantages of a computerized
bibliography -- especially a bibliography produced
by HABS -- is its unique method of analysis, which
makes it possible to produce a wide range of indexes
with relative ease and speed. Of the various indexes
which can be produced, only 13 are presented in this
bibliography. All of these indexes may not be used
at any one time, but in different combinations they
can help the user to retrieve references to a wider
range of topics and to find more relevant and specific information than may be possible with the traditional form of subject indexes.

In order to make full use of the indexes included in this section, the users should be aware of
the following major characteristics of the HABS classification system:

Multidimensional approach. In traditional subject indexing, personal, geographic, and temporal
subject categories are mixed together with more
general topical categories without differentiation.
In this bibliography, however, the subject index contains four different kinds of indexes: topical, personal and corporate subjects, geographic subjects,
and an index by "Publication Years Covered by Bibliographies".

Multiple systems approach. Since no single set
of predetermined classification categories nor any
single principle of topical indexing can be fully
satisfactory for all types of users, several systems
are used together here.

Structured and semistructured classification
approaches. A predetermined set of categories may
make it necessary for a document to be classified
under a category which does not adequately represent
the data. Moreover, it is difficult to classify a

71

document which contains data representing relatively
new social science concepts or one which contains
unique institutional terms, applicable only to a
given culture. For these reasons, we have combined
two different approaches: (1) a structured classification approach, with predetermined subject headings,
such as Major Subjects, with Subdivisions; Outline of
Cultural Materials Category Headings and Subdivisions;
and Library of Congress Subject Headings, and (2) a
semistructured classification approach, which indicates only the type of information being classified
(such as personal subject, temporal coverage, or geographical focus) with the significant key words being supplied by the indexer. (A list of key words
thus derived may then become the basis for future
thesaurus building useful for other bibliographic indexing and retrieval.) The semistructured approach
is also applied in choosing terms that are general
cross-cultural concepts or relate only to a specific
culture.

Generic and specific subject headings approach.
In traditional subject indexing, concepts general to
all cultures are combined with subject categories
unique to a given culture. In this bibliography,
these two different types of concepts are differenti-
ated to produce two different indexes: the Key Words,
General, and the Key Words Specific to Korean Culture.

Further explanation of specific indexes may also
be helpful to the user.

Major Subjects, with Subdivisions. The alphabetical list of major subject categories is similar
to the list of subject headings appearing in Section
I. It is presented here to counteract any bias resulting from the research orientation of the Editor,
which may be reflected in the logical ordering of
these subject categories as presented in Section I.

Some headings appear both with and without the
subheading: "Bibliography", e.g. "Archeology", and
"Archeology--Bibliography". The former term denotes
books which are not bibliographies, but which contain
a substantial amount of bibliographic information
on archeology. The latter indicates that the book or
article is itself a bibliography of archeology.

Outline of Cultural Materials Category Headings
and Subdivisions. This index has been generated according to the OCM classification system now used at
the Human Relations Area Files. The OCM, or Outline
of Cultural Materials (George P. Murdock et al.,
New Haven, HRAF Press, 1965), is designed to cover
"all aspects of man's cultural habitat", and consists
of 711 categories, each with a numeric code. This
classification system has been used at HRAF for the

past 20 years in classifying the ethnographic literature on over 300 cultures. In applying this classification system, the categories now represented by two
and three digit numeric codes have been further subdivided and expanded into five digits (with decimals),
so that more specific topics under each category can
also be identified.

An alphabetical index for the OCM, including
these subcategories, has been generated for this
bibliography and attached to this index for the con-
venience of the users. However, it is strongly urged
that the Outline of Cultural Materials itself also be
consulted, so that the proper meaning of each category can be understood in the total context of the
OCM system and in relation to the other closely related categories.

Researchers may find this OCM index particularly
useful in finding more specific concepts under such
subjects as family and kinship, religion and philosophy, economy, social stratification, and life cycle.
The user can retrieve, for example, annotated bibliographies (113.02), biographical materials (159.04),
references to communication and records (200.00 -
218.00), total culture (180.00 - 186.04), cult of the
dead (760.00 - 769.05), and other such concepts which
would normally be very difficult, if not impossible,
to obtain from other indexes.

Users may further initiate combinations from the
existing OCM index to compile bibliographies on a
wide variety of research topics and policy questions.
For social control, for example, one might combine
the following OCM categories: 670.00 - 698.00,
579.00, 624.00 - 627.00. With imagination and in-
genuity, the users of this bibliography can make up
numerous other similar retrieval combinations to meet
their own specifications and needs.

Library of Congress Subject Headings. This index was compiled from subject headings assigned by a
library cataloger who has followed the Library of
Congress subject headings list. Although it may not
fully represent the usefulness of the present L.C.
classification and indexing system for bibliographic
retrieval, it can aid users who are familiar with this
classification approach to make full use of this
bibliography. Scholars who are not familiar with the
Library of Congress subject headings will find the
index especially helpful in locating library and other
catalogs and in retrieving information on Korean
studies in China, Japan, the U.S. and the U.S.S.R.
In comparison with other systems, there are more subject headings dealing with the forms of recorded data,
e.g. publishers's catalogs, private library catalogs,
bookseller's catalogs, rare book catalogs, etc.

Key Words, General, and Key Words Specific to
Korean Culture. These are two key word indexes, em-
pirically derived from the data using a semistructured approach. The Key Words, General index may be
used when the researcher has been unable to find
references by means of the three previous indexes, or
it may be used as a supplement to these structured
classification indexes. Newly-developed social
science concepts and other general concepts which may
be useful for comparative and cross-cultural research
are included here. Bibliographic references on institutions or events uniquely Korean may be found in the
index of Key Words Specific to Korean Culture.

Three additional subject indexes produced by a
semistructured classification approach included in
this bibliography are: Personal and Corporate Subject, Geographical Subject and Publication Years
Covered by Bibliographies. The first two indexes are
to be used to locate bibliographies containing references to either persons, institutions or places. The
third index will be useful to retrieve bibliographies
covering references issued during particular time
periods.

One of the major advantages of a bibliography
produced by HABS is the generation of additional indexes without any further analysis. By properly
tagging the elements in the descriptive citation, the
following indexes have been produced: author, title,
periodicals, series, and publication year.

Author Index. Includes authors, co-authors,
compilers, editors, translators or any other names
which might normally be listed in the author statement of a library card. Any alternate readings or
spellings of names are also indexed to facilitate
ready retrieval, even at the risk of repetition.

Title Index. Contains titles and alternate ti-
tles. Also appended are titles referring to Section
IV: Serial Publications and the Appendix: Additional
Citations.

Periodicals Index. This index will lead to
periodicals which include bibliographic articles;
whereas the serial publications listed in Section IV
are bibliographies in serial form.

Series Index. Lists the series titles.

Publication Year Index. Through use of this
index, a researcher can not only observe the chronological relationship of various bibliographies but
also ascertain which year produced more bibliographies than others. This index can serve as primary
data for research in the sociology of knowledge, in
publishing, or in the development of science in Korea.

SUBJECT INDEXES

TOPICAL INDEXES

MAJOR SUBJECTS WITH SUBDIVISIONS

ARCHEOLOGY   01077 11726   (2)

ARCHEOLOGY--BIBLIOGRAPHY   00007 00065 00287
    01076 01084 01096 01133   (7)

BIBLIOGRAPHY   00001 00004 00005 00008 00012
    00015 00016 00019 00024 00052 00053 00061 00071
    00080 00088 00118 00120 00121 00125 00132 00139
    00140 00141 00142 00144 00145 00146 00155 00156
    00157 00164 00166 00167 00176 00179 00183 00184
    00199 00300 00346 00389 00424 01004 01007 01008
    01009 01010 01011 01018 01026 01027 01032 01033
    01039 01041 01044 01051 01054 01058 01065 01070
    01072 01074 01075 01078 01079 01080 01082 01092
    01094 01099 01108 01122 01132 01137 01139 01140
    04074 04078 04087 04090 04093 04095 04096 04097
    04100 04115 04118 04119 04120 04121 04122 04128
    04130 04131 04134 04166 04167 04168 06449 07114
    10223 10334 10570 10592 11243 11291 11292 11441
    11442 11445 11450 11558 11559 11572 11590 11654
    11760 11834 11846 11849 11854 11891 11943 11977
                                               (125)

BIBLIOGRAPHY--BIBLIOGRAPHIC ESSAY   00058 00110
    00130 00131 00165 00177 00390 00393 01013 01022
    01034 01036 01090 01095 03724 11241 11440   (17)

BIBLIOGRAPHY--BIBLIOGRAPHIES   01021 01062 04076
    04077 04094 06763 11656   (7)

BIBLIOGRAPHY--CATALOGS--CHINA, REPUBLIC OF
    01123   (1)

BIBLIOGRAPHY--CATALOGS--FRANCE   11928   (1)

BIBLIOGRAPHY--CATALOGS--GREAT BRITAIN   00158
    01028 11945   (3)

BIBLIOGRAPHY--CATALOGS--JAPAN   00065 00067 00116
    00134 00163 00169 00170 00171 00175 00187 00189
    01016 10560 11913 11915 11936   (16)

BIBLIOGRAPHY--CATALOGS--KOREA   00022 00068 00073
    00075 00076 00079 00095 00106 00107 00168 00181

75

INTERCULTURAL RELATIONS--KOREA-CHINA   CO054   (1)

INTERCULTURAL RELATIONS--KOREA-CHINA--BIBLIOGRAPHY
    C1C81   (1)

INTERCULTURAL RELATIONS--KOREA-JAPAN   OCO54
    C1C59 04100   (3)

INTERCULTURAL RELATIONS--KOREA-JAPAN--BIBLIOGRAPHY
    CC116 00128 CO133 00134 00155 C1023 01046 C1C49
    01140 102C7   (10)

INTERCULTURAL RELATIONS--KOREA-MANCHURIA--
    BIBLIOGRAPHY   01081   (1)

INTERCULTURAL RELATIONS--KOREA-RUSSIA/U.S.S.R.--
    BIBLIOGRAPHY   00134   (1)

INTERCULTURAL RELATIONS--KOREA-U.S.A.--BIBLIOGRAPHY
    CO115 00143   (2)

LANGUAGE--BIBLIOGRAPHY   00010 CO050 01C05 01019
    C1C53 01104 C1135   (7)

LAW   0C393   (1)

LAW--BIBLIOGRAPHY   00072 04127 102C6 11440 11451
                                                 (5)

LITERATURE   01101 10334   (2)

LITERATURE--BIBLIOGRAPHY   CC01C 00050 0C058
    CCC67 C0069 CCC76 00107 00185 C1C32 C1033 C1053
    01103 01104 C1112 01121 04092 04124 04125 10754
    11440 11859   (21)

LITERATURE--POETRY--BIBLIOGRAPHY   01052   (1)

MILITARY--BIBLIOGRAPHY   04066   (1)

PERFORMING ARTS   00015   (1)

PERFORMING ARTS--MUSIC--BIBLIOGRAPHY   01105   (1)

PHYSICAL SETTING--GEOGRAPHY   11939 11940   (2)

PHYSICAL SETTING--GEOGRAPHY--BIBLIOGRAPHY   CO123
    0C124 00182 C0390 01042 01088 01089 C1C9C C1C93
    C1110 C1117 01125 04083 04098 04136   (15)

POLITY   01C43 11436 11978   (3)

POLITY--BIBLIOGRAPHY   CC008 COC11 CC023 0CO25
    CCC5C 00128 CC134 00143 01026 01049 01086 C1126

```
        C1127 04111 C6766 07057 10206 1144C 11451 11832
        11904                                        (21)

POPULATION--BIBLIOGRAPHY        01100              (1)

RECREATION--BIBLIOGRAPHY        04086              (1)

RELIGION AND PHILOSOPHY         CC095 1186C        (2)

RELIGION AND PHILOSOPHY--BIBLIOGRAPHY      0C022
      CCC63 C0072 C0107 00118 00120 C0165 CC194 01014
      01C15 01032 C1C33 01048 01064 C1066 C1C67 C1068
      C1C69 01083 C1C85 01116 11440 11447 11856 11857
                                                   (25)

SOCIOCULTURAL PATTERN           C0015              (1)

SOCIOCULTURAL PATTERN--BIBLIOGRAPHY        C0C01 C0002
      C0C03 C0C07 C0008 0C010 0C011 C0020 CCC25 C0C62
      C0117 01134 01138 06761 06762 06766 102C7 11436
      11437 11452 11453 11852 11853                (23)

VISUAL ARTS         0CC15 00346 01C54              (3)

VISUAL ARTS--CERAMICS--BIBLIOGRAPHY        01017 C1060
                                                   (2)

VISUAL ARTS--PAINTING           01072 11726        (2)

VISUAL ARTS--POTTERY--BIBLIOGRAPHY         01115   (1)

WELFARE--DISEASE--BIBLIOGRAPHY       01141         (1)

WELFARE--MEDICINE--BIBLIOGRAPHY      01016 01020
      01C24 01073 C1141                            (5)
```

OUTLINE OF CULTURAL MATERIALS

CATEGORY HEADINGS AND SUBDIVISIONS

000.00 Material Not Categorized

100.00 ORIENTATION
101.00 Identification
102.00 Maps
    00008 00012 00015 00025 00050 00058 00061 00062
    00073 00110 00155 00182 01080 01125 04077 04078
    04083 04098 10560   (19)
103.00 Place Names
    01096 11291   (2)
104.00 Glossary
105.00 Cultural Summary
    00012 00016 00019 00024 00120 01139   (6)

110.00 BIBLIOGRAPHY
    00004 00005 00006 00023 00052 00053 00058 00063
    00065 00068 00070 00071 00072 00073 00075 00076
    00079 00080 00087 00088 00091 00100 00107 00108
    00109 00116 00118 00120 00121 00123 00124 00125
    00129 00131 00132 00133 00134 00138 00139 00140
    00141 00143 00145 00146 00156 00157 00158 00163
    00164 00166 00167 00168 00169 00170 00175 00179
    00180 00181 00182 00183 00184 00185 00186 00189
    00192 00194 00197 00199 00300 00346 00389 00390
    00393 00424 01003 01004 01005 01006 01007 01008
    01009 01010 01013 01015 01016 01019 01021 01024
    01026 01028 01033 01037 01039 01041 01042 01044
    01045 01048 01049 01051 01052 01053 01057 01060
    01062 01066 01068 01070 01073 01074 01076 01078
    01079 01080 01081 01082 01084 01085 01093 01094
    01096 01097 01104 01108 01110 01114 01115 01116
    01119 01120 01121 01122 01123 01125 01132 01133
    01134 01135 01139 01141 03066 03723 03724 04066
    04074 04075 04076 04077 04078 04082 04084 04085
    04086 04090 04094 04095 04096 04097 04100 04111
    07057 09105 10204 10207 10223 10560 10576 10592
    10754 11241 11292 11293 11425 11436 11440 11442
    11447 11448 11558 11559 11560 11726 11760 11787
    11788 11795 11849 11853 11860 11885 11888 11891
                               (192)
111.00 Sources Processed
112.00 Sources Consulted
113.00 Additional References
113.02 Annotated bibliographies
    00001 00002 00003 00007 00008 00010 00011 00012
    00015 00016 00019 00020 00022 00024 00025 00050
    00061 00062 00067 00069 00115 00117 00128 00130
    00142 00155 00171 00187 00287 01011 01017 01018

```
          01022 01023 01027 01032 01034 01036 01046 01058
          01059 01064 01065 01072 01075 01077 01083 01089
          01090 01095 01099 01103 01109 01112 01128 01137
          01138 06766 10205 10334 10582 11177 11424 11590
          11654 11656 11761 11852 11898 11907 11976   (71)
114.00 Comments
115.00 Informants
116.00 Texts
117.00 Field Data

120.00 METHODOLOGY
121.00 Theoretical Orientation
122.00 Practical Preparations
123.00 Observational Role
124.00 Interviewing
125.00 Tests and Schedules
126.00 Recording and Collecting
          10204                                        (1)
127.00 Historical Research
128.00 Organization and Analysis

130.00 GEOGRAPHY
          00005 00011 00012 00016 00020 00025 00050 00058
          00061 00065 00067 00073 00087 00088 00107 00117
          00131 00155 00390 01004 01011 01032 01033 01062
          01090 01123 01129 01139 10560 11291 11440 11452
          11453                                       (33)
131.00 Location
          00008                                        (1)
132.00 Climate
          00008 00012 00016 00124                      (4)
133.00 Topography and Geology
          00012 00123                                  (2)
134.00 Soil
          01127                                        (1)
135.00 Mineral Resources
          00008 00016 01127                            (3)
136.00 Fauna
          00019 00129                                  (2)
137.00 Flora
          00012 00129                                  (2)

140.00 HUMAN BIOLOGY
          00183 00184                                  (2)
141.00 Anthropometry
          01096                                        (1)
142.00 Descriptive Somatology
          01096                                        (1)
143.00 Genetics
144.00 Racial Affinities
          00008 00131 11440                            (3)
145.00 Ontogenetic Data
146.00 Nutrition
147.00 Physiological Data
```

150.00 BEHAVIOR PROCESSES AND PERSONALITY
151.00 Sensation and Perception
152.00 Drives and Emotions
153.00 Modification of Behavior
154.00 Adjustment Processes
155.00 Personality Development
156.00 Social Personality
157.00 Personality Traits
158.00 Personality Disorders
159.00 Life History Materials
      01140 04077   (2)
159.04 Biographical materials
      00019 00020 00022 00050 00062 00067 00121 00133
      01023 01049 01062 01103 01121 01126 01133 04076
      04078 06449 10207 11291 11293 11424 11452 11453
      11860 11898 11976   (27)
159.06 Acquired behavior and personality--test results
      11425   (1)

160.00 DEMOGRAPHY
      00012 00073 00087 00117 00155 01080 01100 10269
      11425   (9)
161.00 Population
      00070 10205 11424   (3)
162.00 Composition of Population
      00070 00129 11425   (3)
163.00 Birth Statistics
      00005   (1)
164.00 Morbidity
165.00 Mortality
166.00 Internal Migration
      00070   (1)
167.00 Immigration and Emigration
      00012 01023 01050   (3)
167.02 Emigration--extent and destination
      00117   (1)
168.00 Population Policy

170.00 HISTORY AND CULTURE CHANGE
      00005 00121 04074 04076 04077 04078   (6)
171.00 Distributional Evidence
      01135 10206 11860   (3)
172.00 Archeology
      00004 00011 00022 00050 00063 00107 00117 00120
      00131 00287 01006 01084 01134 11436 11452 11453
      11726   (17)
172.05 ... archeological sites or artifacts
      01017 01138   (2)
173.00 Traditional History
      00004 00005 00019 00067 00121 00131 00287 10334
      11451   (9)
173.02 Dynastic lists and genealogies
      00015 00022 01139   (3)

174.00 Historical Reconstruction
       00004 (1)
175.00 Recorded History
       00001 00002 00004 00005 00006 00008 00010 00016
       00020 00024 00050 00053 00062 00063 00065 00070
       00073 00075 00076 00087 00088 00118 00120 00128
       00134 00379 00424 01004 01006 01011 01044 01049
       01062 01078 01080 01084 01096 01103 01119 01120
       01123 01129 01133 01134 01139 01140 04084 10207
       10560 11291 11293 11440 11448 11451 11452 11453
       11566 (57)
175.01 Written sources and their evaluation
       01003 01022 06021 (3)
176.00 Innovation
177.00 Acculturation and Culture Contact
       00008 00117 01103 10205 10269 11451 11860 (7)
178.00 Socio-cultural Trends
       00004 01023 01140 07055 (4)

180.00 TOTAL CULTURE
181.00 Ethos
       00004 00117 06761 10269 (4)
181.04 ... national character
       11436 (1)
182.00 Function
182.03 Adjustments of parts of culture to one another
       11241 (1)
183.00 Norms
       00004 00005 00019 00072 00075 00121 00131 00155
       01096 04074 04077 10269 11291 11424 (14)
184.00 Cultural Participation
185.00 Cultural Goals
       00005 00016 00058 00072 00087 00116 00131 01049
       11291 11293 11448 (11)
186.00 Ethnocentrism
       00012 00072 00155 10269 (4)
186.04 Ethnocentrism--symbolic representation (e.g.
       flags)
       11425 (1)

190.00 LANGUAGE
       00001 00002 00004 00005 00008 00010 00011 00012
       00016 00019 00020 00023 00025 00058 00072 00073
       00087 00088 00118 00120 00121 00131 00155 01004
       01005 01011 01019 01032 01033 01034 01036 01095
       01096 01103 01129 01134 01135 04077 10560 11293
       11424 11425 11436 11440 11447 11448 11452 11453
       11566 (49)
191.00 Speech
192.00 Vocabulary
193.00 Grammar
194.00 Phonology
195.00 Stylistics
196.00 Semantics

```
197.00 Linguistic Identification
198.00 Special Languages


200.00 COMMUNICATION
       00012 10206 10207 11425                              (4)
201.00 Gestures and Signs
202.00 Transmission of Messages
203.00 Dissemination of News and Information
204.00 Press
       00004 00016 00024 00072 00073 00075 00118 00120
       00128 00129 00180 00346 01009 01062 01080 01126
       04074 04075 04077 04078 04097 10207 10269 10560
       10592 11291 11424 11425 11448 11452 11453 11569
                                                           (32)
204.01 Newspapers and magazines
       01049 04170 11914                                    (3)
205.00 Postal System
       00131 10205 11424                                    (3)
206.00 Telephone and Telegraph
207.00 Radio and Television
       00005                                                (1)
208.00 Public Opinion
       01127 10269                                          (2)


210.00 RECORDS
211.00 Mnemonic Devices
212.00 Writing
       00005 00008 00022 00058 00075 00121 11241            (7)
212.09 Writing--description of output
       11241                                                (1)
213.00 Printing
       00072 01013 01062 01080 01103 04074 04076 04077
       11241 11291 11846                                   (11)
213.01 Printing--methods
       00050                                                (1)
213.05 Printing--description of output
       11903                                                (1)
214.00 Publishing
       00015 00164 01013 01032 01034 01036 01095 04076
       04077 11424 11849                                   (11)
215.00 Photography
216.00 Sound Records
217.00 Archives
       00005 00116 00128 00134 01021 01022 01032 01034
       01036 01062 01080 01095 04135 06766 11424          (15)
217.01 Repositories of records
       11425                                                (1)
217.02 State archives
       00016 00019 00058 00072 00121 00131 01085 04074
       04076 04077 04078 10204                             (12)
217.03 Archives--making collections
       11241                                                (1)
217.04 Archives--accessions
       11241                                                (1)
```

217.05 Archives--filing and indexing
      00053 (1)
218.00 Writing and Printing Supplies

220.00 FOOD QUEST
221.00 Annual Cycle
222.00 Collecting
223.00 Fowling
224.00 Hunting and Trapping
225.00 Marine Hunting
226.00 Fishing
      00008 (1)
227.00 Fishing Gear
      00131 (1)
228.00 Marine Industries
      00005 01127 10207 11425 (4)

230.00 ANIMAL HUSBANDRY
      00129 (1)
231.00 Domesticated Animals
232.00 Applied Animal Science
233.00 Pastoral Activities
234.00 Dairying
235.00 Poultry Raising
236.00 Wool Production
237.00 Animal By-products

240.00 AGRICULTURE
      00004 00005 00012 00058 00129 (5)
241.00 Tillage
      00019 00129 00186 10207 11424 11446 (6)
242.00 Agricultural Science
243.00 Cereal Agriculture
      10207 (1)
244.00 Vegetable Production
245.00 Arboriculture
246.00 Forage Crops
247.00 Floriculture
248.00 Textile Agriculture
249.00 Special Crops

250.00 FOOD PROCESSING
251.00 Preservation and Storage of Food
      11425 (1)
252.00 Food Preparation
      00019 11424 11425 (3)
253.00 Meat Packing Industry
254.00 Refrigeration Industry
255.00 Canning Industry
256.00 Cereal Industry
257.00 Confectionery Industries
258.00 Miscellaneous Food Processing and Packing
      Industries

```
260.00 FOOD CONSUMPTION
       00012                                              (1)
261.00 Gratification and Control of Hunger
262.00 Diet
       00129 01096                                        (2)
264.00 Eating
263.00 Condiments
265.00 Food Service Industries
266.00 Cannibalism


270.00 DRINK, DRUGS, AND INDULGENCE
       10207                                              (1)
271.00 Water and Thirst
272.00 Nonalcoholic Beverages
273.00 Alcoholic Beverages
274.00 Beverage Industries
275.00 Drinking Establishments
276.00 Narcotics and Stimulants
277.00 Tobacco Industry
278.00 Pharmaceuticals
       00072                                              (1)


280.00 LEATHER, TEXTILES, AND FABRICS
281.00 Work in Skins
282.00 Leather Industry
283.00 Cordage
284.00 Knots and Lashings
285.00 Mats and Basketry
286.00 Woven Fabrics
287.00 Nonwoven Fabrics
288.00 Textile Industries
       00005 10207                                        (2)
289.00 Paper Industry
       04075                                              (1)


290.00 CLOTHING
       00004 00012 00073 11425                            (4)
291.00 Normal Garb
       01096 11424                                        (2)
292.00 Special Garments
293.00 Paraphernalia
294.00 Clothing Manufacture
295.00 Special Clothing Industries
296.00 Garment Care


300.00 ADORNMENT
301.00 Ornament
302.00 Toilet
       10207                                              (1)
302.01 Shaving and depilation
       01096                                              (1)
303.00 Manufacture of Toilet Articles
304.00 Mutilation
305.00 Beauty Specialists
```

```
306.00  Jewelry Manufacture

310.00  EXPLOITATIVE ACTIVITIES
311.00  Land Use
        00129                                                 (1)
312.00  Water Supply
        00005 00120 00129                                     (3)
313.00  Lumbering
        00005 00129 00131 01127 10205 10207 11293             (7)
314.00  Forest Products
        00129 10207                                           (2)
315.00  Oil and Gas Wells
316.00  Mining and Quarrying
        00120 00128 00131 00155 10205 10207                   (6)
317.00  Special Deposits
        10207                                                 (1)

320.00  PROCESSING OF BASIC MATERIALS
321.00  Work in Bone, Horn, and Shell
322.00  Woodworking
323.00  Ceramic Industries
        00117 00287 01017 01060 01115                         (5)
324.00  Stone Industry
325.00  Metallurgy
326.00  Smiths and Their Crafts
327.00  Iron and Steel Industry
328.00  Nonferrous Metal Industries

330.00  BUILDING AND CONSTRUCTION
331.00  Construction
332.00  Earth Moving
333.00  Masonry
334.00  Structural Steel Work
335.00  Carpentry
336.00  Plumbing
337.00  Electrical Installation
338.00  Miscellaneous Building Trades
339.00  Building Supplies Industries

340.00  STRUCTURES
341.00  Architecture
        00072 00117 01080 01096                               (4)
342.00  Dwellings
343.00  Outbuildings
344.00  Public Structures
344.01  ... public buildings
        11425                                                 (1)
345.00  Recreational Structures
346.00  Religious and Educational Structures
        01080 01096 04076 11291 11425                         (5)
347.00  Business Structures
348.00  Industrial Structures
349.00  Miscellaneous Structures
```

350.00 EQUIPMENT AND MAINTENANCE OF BUILDINGS
351.00 Grounds
352.00 Furniture
353.00 Interior Decoration and Arrangement
354.00 Heating and Lighting Equipment
        04119 04130   (2)
355.00 Miscellaneous Building Equipment
356.00 Housekeeping
357.00 Domestic Service
358.00 Maintenance of Nondomestic Buildings

360.00 SETTLEMENTS
        00155   (1)
361.00 Settlement Patterns
        00012   (1)
362.00 Housing
        01096   (1)
363.00 Streets and Traffic
364.00 Sanitary Facilities
365.00 Public Utilities
366.00 Commercial Facilities
367.00 Parks
        10269   (1)
368.00 Miscellaneous Urban Facilities
368.01 Fire protection services
        00072   (1)
369.00 Urban and Rural Life
        00004 00005 00012 00070 00072 00075 00087 00117
        00129 00131 01096 01103 01127 04075 04076 06761
        07055 10269 10560 11425 11448 11451   (22)

370.00 ENERGY AND POWER
        10207   (1)
371.00 Power Development
372.00 Fire
373.00 Light
        04074 04119 04130   (3)
374.00 Heat
375.00 Thermal Power
376.00 Water Power
377.00 Electric Power
        00005 04076 11425   (3)
378.00 Atomic Energy
        01127   (1)
379.00 Miscellaneous Power Production

380.00 CHEMICAL INDUSTRIES
381.00 Chemical Engineering
382.00 Petroleum and Coal Products Industries
383.00 Rubber Industry
384.00 Synthetics Industry
385.00 Industrial Chemicals
386.00 Paint and Dye Manufacture
        10207   (1)

387.00 Fertilizer Industry
388.00 Soap and Allied Products
389.00 Manufacture of Explosives

390.00 CAPITAL GOODS INDUSTRIES   (1)
       11425
391.00 Hardware Manufacture
392.00 Machine Industries
393.00 Electrical Supplies Industry
394.00 Manufacture of Heating and Lighting Appliances
395.00 Manufacture of Optical and Photographic
       Equipment
396.00 Shipbuilding
397.00 Railway Equipment Industry
398.00 Manufacture of Vehicles
399.00 Aircraft Industry

400.00 MACHINES
401.00 Mechanics
402.00 Industrial Machinery
403.00 Electrical Machines and Appliances
404.00 Household Machines and Appliances
405.00 Weighing, Measuring, and Recording Machines
406.00 Weight-moving Machinery
407.00 Agricultural Machinery

410.00 TOOLS AND APPLIANCES
411.00 Weapons
412.00 General Tools
413.00 Special Tools
414.00 Miscellaneous Hardware
415.00 Utensils
416.00 Appliances
417.00 Apparatus

420.00 PROPERTY   (1)
       00131
421.00 Property System
422.00 Property in Movables
423.00 Real Property
       00004 00005 00016 01127 10205 10207 10269 11291
       11425   (9)
424.00 Incorporeal Property
425.00 Acquisition and Relinquishment of Property
426.00 Borrowing and Lending
       11425   (1)
427.00 Renting and Leasing
       10207   (1)
428.00 Inheritance
       00005 00131 01096 07055   (4)
429.00 Administration

430.00 EXCHANGE
       00005 00070 10207   (3)

88

```
431.00  Gift Giving
432.00  Buying and Selling
433.00  Production and Supply
        00053 00062 00070 00129 10207 11177 11446 11452
        11453                                              (9)
434.00  Income and Demand
435.00  Price and Value
436.00  Medium of Exchange
        00075 00131 01049 04132                            (4)
436.05  Coinage and mints
        00117                                              (1)
437.00  Exchange Transactions
438.00  Domestic Trade
439.00  Foreign Trade
        00012 00016 01127 11425 11446                      (5)

440.00  MARKETING
        00070 00131 10205 10207                            (4)
441.00  Mercantile Business
442.00  Wholesale Marketing
443.00  Retail Marketing
        01032 01034 01036 01095                            (4)
444.00  Retail Businesses
445.00  Service Industries
446.00  Sales Promotion
447.00  Advertising

450.00  FINANCE
        00005 00012 00019 00070 00072 00075 00087 00120
        00131 01127 10205 10207 11425                      (13)
451.00  Accounting
        00004                                              (1)
452.00  Credit
453.00  Banking
        00004 00016 00075 01127                            (4)
454.00  Saving and Investment
455.00  Speculation
        11425                                              (1)
456.00  Insurance
        00070                                              (1)
457.00  Foreign Exchange
        00005 10560 11425                                  (3)
457.02  Foreign exchange--role of invisible factors
        11424                                              (1)
458.00  Business Cycles

460.00  LABOR
        00004 00005 00073 01080 01100 01127 10269          (7)
461.00  Labor and Leisure
462.00  Division of Labor by Sex
463.00  Occupational Specialization
        00070                                              (1)
464.00  Labor Supply and Employment
        11425                                              (1)
```

```
465.00  Wages and Salaries
466.00  Labor Relations
        11446                                               (1)
467.00  Labor Organization
468.00  Collective Bargaining


470.00  BUSINESS AND INDUSTRIAL ORGANIZATION
        00070 10205 10207                                   (3)
471.00  Ownership and Control of Capital
472.00  Individual Enterprise
        04076                                               (1)
473.00  Corporate Organization
474.00  Cooperative Organization
        00004 00129 11446                                   (3)
475.00  State Enterprise
476.00  Mutual Aid
477.00  Competition


480.00  TRAVEL AND TRANSPORTATION
        10205 10560                                         (2)
481.00  Locomotion
        00005                                               (1)
482.00  Burden Carrying
483.00  Weight Moving
484.00  Travel
        11425                                               (1)
485.00  Travel Services
485.01  Travel services--accommodations
        11425                                               (1)
486.00  Regulation of Travel
487.00  Routes
488.00  Warehousing
489.00  Transportation
        00019 00050 00073 00075 00128 00134 00138 00155
        01127 10207 11451                                  (11)


490.00  LAND TRANSPORT
491.00  Highways
        00155                                               (1)
492.00  Animal Transport
493.00  Vehicles
494.00  Highway Transport
495.00  Auxiliary Highway Services
496.00  Railways
        00012 00072 00120 00131 00134 11425                 (6)
497.00  Rail Transport
498.00  Terminal Facilities
499.00  Highway and Railway Construction


500.00  WATER AND AIR TRANSPORT
501.00  Boats
502.00  Navigation
503.00  Waterways Improvements
        00128                                               (1)
```

```
504.00  Port Facilities
        00012 00016 00128 00155                        (4)
505.00  Water Transport
506.00  Aircraft
507.00  Aviation
508.00  Airport Facilities
509.00  Air Transport


510.00  LIVING STANDARDS AND ROUTINES
511.00  Standard of Living
        00121 10269                                    (2)
512.00  Daily Routine
513.00  Sleeping
514.00  Elimination
515.00  Personal Hygiene
516.00  Postures
517.00  Leisure Time Activities


520.00  RECREATION
521.00  Conversation
522.00  Humor
523.00  Hobbies
        00073 00075                                    (2)
524.00  Games
        10560 11425                                    (2)
524.04  Games of calculation
        04086                                          (1)
525.00  Gambling
526.00  Athletic Sports
        10269 11291 11425                              (3)
527.00  Rest Days and Holidays
        00005 00012 00117 01096 11291 11425            (6)
528.00  Vacations
529.00  Recreational Facilities


530.00  FINE ARTS
        00012 00016 00020 00024 00117 00118 00120 00121
        00287 01096 01121 01133 10560 10754 11291 11293
        11424 11425 11436 11448                        (20)
531.00  Decorative Art
        00004                                          (1)
532.00  Representative Art
        00008 00019 00087 01072 10269 11241 11726      (7)
533.00  Music
        00008 00010 00019 00050 00072 00073 00075 01105
        01129 11440                                    (10)
534.00  Musical Instruments
        01105                                          (1)
535.00  Dancing
536.00  Drama
        00005 00019 01105 01129                        (4)
537.00  Oratory
        00019                                          (1)
538.00  Literature
```

```
         00001 00002 00004 00005 00008 00010 00011 00012
         00019 00020 00022 00023 00025 00058 00062 00065
         00072 00073 00075 00076 00087 00088 00131 01004
         01011 01032 01034 01036 01052 01062 01095 01103
         01105 01112 01129 01134 01139 04074 04076 04077
         04078 04092 04125 10269 10334 10754 11241 11424
         11436 11452 11453 11566                      (52)
539.00 Literary Texts
         01062 01103 04074 04076 04077 04078           (6)

540.00 ENTERTAINMENT
541.00 Spectacles
542.00 Commercialized Sports
543.00 Exhibitions
544.00 Public Lectures
545.00 Musical and Theatrical Productions
546.00 Motion Picture Industry
         00005 00346 11425                             (3)
547.00 Night Clubs and Cabarets
         11425                                         (1)
548.00 Organized Vice
549.00 Art and Recreational Supplies Industries

550.00 INDIVIDUATION AND MOBILITY
551.00 Personal Names
         00121 01096 10204 11425                       (4)
552.00 Names of Animals and Things
         01103                                         (1)
553.00 Naming
554.00 Status, Role, and Prestige
554.06 Symbolic tokens of achievement of prestige
         11425                                         (1)
555.00 Talent Mobility
556.00 Accumulation of Wealth
557.00 Manipulative Mobility
558.00 Downward Mobility

560.00 SOCIAL STRATIFICATION
         01103 11291                                   (2)
561.00 Age Stratification
         10269                                         (1)
562.00 Sex Status
         00073 01096 07055 10269                       (4)
563.00 Ethnic Stratification
         01050 10207                                   (2)
563.01 Alien and immigrant subgroups
         01023                                         (1)
564.00 Castes
         00008                                         (1)
565.00 Classes
         00022 00117 01140 06761 06762 06766 10269     (7)
566.00 Serfdom and Peonage
567.00 Slavery
         00063 00117 00121 10205 11436                 (5)
```

                    00067 00121 01096 04077 07055   (5)
602.00 Kin Relationships
603.00 Grandparents and Grandchildren
604.00 Avuncular and Nepotic Relatives
605.00 Cousins
606.00 Parents-in-law and Children-in-law
607.00 Siblings-in Law
608.00 Artificial Kin Relationships
609.00 Behavior Toward Nonrelatives

610.00 KIN GROUPS
611.00 Rule of Descent
612.00 Kindreds and Ramages
613.00 Lineages
                    00131   (1)
614.00 Sibs
615.00 Phraties
616.00 Moieties
617.00 Bilinear Kin Groups
618.00 Clans
619.00 Tribe and Nation

620.00 COMMUNITY
                    01080 11291 11451   (3)
621.00 Community Structure
                    01096 04074 07055   (3)
622.00 Headmen
623.00 Councils
624.00 Local Officials
                    11451   (1)
625.00 Police
                    00072 10206 10207 11425 11451   (5)
626.00 Social Control
627.00 Informal Ingroup Justice
628.00 Inter-community relations

630.00 TERRITORIAL ORGANIZATION
                    04076 10206 10207 11451   (4)
631.00 Territorial Hierarchy
                    00062   (1)
632.00 Towns
633.00 Cities
634.00 Districts
635.00 Provinces
636.00 Dependencies

640.00 STATE
                    00128 10207 11425 11436   (4)
641.00 Citizenship
642.00 Constitution
                    00050   (1)
643.00 Chief Executive
                    00134 01062 11291 11425   (4)
644.00 Executive Household

```
                  00117 00131 01062 01096 11291              (5)
645.00 Cabinet
       10204                                                 (1)
646.00 Parliament
       00005 00075 00192                                     (3)
647.00 Administrative Agencies
       00005 00062 00087 00121 01127 04077 04078 10206
       11424 11451                                          (10)
647.04 Civil service
       00005                                                 (1)
648.00 International Relations
       00004 00005 00008 00012 00016 00054 00062 00063
       00070 00072 00108 00116 00117 00121 00128 00134
       00379 01004 01023 01049 01050 01062 01080 01081
       01126 01127 04074 04076 04077 04078 04100 10204
       10207 10560 11177 11291 11293 11448 11450 11451
                                                            (40)

650.00 GOVERNMENT ACTIVITIES
       00128 00131 01054 01126 01127 10206 11291 11425
                                                             (8)
651.00 Taxation and Public Income
       00004 00016 00070 00117 01127 10205                   (6)
652.00 Public Finance
       00005 00070 00075 11446 11451                         (5)
653.00 Public Works
654.00 Research and Development
       00008 00070                                           (2)
655.00 Government Enterprises
       11451                                                 (1)
656.00 Government Regulation
       00019 00164 10207                                     (3)
657.00 Public Welfare
658.00 Public Education
659.00 Miscellaneous Government Activities
       00012                                                 (1)

660.00 POLITICAL BEHAVIOR
       00053 00128 11291 11425                               (4)
661.00 Exploitation
662.00 Political Intrigue
663.00 Public Service
664.00 Pressure Politics
665.00 Political Parties
       00087 00116 01049 01126                               (4)
666.00 Elections
       11451                                                 (1)
667.00 Political Machines
668.00 Political Movements
       00012 00016 00116 00134 01086 01140 04074 04077
       10207 11448                                          (10)
669.00 Revolution
       00016 00116 01049 10207                               (4)
```

```
670.00 LAW
       00002 00004 00005 00012 00020 00023 00050 00058
       00073 00087 00117 00120 00121 00131 01004 01127
       10269 10560 11291 11436 11452 11453            (22)
671.00 Legal Norms
       00053 00075 07055 10207                          (4)
671.05 Law codes
       00346 04127                                      (2)
672.00 Liability
673.00 Wrongs
674.00 Crime
675.00 Contracts
676.00 Agency


680.00 OFFENSES AND SANCTIONS
681.00 Sanctions
682.00 Offenses Against Life
683.00 Offenses Against the Person
684.00 Sex And Marital Offenses
685.00 Property Offenses
686.00 Nonfulfillment of Obligations
687.00 Offenses Against the State
688.00 Religious Offenses
689.00 Social Offenses


690.00 JUSTICE
691.00 Litigation
692.00 Judicial Authority
       00393                                            (1)
693.00 Legal and Judicial Personnel
694.00 Initiation of Judicial Proceedings
695.00 Trial Procedure
696.00 Execution of Justice
697.00 Prisons and Jails
698.00 Special Courts


700.00 ARMED FORCES
       00016 00058 00073 00088 00128 01023 04078 11291
       11425 11573                                     (10)
701.00 Military Organization
702.00 Recruitment and Training
       11425                                            (1)
703.00 Discipline and Morale
704.00 Ground Combat Forces
705.00 Supply and Commissariat
706.00 Navy
707.00 Air Forces
708.00 Auxiliary Corps


710.00 MILITARY TECHNOLOGY
       11573                                            (1)
711.00 Military Engineering
712.00 Military Installations
713.00 Ordnance
```

714.00 Uniform and Accouterment
715.00 Military Vehicles
716.00 Naval Vessels
717.00 Military Aircraft
718.00 Special Military Equipment
719.00 Munitions Industries

720.00 WAR
       00016 00115 01023 04082 04085 11573 11761 11795
                                                    (8)
721.00 Instigation of War
722.00 Wartime Adjustments
       11425   (1)
723.00 Strategy
       00022   (1)
723.05 ... propaganda and pschological warfare
       11573   (1)
724.00 Logistics
725.00 Tactics
       00022   (1)
726.00 Warfare
       11425   (1)
727.00 Aftermath of Combat
727.05 Treatment of captives and prisoners
       01023 11573   (2)
728.00 Peacemaking
       00120   (1)
729.00 War Veterans

730.00 SOCIAL PROBLEMS
731.00 Disasters
732.00 Defectives
733.00 Alcoholism and Drug Addiction
734.00 Invalidism
       10269   (1)
735.00 Poverty
736.00 Dependency
736.01 Dependency--incidence
       11425   (1)
737.00 Old Age Dependency
738.00 Delinquency
       10269   (1)

740.00 HEALTH AND WELFARE
       01023 10206   (2)
741.00 Philanthropic Foundations
742.00 Medical Research
743.00 Hospitals and Clinics
       11425   (1)
744.00 Public Health and Sanitation
       00004 00016 00050 00062 00072 00117 00155 11451
                                                    (8)
745.00 Social Insurance
746.00 Public Assistance

```
747.00 Private Welfare Agencies
       00072                                              (1)
748.00 Social Work

750.00 SICKNESS
       00061 00120 01016 11448                            (4)
751.00 Preventive Medicine
       00019                                              (1)
752.00 Bodily Injuries
753.00 Theory of Disease
754.00 Sorcery
755.00 Magical and Mental Therapy
756.00 Psychotherapists
       11291                                              (1)
757.00 Medical Therapy
       01134                                              (1)
758.00 Medical Care
       00058                                              (1)
759.00 Medical Personnel

760.00 DEATH
761.00 Life and Death
762.00 Suicide
763.00 Dying
764.00 Funeral
       01139 07055 11425                                  (3)
764.04 Funeral--preservative techniques (e.g.
       embalming)
       01096 11291                                        (2)
764.05 Determination of time, place, and mode of burial
       11726                                              (1)
764.15 Funerary mounds, monuments and memorials
       00005 00008 00117 00118 00120 00287 10269 10334
                                                          (8)
765.00 Mourning
       01096 11291 11440                                  (3)
766.00 Deviant Mortuary Practices
767.00 Mortuary Specialists
768.00 Social Readjustments to Death
769.00 Cult of the Dead
769.04 Maintaining relations with the long dead
       11291                                              (1)
769.05 Ancestor worship
       00117 01096                                        (2)

770.00 RELIGIOUS BELIEFS
       01096 11291                                        (2)
771.00 General Character of Religion
       00020 00062 00087 00088 00121 00155 01129 01134
                                                          (8)
772.00 Cosmology
773.00 Mythology
       00005 00117                                        (2)
774.00 Animism
```

```
775.00 Eschatology
       06449 11291                                            (2)
776.00 Spirits and Gods
       00121                                                  (1)
777.00 Luck and Chance
       04074 10269                                            (2)
778.00 Sacred Objects and Places
779.00 Theological Systems
       01066 01067 01068 01069 11452 11453                   (6)
779.04 Sacred books
       01014                                                  (1)

780.00 RELIGIOUS PRACTICES
       01096                                                  (1)
781.00 Religious Experience
782.00 Propitiation
783.00 Purification and Expiation
784.00 Avoidance and Taboo
785.00 Asceticism
786.00 Orgies
787.00 Revelation and Divination
       00022                                                  (1)
788.00 Ritual
789.00 Magic

790.00 ECCLESIASTICAL ORGANIZATION
791.00 Magicians and Diviners
792.00 Holy Men
       00004                                                  (1)
793.00 Priesthood
794.00 Congregations
       00194                                                  (1)
795.00 Sects
       11860                                                  (1)
796.00 Organized Ceremonial
797.00 Missions
       00006 00012 00016 00023 00050 00117 00118 00120
       01015 01064 01123 01139 11856 11857                  (14)
798.00 Religious Intolerance
       01049                                                  (1)

800.00 NUMBERS AND MEASURES
801.00 Numerology
802.00 Numeration
803.00 Mathematics
       00058                                                  (1)
804.00 Weights and Measures
       00012                                                  (1)
805.00 Ordering of Time
       00058 10204                                            (2)

810.00 EXACT KNOWLEDGE
       00020 10269                                            (2)
811.00 Logic
```

```
812.00 Philosophy
       00020 00087 00121 01134 11425 11452 11453    (7)
813.00 Scientific Method
       01127 04077 11241                            (3)
814.00 Humanistic Studies
       00131 06766 11241                            (3)
814.01 Historiography
       01022 11898                                  (2)
814.05 Research in literature and fine arts
       00058 00061 10334                            (3)
815.00 Pure Science
       00016 00061 00118 00120 01008 01009 01132 06766
       10560 11424                                 (10)
816.00 Applied Science
       11241                                        (1)

820.00 IDEAS ABOUT NATURE AND MAN
       00020                                        (1)
821.00 Ethnometeorology
       00022 00058 00107 00117 11293 11440          (6)
822.00 Ethnophysics
823.00 Ethnogeography
       00058 01096                                  (2)
824.00 Ethnobotany
       00019 11425                                  (2)
825.00 Ethnozoology
       11291                                        (1)
826.00 Ethnoanatomy
827.00 Ethnophysiology
828.00 Ethnopsychology
829.00 Ethnosociology
       00131 06761                                  (2)

830.00 SEX
831.00 Sexuality
832.00 Sexual Stimulation
833.00 Sexual Intercourse
834.00 General Sex Restrictions
835.00 Kinship Regulation of Sex
836.00 Premarital Sex Relations
837.00 Extramarital Sex Relations
838.00 Homosexuality
839.00 Miscellaneous Sex Behavior

840.00 REPRODUCTION
       11291                                        (1)
841.00 Menstruation
842.00 Conception
       00073 11425                                  (2)
843.00 Pregnancy
844.00 Childbirth
       01096                                        (1)
845.00 Difficult and Unusual Births
846.00 Postnatal Care
```

847.00 Abortion and Infanticide
848.00 Illegitimacy

850.00 INFANCY AND CHILDHOOD
851.00 Social Placement
852.00 Ceremonial During Infancy and Childhood
853.00 Infant Feeding
854.00 Infant Care
855.00 Child Care
856.00 Development and Maturation
857.00 Childhood Activities
858.00 Status of Children

860.00 SOCIALIZATION
861.00 Techniques of Inculcation
862.00 Weaning and Food Training
863.00 Cleanliness Training
864.00 Sex Training
865.00 Aggression Training
866.00 Independence Training
867.00 Transmission of Cultural Norms
868.00 Transmission of Skills
869.00 Transmission of Beliefs

870.00 EDUCATION
       00002 00003 00004 00005 00008 00011 00012 00016
       00020 00025 00050 00065 00067 00072 00073 00087
       00117 00155 01011 01049 01134 04077 10269 10560
       11291 11424 11440 11448 11451   (29)
871.00 Educational System
       00062 10207 10223 11425 11452 11453   (6)
872.00 Elementary Education
873.00 Liberal Arts Education
873.10 Liberal arts education--degrees
       00087   (1)
874.00 Vocational Education
875.00 Teachers
876.00 Educational Theory and Methods

880.00 ADOLESCENCE, ADULTHOOD, AND OLD AGE
881.00 Puberty and Initiation
882.00 Status of Adolescents
883.00 Adolescent Activities
884.00 Majority
885.00 Adulthood
886.00 Senescence
887.00 Activities of the Aged
888.00 Status and Treatment of the Aged

Accounting, 451.00
Acculturation and culture
  contact, 177.00
Administrative agencies,
  647.00
Adoption, 597.00
Age stratification,
  561.00
Agriculture, 240.00
Agriculture, cereal,
  243.00
Alien and immigrant
  subgroups, 563.01
Ancestor worship, 769.05
Animal husbandry, 230.00
Animals and things,
  names of, 552.00
Annotated bibliographies,
  113.02
Antagonisms, ingroup,
  578.00
Anthropometry, 141.00
Archaeological sites or
  artifacts, 172.05
Archeology, 172.00
Architecture, 341.00
Archives, 217.00
Archives--accessions,
  217.04
Archives--filing and
  indexing, 217.05
Archives--making collec-
  tions, 217.03
Archives, state, 217.02
Armed forces, 700.00
Armed forces--recruit-
  ment and training,
  702.00
Art, decorative, 531.00
Art, representative,
  532.00
Arts, fine, 530.00
Arts, research in,
  814.05
Athletic sports, 526.00
Atomic energy, 378.00

B

Banditry, 579.00
Banking, 453.00

Behavior and personality--
  test results, 159.06
Bibliographies, annotated,
  113.02
Bibliography, 110.00
Biographical materials,
  159.04
Biology, human, 140.00
Birth statistics, 163.00
Books, sacred, 779.04
Borrowing and lending,
  426.00
Botany--ethnobotany,
  824.00
Brawls, riots, and banditry,
  579.00
Business and industrial
  organization, 470.00

C

Cabarets and night clubs,
  547.00
Cabinet, 645.00
Capital goods industries,
  390.00
Captives and prisoners, treat-
  ment of, 727.05
Castes, 564.00
Ceramic industries, 323.00
Cereal agriculture, 243.00
Chance and luck, 777.00
Chief executive, 643.00
Childbirth, 844.00
Civil service, 647.04
Classes, 565.00
Climate, 132.00
Clinics and hospitals,
  743.00
Clothing, 290.00
Clothing--normal garb,
  291.00
Coinage and mints,
  436.05
Communication, 200.00
Community, 620.00
Community structure,
  621.00
Conception, 842.00
Congregations, 794.00
Constitution, 642.00
Cooperative organization,
  474.00

Funeral, 764.00
Funeral--determination of
time, place, and mode
of burial, 764.05
Funeral--preservative
techniques (e.g. em-
balming), 764.04
Funerary mounds, monu-
ments and memorials,
764.15

G

Games, 524.00
Games of calculation,
524.04
Genealogies, 173.02
Geography, 130.00
Geography--ethnogeography,
823.00
Geology and topography,
133.00
Gods and spirits,
776.00
Government activities,
650.00
Government activities,
miscellaneous,
659.00
Government activities--
research and development,
654.00
Government enterprises,
655.00
Government regulation,
656.00

H

Health, public, 744.00
Health and welfare,
740.00
Heating and lighting,
equipment, 354.00
Highways, 491.00
Historical reconstruction,
174.00
Historical sources and
their evaluation,
175.01
Historiography, 814.01
History, 170.00

History, recorded, 175.00
History, traditional, 173.00
Hobbies, 523.00
Holidays, 527.00
Holy men, 792.00
Hospitals and clinics,
743.00
Household, 592.00
Household, executive,
644.00
Housing, 362.00
Human biology, 140.00
Humanistic studies, 814.00

I

Ideas about nature and man,
820.00
Immigrant and alien subgroups,
563.01
Immigration and emigration,
167.00
Income, public, 651.00
Industrial organization,
470.00
Ingroup antagonisms,
578.00
Inheritance, 428.00
Insurance, 456.00
International relations,
648.00
Invalidism, 734.00

J

Judicial authority,
692.00

K

Kinship, 600.00
Kinship terminology,
601.00
Knowledge, exact, 810.00

L

Labor, 460.00
Labor relations, 466.00
Labor supply and employ-
ment, 464.00
Land use, 311.00

Language, 190.00
Law, 670.00
Law codes, 671.05
Leasing, 427.00
Legal norms, 671.00
Lending, 426.00
Liberal arts education,
873.10
Life history materials,
159.00
Light, 373.00
Lighting equipment,
354.00
Lineages, 613.00
Literary texts, 539.00
Literature, 538.00
Literature, research in,
814.05
Local officials, 624.00
Location, 131.00
Locomotion, 481.00
Luck and chance, 777.00
Lumbering, 313.00

M

Magazines and newspapers,
204.01
Maps, 102.00
Marine industries,
228.00
Marketing, 440.00
Marketing, retail,
443.00
Marriage, 580.00
Marriage, mode of,
583.00
Marriage, regulation of,
582.00
Marriage, secondary,
587.00
Marriage, termination of,
586.00
Mathematics, 803.00
Measures and weights,
804.00
Medical care, 758.00
Medical therapy, 757.00
Medicine, preventive,
751.00
Memorials, funerary,
764.15

Meteorology--ethnometeorology,
821.00
Methodology--recording and
collecting, 126.00
Migration, internal, 166.00
Military technology, 710.00
Mineral resources, 135.00
Mining and quarrying,
316.00
Mints, 436.05
Missions, 797.00
Monuments, funerary, 764.15
Motion picture industry,
546.00
Mounds, funerary, 764.15
Mourning, 765.00
Music, 533.00
Musical instruments,
534.00
Mythology, 773.00

N

Names of animals and things,
552.00
Names of places, 103.00
Names, personal, 551.00
National character,
181.04
Nature and man, ideas
about, 820.00
Newspapers and magazines,
204.01
Night clubs and cabarets,
547.00
Normal garb, 291.00
Norms, 183.00
Norms, legal, 671.00
Nuptials, 585.00

O

Occupational specialization,
463.00
Officials, local 624.00
Oratory, 537.00

P

Paint and dye manufacture,
386.00
Paper industry, 289.00

Parks, 367.00
Parliament, 646.00
Parties, political,
  665.00
Peacemaking, 728.00
Personality and be-
  havior--test results,
  159.06
Pharmaceuticals,
  278.00
Philosophy, 812.00
Place names, 103.00
Police, 625.00
Political behavior,
  660.00
Political movements,
  668.00
Political parties,
  665.00
Population, 161.00
Population, composition
  of, 162.00
Port facilities,
  504.00
Postal system, 205.00
Preservation and storage
  of food, 251.00
Press, 204.00
Prestige, symbolic tokens
  of achievement of,
  554.06
Preventive medicine,
  751.00
Printing, 213.00
Printing--description
  of output, 213.05
Printing--methods,
  213.01
Production and supply,
  433.00
Propaganda and psycho-
  logical warfare,
  723.05
Property, 420.00
Property, real, 423.00
Psychological warfare,
  723.05
Psychotherapists,
  756.00
Public buildings,
  344.01
Public finance, 652.00

Public health and sanitation,
  744.00
Public income, 651.00
Public opinion, 208.00
Publishing, 214.00

Q

Quarrying, 316.00

R

Racial affinities,
  144.00
Radio and television,
  207.00
Railways, 496.00
Real property, 423.00
Religion, general
  character of, 771.00
Religious and educational
  structures, 346.00
Religious beliefs,
  770.00
Religious intolerance,
  798.00
Religious practices,
  780.00
Renting and leasing,
  427.00
Repositories of records,
  217.01
Representative art,
  532.00
Reproduction, 840.00
Research in literature and
  fine arts, 814.05
Retail marketing, 443.00
Revelation and divination,
  787.00
Revolution, 669.00
Riots, 579.00
Rural and urban life,
  369.00

S

Sacred books, 779.04
Sanitation, public,
  744.00
Science, applied,
  816.00

Science--ethnobotany,
824.00
Science--ethnogeography,
823.00
Science--ethnometeorology,
821.00
Science--ethnoscience,
820.00
Science--ethnosociology,
829.00
Science--ethnozoology,
825.00
Science, pure, 815.00
Scientific method,
813.00
Secondary marriages,
587.00
Sects, 795.00
Settlement patterns,
361.00
Settlements, 360.00
Sex status, 562.00
Shaving and depilation,
302.01
Sickness, 750.00
Slavery, 567.00
Social groups, 571.00
Social relationships
and groups, 571.00
Social stratification,
560.00
Socio-cultural trends,
178.00
Sociology--ethno-
sociology, 829.00
Sodalities, 575.00
Soil, 134.00
Somatology, descriptive,
142.00
Specialization, occupa-
tional, 463.00
Speculation, 455.00
Spirits and gods,
776.00
Sports, athletic,
526.00
Standard of living,
511.00
State, 640.00
State archives, 217.02
Statistics, birth, 163.00

Status, sex, 562.00
Status symbols, 554.06
Strategy, 723.00
Stratification, age,
561.00
Stratification, ethnic,
563.00
Stratification, social,
560.00
Symbolic tokens of
achievement of prestige,
554.06

T

Tactics, 725.00
Taxation and public
income, 651.00
Television and radio,
207.00
Territorial hierarchy,
631.00
Territorial organiza-
tion, 630.00
Textile industries,
288.00
Theological systems,
779.00
Therapy, medical,
757.00
Tillage, 241.00
Time, ordering of,
805.00
Toilet, 302.00
Topography and geology,
133.00
Trade, foreign,
439.00
Traditional history,
173.00
Transportation,
489.00
Travel, 484.00
Travel services--
accommodations,
485.01
Travel and transporta-
tion, 480.00

U

Urban and rural life,
369.00

V

Vocabulary--kinship
terminology,   601.00

W

War,   720.00
Warfare,   726.00
Warfare, psychological,
723.05
Wartime adjustments,
722.00
Water supply,   312.00
Waterways improvements,
503.00
Weights and measures,
804.00
Welfare,   740.00
Welfare agencies,
private,   747.00
Worship ancestor,
769.05
Writing,   212.00
Writing--description of
output,   212.09

Z

Zoology--ethnozoology,
825.00

ADMINISTRATIVE AND POLITICAL DIVISIONS   01042
                                                      (1)
AGRICULTURE--BIBLIOGRAPHY   00129   (1)
AGRICULTURE--ECONOMIC ASPECTS   00186   (1)
ANTHROPOLOGY--BIBLIOGRAPHY   CC183   (1)
ANTHROPOLOGY--INDEXES   00197   (1)
ANTIQUITIES--CATALOGS   C1C54   (1)
ART TREASURES--CATALOGS   01C54   (1)
ASIA--BIBLIOGRAPHY   00108   (1)
ASSOCIATIONS, INSTITUTIONS, ETC.--DIRECTORIES
     C0346   (1)
BIBLIOGRAPHICAL EXHIBITIONS   00171 C0182 09105
                                                      (3)
BIBLIOGRAPHICAL EXHIBITIONS--BIBLICGRAPHY   C1015
                                                      (1)
BIBLIOGRAPHY   11446   (1)
BIBLIOGRAPHY--ADDRESSES, ESSAYS, LECTURES   01079
                                                      (1)
BIBLIOGRAPHY--COLLECTIONS   CC065 00175   (2)
BIBLIOGRAPHY--HISTORY--SOURCES   11243   (1)
BIBLIOGRAPHY--RARE BOOKS   C1C39 01108 11243   (3)
BIO-BIBLIOGRAPHY   01065   (1)
BUSINESS--BIBLIOGRAPHY   00070   (1)
CATALOG, PUBLISHER   C0167   (1)
CATALOGS   CC166 00179 C0185 C03C0 01008 C1010
     11849   (7)
CATALOGS--BOOK EXHIBITIONS   09105   (1)
CATALOGS--CULTURAL PROPERTIES   C1054   (1)
CATALOGS--PERIODICALS   C1C09   (1)
CATALOGS, BOOK   C0005 00117 00118 00120 03066
     1C570   (6)
CATALOGS, CLASSIFIED   C017C CC192   (2)
CATALOGS, COLLEGE   0C065 CC175   (2)
CATALOGS, PERIODICAL   00346 04170   (2)
CATALOGS, PRIVATE LIBRARY   CCC95 C0168 00169
     CC17C C1026   (5)
CATALOGS, RARE BOOK   01011   (1)
CATALOGS, SUBJECT   00158   (1)
CATALOGS, UNIVERSITY LIBRARY   C0181   (1)
CENSORSHIP OF THE PRESS   C0164   (1)
CHEJUDO--BIBLICGRAPHY   CCG01   (1)
CLIMATCLOGY--BIBLICGRAPHY   00124   (1)
DISSERTATIONS, ACADEMIC--ABSTRACTS   11654   (1)
DOCUMENTS, DIPLOMATIC--BIBLIOGRAPHY   00054 00128
     C0134   (3)
ECONOMIC CONDITICNS--BIBLICGRAPHY   11446 11572
     11590   (3)
ECONOMIC CONDITICNS--INDEXES   C0180   (1)
ECONOMICS--BIBLICGRAPHY   CCC70 11446   (2)
EXHIBITIONS--BIBLICGRAPHY   C0171   (1)
EXHIBITIONS--CATALCGS   01066 C1068   (2)

```
ADMINISTRATION      11450 11572                          (2)
ADMINISTRATION, LOCAL      11451                         (1)
AGRICULTURE      CCC01 00008 0CC16 C0022 00023 C0050
     CCC72 CC073 CCC88 C01C7 0C120 C0129 C0131 01127
     1C560 11436 11440                                  (17)
ALPHABET      11436                                      (1)
ANTHROPOLOGY      CC023                                  (1)
ARCHEOLOGY      0CC15 01006 01123 01138 01139 11450
                                                         (6)
ARTS      CC011 00022 00025 C0C5C C0065 00067 0CC73
     C0117 C1CC6 C1C11 01032 01C33 01137 01138 C6766
     1C207 10269 1C754 11436 1144C 11452 11453 11859
                                                         (23)
ASIAN STUDIES      C1051                                 (1)
ASTRONCMY      01032                                     (1)
BAMBCO      11425                                        (1)
BIBLIOGRAPHIES      00001 00011 00025 00117 01021
     01C80 01128 C4074 04076 04077 C4094 C6763 11656
                                                         (13)
BIOGRAPHY      00022 00065 C007C CC073 00075 00133
     01C32 01033 C1064 01123 01128 01139 06449 10269
     1C334 11436 11437 11898                             (18)
BIOLOGY      0CC63                                       (1)
BLOOD BANK      11425                                    (1)
BUDDHISM      C0004 00005 00008 0CC15 00019 00022
     0CC58 00063 C0C65 00C72 CC073 CCC75 00088 C0095
     00117 C0121 CC165 01014 01032 C1048 01066 01067
     01C68 C1069 01C80 01083 01085 01103 C1116 01123
     04C76 C4077 11291 11436 1144C 11860                (36)
BULLFIGHT      11291                                     (1)
BUSINESS      11425                                      (1)
BUSINESS POLICY      00070                               (1)
BUTCHERS      CCC08 11447                                (2)
CALENDAR      C1032                                      (1)
CALLIGRAPHY      C0C22                                   (1)
CEMENT      0CCC5                                        (1)
CHILDREN      00117 04076 04077 11448                    (4)
CHINESE CLASSICS      01123                              (1)
CHRISTIANITY      CC006 CCCC8 C0012 C0015 00063
     CCC72 C0073 CC075 00117 00128 10560 11291          (12)
CHRISTIANITY--METHCDISTS      CC05C                      (1)
CHRISTIANITY--PROTESTANTS      00118 0012C 01049    (3)
CHRISTIANITY--ROMAN CATHOLICISM      0CC05 00019
     CCC5C C0118 C0120 01015 01032 01049 C1062 01064
     04C76 04077 11436 11856 11857                      (15)
CHRONOLOGY      CCC22                                    (1)
CLANS      00121 07055                                   (2)
CLASSICS      CC022 00061 CC067 00C91 C0107 00176
     C1018 C1C39 C1C41 01C46 01C58 01062 01080 01094
     01103 01112 01121 03066 04C74 04076 C4077 04078
     04121 04122 04128 1C334 11291 11293 11440 11452
```

```
PHILOSOPHY        CCCC2 C0003 C0067 C0073 01011 03066
     10207                                              (7)
PHYSICAL ANTHROPOLOGY         C0007 00183 00184 01138
                                                       (4)
POETRY       10269                                     (1)
POLITICAL DEVELOPMENT        C1126                     (1)
POLITICAL IDEOLOGY       11832                         (1)
POLITICAL SCIENCE        04111                         (1)
POLITY       CCCC1 CC002 C0CC4 C0CC5 C0012 00016
     C0022 CC024 C0C72 00C73 0C075 C0087 00118 00120
     00155 01046 C4C77 10207 10560 11293 11437 11448
     11452 11453                                      (24)
POPULATION       CC075 06761 06762                     (3)
PRINTING CULTURE        00165 11241                    (2)
PUBLIC ADMINISTRAT.ION        01127 07057 10206 11451
                                                       (4)
RARE BOOKS       CCC58 00061 C0067 CC069 00080 0C088
     CCC91 CC095 C0165 00168 C1011 C1018 C1027 01C39
     01C41 01072 C1C80 01085 01094 C11C3 01108 01121
     04C74 04C76 C4C77 04078 1C576 11290 11291 11293
     11440 11566 11846                                (33)
RECREATION       0C072 00117 11447                     (3)
REFERENCE WORKS         00015 C0016 CC019 01C04 01026
     C1137                                             (6)
RELIGION       CCCC1 C0003 CCCC5 CCC11 CC023 00025
     0CC50 C0065 C0073 01C11 01137 C4078 06762 06766
     1C207 10269 1C560 11293 11425 11448 11450   (21)
RITES       C0117                                      (1)
RURAL SOCIOLOGY        06761 C6762                     (2)
SALT       C0CC5                                        (1)
SCIENCE       0C012 C1033                              (2)
SHAMANISM       CCC15 00063 C0117 0C121 C6449 11447
                                                       (6)
SHAMANS       01C62                                    (1)
SLAVERY       11436                                    (1)
SOCIAL CHANGE       C0117                              (1)
SOCIAL CONDITIONS        00155 1C269                   (2)
SOCIAL GROUPINGS        06449 11447                    (2)
SOCIAL PATHOLOGY        06761                          (1)
SOCIAL POLICY       C0070                              (1)
SOCIAL PSYCHOLOGY        06761                         (1)
SOCIAL SCIENCES       00004 C0005 0C167 01078    (4)
SOCIAL STRATIFICATION       11436                      (1)
SOCIETY       0C117 10207                              (2)
SOCIOCULTURAL CHANGE        C0007 00C16 00120 01138
     06761 C6762 1C207 11436 11852                     (9)
SOCIOLOGY       C0C23 00117 01133 01134 01137 06761
     06762 11452 11453                                 (9)
SOCIOLOGY OF KNOWLEDGE       11241                     (1)
SOCIOLOGY OF LAW       06761                           (1)
STATISTICS       0C004 00005 00012 C0075 00144 11451
     11572                                             (7)
SURNAMES       CC063 01096 C7055                       (3)
SUTRAS       C0C22 CC067                               (2)
```

```
TAOISM        00022 01032 11440                          (3)
TECHNOLOGY      00061 00073 10269 11448                  (4)
THEORY        00058                                      (1)
TOBACCO       CCC05                                      (1)
TOMBS         00121                                      (1)
TRADE         C0019 C0121 01046 01129 10269 11448        (6)
TRAVELERS' ACCOUNTS      C0011 C0012 00016 00050
      CC075 00117 C0118 00120 00121 C0155 01044 01059
      C1123 01139 04076 04077 04078 10207 10269 10560
      11450                                              (21)
TRIBUTE       01139                                      (1)
TUBERCULOSIS     C0050                                   (1)
URBAN SOCIOLOGY      06761                               (1)
VALUES        11177                                      (1)
WELFARE       CCC50 11440                                (2)
WOMEN         CC050 C0C72 00117 00121 C0155 01049 01096
      04077 10560 11291 11448                            (11)
```

KEY WORDS SPECIFIC TO KOREAN CULTURE

```
AJIA-SHUGI      1C207                                    (1)
APRIL REVOLUTION      01126                              (1)
ASIANISM      1C207                                      (1)
ASSASSINATION OF THE QUEEN      00012                    (1)
CH'ONDO KYO      CC072 00194 01062 04076 10269           (5)
CHANGGI       04C86                                      (1)
CHODANGJIP       11860                                   (1)
CHOGYE        11860                                      (1)
CHOSEN SOTOKUFU      04100 10207                         (2)
CHULDARIGI       11291                                   (1)
DEMOCRATIC PEOPLE'S REPUBLIC OF KCREA       00016
      CCC52 00180 01C86 1159C                            (5)
GOVERNMENT-GENERAL OF KOREA      10207                   (1)
HALLYANG      11291                                      (1)
HAN'GUL       CCC58 11291                                (2)
HANMUN        11436                                      (1)
HARBIN INCIDENT      00128                               (1)
HIDEYOSHI'S INVASIONS      C0117                         (1)
HUNMIN CHONGUM      00058 01103 04C76                    (3)
HYANGGA       01C96 11291                                (2)
IMO KULLAN       01C49                                   (1)
INDEPENDENCE MOVEMENT      00012 C0016 00019 01C49
      10269 10560                                        (6)
JAPANESE ARMY      C0116                                 (1)
JAPANESE COLONIALISM      10207                          (1)
JAPANESE EDUCATICN      11443                            (1)
```

116

```
JAPANESE IMPERIALISM        10207                    (1)
JAPANESE IN KOREA        00133 10207                 (2)
JAPANESE LEGATION (SEOUL)        00128              (1)
JAPANESE MILITARY IN KOREA        10207            (1)
JAPANESE MINISTRY OF FOREIGN AFFAIRS        00134   (1)
JAPANESE NATIONALISM        10207                   (1)
JAPANESE NAVY        00116                          (1)
JAPANESE OCCUPATION        00008 00024             (2)
JAPANESE RESIDENCY-GENERAL IN KOREA        00128   (1)
KABO KYONGJANG        01049                         (1)
KAPSIN CHONGBYON        01049                       (1)
KHITAN        01081                                 (1)
KOREAN WAR        00008 00016 00019 00050 00115 01023
     01049 01126 04076 04077 04082 04085 10560 11424
     11451 11573 11761 11795                       (18)
KUT        00005                                    (1)
KWAGO        00005 11291 11451                      (3)
KYE        00087                                    (1)
LIAO        01081                                   (1)
MOSUM        11291                                  (1)
MUDANG        01096 11291                           (2)
MYON        00131                                   (1)
ONDOL        01096 11291                            (2)
OVERSEAS KOREANS        00012 00016 00072 00116 00117
     00128 00134 01126 10207 10269                 (10)
PAEKCHONG        07055 11291                        (2)
POBUSANG        10205                               (1)
SIRHAK        00005 00019 10334                     (3)
TAEJANGGYONG        11291                           (1)
TOKANFU        10207                                (1)
TONGHAK        00005                                (1)
TONGHAK REVOLT        00128 01049                   (2)
TONGNIP HYOPHOE        01049                        (1)
TONGNIP MOVEMENT        01049                       (1)
U.S. MARINES        00115                           (1)
UNIFICATION        01126                            (1)
YANGBAN        11291 11436                          (2)
YEJO        10204                                   (1)
ZEN        11860                                    (1)
```

AN, CHUNG-GUN   C0128   (1)
ASAMI LIBRARY. UNIVERSITY CF CALIFCRNIA (BERKELEY)
      11898   (1)
BIBLIOTHEQUE NATIONALE   11928   (1)

BRITISH MUSEUM. LONDON. DEPARTMENT OF ORIENTAL
      PRINTED BOOKS AND MANUSCRIPTS   11945   (1)
BROOKLYN PUBLIC LIBRARY   11933   (1)
CHOSEN CHRISTIAN COLLEGE LIBRARY   03066   (1)
COLUMBIA UNIVERSITY. EAST ASIATIC LIBRARY   00100
                                                               (1)
ESSEX INSTITUTE. SALEM, MASS   11935   (1)
FUJITA, RYOSAKU   01133   (1)
GOVERNMENT-GENERAL LIBRARY   C0C22 00107 00192
      11937   (4)
GREAT BRITAIN. WAR OFFICE LIBRARY   01028   (1)
HARVARD-YENCHING LIBRARY   11452 11453   (2)
HOSA BUNKO   C0187   (1)
HOSEKO, SHIGEKATSU   01005   (1)
ILSA AND GARAM COLLECTIONS. SEOUL NATIONAL
      UNIVERSITY LIBRARY   11293   (1)
IMANISHI COLLECTION. TENRI UNIVERSITY   00065
      C0175   (2)
IMANISHI, RYU (1875-1932)   00065 00175   (2)
ITO, HIROBUMI   C0128   (1)
ITO, MARQUIS   10207   (1)
JAPANESE ARMY AND NAVY ARCHIVES   00116   (1)
JAPANESE MINISTRY CF FOREIGN AFFAIRS   00134   (1)
KANASEKI COLLECTION, STANFORD UNIVERSITY LIBRARY
      CCCO7   (1)
KEIJO FURITSU TOSHOKAN   C0C68   (1)
KEIJO IMPERIAL UNIVERSITY LIBRARY   C0181   (1)
KEIJO TEIKOKU DAIGAKU   C0181 CC182   (2)
KOREAN RESEARCH CENTER. KOREANA CCLLECTICN
      11787   (1)
KUKKA CHAEGON CH'OEGO HOEUI TOSOGWAN   C0075   (1)
KUNGNIP CHUNGANG TOSOGWAN   00068 00073   (2)
KUNGNIP TOSOGWAN   00079 10576   (2)
KYOTO DAIGAKU. JINBUN KAGAKU KENKYUJO   00189   (1)
KYUJANGGAK   0C076 00106 01022 11948 11950 11962
                                                               (6)
LANDIS LIBRARY   04182   (1)
LAUTENSACH, HERMANN   01090   (1)
LENINGRAD STATE UNIVERSITY. ORIENTAL INSTITUTE
      11788   (1)
LIBRARY OF CONGRESS   00020   (1)
MAEMA COLLECTICN   C0067   (1)
NAIKAKU BUNKO   11913   (1)
NATIONAL AGRICULTURAL LIBRARY   00129   (1)

```
NATIONAL ASSEMBLY LIBRARY      C0075                    (1)
NATIONAL CENTRAL LIBRARY       C0073 C0079 10576        (3)
NATIONAL DIET LIBRARY          10560 11913              (2)
ODAESAN SAGO      11949                                 (1)
OSAKA FURITSU TOSHOKAN      00163                       (1)
OSAKA PREFECTURAL LIBRARY      C0163                    (1)
PAK, YONG-HYO      C0128                                (1)
PANG, CHONG-HYON      11293                             (1)
RIOKE ZOSHOKAKU      00168                              (1)
ROYAL EMPIRE SOCIETY. LONDON. LIBRARY      00158    (1)
SEIKADO BUNKO      11915                                (1)
SEOUL NATIONAL UNIVERSITY LIBRARY      11293        (1)
SONKEIKAKU BUNKO      11915                             (1)
SOUL TAEHAKKYO      11293                               (1)
SUNGMYONG WOMEN'S UNIVERSITY      119CC              (1)
TAKAHASHI, TORU      01134                              (1)
TAKASHI, AKIBA      06449                               (1)

TERAUCHI COLLECTION. YAMAGUCHI WOMEN'S JUNIOR
     COLLEGE      CC169                                 (1)
TOKSINDANG      0C095                                   (1)
TOKYO DAIGAKU. TOYO BUNKA KENKYUJC      00189       (1)
TONGGUK TAEHAKKYO      01066 01067 C1068 01069 11566
                                                       (5)
TOYO BUNKO      CC170 C0171 11936                      (3)
TOYO BUNKO, TOKYO      00189                           (1)
U.S. NATIONAL ARCHIVES      11946                      (1)
WANG, YANG-MING      10334                             (1)
YI WANGJIK. SOMUKWA      00168                         (1)
YI, PYONG-GI      11293                                (1)
YI, SUNSIN      CCC16                                  (1)
YOAN-IN LIBRARY      01016                             (1)
YONGSAN SPECIAL SERVICE LIBRARY      11424         (1)
YONGSAN SPECIAL SERVICES LIBRARY      11425        (1)
YONSEI UNIVERSITY LIBRARY      03C66               (1)
```

GEOGRAPHICAL SUBJECTS

```
CHEJUDO      CCC01 C0117                               (2)
DAGELET      00117                                     (1)
DIAMOND MOUNTAINS      00117                           (1)
KUMGANG-SAN      CC117                                 (1)
KYONGJU      11726                                     (1)
KYONGSANG NAMDO      01104                             (1)
QUELPART      CC117                                    (1)
ULLUNGDO      CC117                                    (1)
```

PUBLICATION YEARS COVERED BY BIBLIOGRAPHIES

BIBLIOGRAPHY-- UP TO 1870	01045	(1)
BIBLIOGRAPHY-- UP TO 1890	C1032	(1)
BIBLIOGRAPHY-- UP TO 1899	01033	(1)
BIBLIOGRAPHY-- UP TO 1900	C0156	(1)
BIBLIOGRAPHY-- UP TO 1945	01092	(1)
BIBLIOGRAPHY-- UP TO 1961	C0075	(1)
BIBLIOGRAPHY-- UP TO 1967	04076 04077	(2)
BIBLIOGRAPHY--0918-1392	01121	(1)
BIBLIOGRAPHY--0918-1933	03066	(1)
BIBLIOGRAPHY--1392-1941	01027	(1)
BIBLIOGRAPHY--1420-1858	11846	(1)
BIBLIOGRAPHY--1477-1859	00157	(1)
BIBLIOGRAPHY--1576-1965	01062	(1)
BIBLIOGRAPHY--1588-1950	C0117	(1)
BIBLIOGRAPHY--1594-1930	00120	(1)
BIBLIOGRAPHY--1725-1800	10334	(1)
BIBLIOGRAPHY--1800-1909	01064	(1)
BIBLIOGRAPHY--1818-1935	0C118	(1)
BIBLIOGRAPHY--1832-1944	01096	(1)
BIBLIOGRAPHY--1834-1943	00155	(1)
BIBLIOGRAPHY--1850-1956	0C016	(1)
BIBLIOGRAPHY--1859-1893	00157	(1)
BIBLIOGRAPHY--1868-1912	00062	(1)
BIBLIOGRAPHY--1868-1931	01131	(1)
BIBLIOGRAPHY--1870-1912	01045	(1)

BIBLIOGRAPHY--1877-1969	11976	(1)
BIBLIOGRAPHY--1883-1945	11448	(1)
BIBLIOGRAPHY--1886-1935	CC197	(1)
BIBLIOGRAPHY--1886-1962	01049	(1)
BIBLIOGRAPHY--1887-1948	CC183	(1)
BIBLIOGRAPHY--1890-1940	0CC06	(1)
BIBLIOGRAPHY--1893-1902	11939	(1)
BIBLIOGRAPHY--1894-1906	11891	(1)
BIBLIOGRAPHY--1895-1910	00192	(1)
BIBLIOGRAPHY--1896-1910	10592	(1)
BIBLIOGRAPHY--1896-1945	CC072	(1)
BIBLIOGRAPHY--1900-1931	00176	(1)
BIBLIOGRAPHY--19C0-1936	03723	(1)
BIBLIOGRAPHY--19C0-1965	07055	(1)
BIBLIOGRAPHY--19C0-1966	11291	(1)
BIBLIOGRAPHY--1903-1912	11940	(1)
BIBLIOGRAPHY--1905-1938	04075	(1)
BIBLIOGRAPHY--1906-1926	00125	(1)
BIBLIOGRAPHY--1906-1929	CC140	(1)
BIBLIOGRAPHY--1906-1932	CC141	(1)
BIBLIOGRAPHY--1906-1935	00145	(1)
BIBLIOGRAPHY--1906-1937	CC146	(1)
BIBLIOGRAPHY--1909-1959	01134	(1)
BIBLIOGRAPHY--1910-1945	04170	(1)
BIBLIOGRAPHY--1910-1958	CC019	(1)
BIBLIOGRAPHY--1911-1935	C1130	(1)
BIBLIOGRAPHY--1912-1926	01099	(1)

BIBLIOGRAPHY--1916-1945	0CC07	(1)
BIBLIOGRAPHY--1917-1961	01133	(1)
BIBLIOGRAPHY--1920-1949	10269	(1)
BIBLIOGRAPHY--1921-1961	0C071	(1)
BIBLIOGRAPHY--1925-1959	11447	(1)
BIBLIOGRAPHY--1926-1936	01089	(1)
BIBLIOGRAPHY--1927-1953	0CC63	(1)
BIBLIOGRAPHY--1930-1949	0C025	(1)
BIBLIOGRAPHY--1932-1937	C0121	(1)
BIBLIOGRAPHY--1933-1958	00109	(1)
BIBLIOGRAPHY--1933-1962	0C023	(1)
BIBLIOGRAPHY--1934-1963	01129	(1)
BIBLIOGRAPHY--1937-1940	04074	(1)
BIBLIOGRAPHY--1940-1950	00389	(1)
BIBLIOGRAPHY--1941-1942	C1080	(1)
BIBLIOGRAPHY--1943-1968	11560	(1)
BIBLIOGRAPHY--1944-1950	00143	(1)
BIBLIOGRAPHY--1945-1954	11443	(1)
BIBLIOGRAPHY--1945-1958	CCC02 01097	(2)
BIBLIOGRAPHY--1945-1959	0CC10 C0C20	(2)
BIBLIOGRAPHY--1945-1960	0CC70 CC087 C0166 C0179	(4)
BIBLIOGRAPHY--1945-1961	0CC04 CC0C5	(2)
BIBLIOGRAPHY--1945-1962	00073	(1)
BIBLIOGRAPHY--1945-1964	06761 11885	(2)
BIBLIOGRAPHY--1945-1966	10206 11423 11451 11559	(4)
BIBLIOGRAPHY--1946-1950	01C06	(1)

BIBLIOGRAPHY--1948-1965	11849	(1)
BIBLIOGRAPHY--1950-1956	04167	(1)
BIBLIOGRAPHY--1950-1958	0C050	(1)
BIBLIOGRAPHY--1954-1964	11177	(1)
BIBLIOGRAPHY--1954-1966	11902	(1)
BIBLIOGRAPHY--1957-1963	01C86	(1)
BIBLIOGRAPHY--1959-1962	0CC03	(1)
BIBLIOGRAPHY--1959-1963	11437	(1)
BIBLIOGRAPHY--1963-1964	11441	(1)
BIBLIOGRAPHY--1964-1965	06762	(1)
BIBLIOGRAPHY--1965	11442	(1)
BIBLIOGRAPHY--1967	04090	(1)

AKADEMIIA NAUK SSSR. INSTITUT NARCDOV AZII
    11788
ALLIED FORCES. SCUTHWEST PACIFIC AREA   00155
AMERICAN HISTORICAL ASSOCIATION, CCMP   01037
AN, CH'UN-GUN   04086
ASAMI, RINTARC   11859
ASIATIC RESEARCH CENTER, KOREA UNIVERSITY   01049
ASO, TAKEKAME   04127
BACKUS, ROBERT L.   00016
BARK, DONG-SUH   10206 11451
BEAL, EDWIN G.   00011 00134
BERTCN, PETER A   00128
BLANCHARD, CARROLL HENRY   11573
BRITISH MUSEUM. LONDON. (DEPARTMENT OF ORIENTAL
    PRINTED BOOKS AND MANUSCRIPTS)   11945
BUDDHIST LODGE, LONDON   01116
BURR, NELSCN R.   00133
CALIFORNIA. UNIVERSITY. EAST ASIATIC STUDIES
    COC16
CALIFORNIA. UNIVERSITY. INSTITUTE CF EAST ASIATIC
    STUDIES   CC015
CAMMAERTS, EMILE   01110
CEADEL, E. B.   01081 01082
CENTRE FOR EAST ASIAN CULTURAL STUDIES, COMP
    01021
CH'OE, CHAE-SOK   06761 06762 07055
CH'OE, SUN-JA   00072
CHANG, KI-GUN   04092
CHANG, TOK-SUN   04093
CHO, LEE-JAE   CC144
CHOI, SOON JA   C0072
CHON, HAE-JONG   10204
CHON, MUNAM   11423
CHONG, CH'OL   1C329
CHONG, IN-BO   1C334
CHONG, JOSEPH SANG-HUN   11446
CHONG, YONG-SUN   11437
CHOSEN GAKKAI   04073
CHOSEN KEIZAI KENKYUJO   11572
CHOSEN KOSHO KANKOKAI   11440
CHOSEN SOTOKUFU   00107
CHOSEN SOTOKUFU CHOSENSHI HENSHU-KAI   11888
CHOSEN SOTOKUFU KAMBO BUNSHOKA, EC   01130
CHOSEN SOTCKUFU. KEIMUKYOKU   00164
CHOSEN SOTOKUFU TOSHO-KAN, ED   11854
CHOSENSHI HENSHUKAI, ED   11855
CHOSCN KOSO KANHAENGHOE. SEOUL, KCREA   01108
CHOSON MINJUJUUI INMIN KONGHWAGUK KWAHAGWCN
    C1C08 C1009
CHOSON MINJUJUUI INMIN KONGHWAGUK SAHCE KWAHAGWON.
    KOJON YON'GUSO. P'YONGYANG, KCREA.   CCC61

CHUN, HAE-JONG   10204
CHUNG, DA-SAN   10334
CHUNG, JOSEPH SANG-HOON   11446
CHUNG, YONG-SUN   11437
COLUMBIA UNIVERSITY   00100
CONOVER, HELEN F.   00139
CORDIER, HENRI   00156 01045
CORNELL UNIVERSITY. DEPT. OF FAR EASTERN STUDIES.
    SOUTHEAST ASIA PROGRAM   00109
COUNCIL FOR OLD WORLD ARCHAEOLOGY   01077
COURANT, MAURICE (AUGUSTE LOUIS MARIE)   01032
    01033 01034 01036 01095 01117 11241 11928
DENNEY, RUTH N.   11916
DINDINGER, P. JOHANNES   01064
DOROSH, ELIZABETH GARDNER   00012
DOROSH, JOHN T.   00012
EELLS, WALTER CROSBY   11443
EHRMAN, EDITH   11834
ELROD, JEFFERSON MCREE   00006
EN'O-SEI   04128
ENDO, MOTOO   01046
EVANS, LEWIN   00158
FANG, CHAO-YING   11898
FITZGERALD, JAMES S   00144
FUJII, SOJU   01014
FUKUDA, TOKUZO   01078
FURUKAWA, KANEHICE   01079
FURUTANI, KIYOSHI   04115
FURUYA, KIYOSHI   01013
GEORGE PEABODY COLLEGE FOR TEACHERS   00019
GEROW, BERT A   00007
GOMPERTZ, E   00118
GOMPERTZ, G.   00118
GOMPERTZ, G. ST.G. M   00117
GOTO, KIMPEI   01021
GREAT BRITAIN. IMPERIAL WAR MUSEUM. LIBRARY
    11795
GREAT BRITAIN. WAR OFFICE. LIBRARY   01028
GRIFFIN, APPLETON PRENTISS CLARK   11943
GRINSTEAD, E. D.   11945
HA, YUN-DO   00061
HAENISCH, WOLF   00145 00146
HAMMOND, THOMAS T.   11761
HAN, U-GUN   10205
HAN, WOO-KEUN   10205
HAN'GUK PAN'GONG YONMAENG   04082
HAN'GUK TOSOGWAN HYOPHOE   04090
HAN'GUK YON'GU TOSOGWAN   00087
HAN'GUK YON'GU TOSOGWAN. SEOUL, KOREA   11787
HAN'GUK YON'GUWON   00087
HAN'GUK YON'GUWON. SEOUL, KOREA   11423
HANAYAMA, SHINSHO   01048
HARA, SANSHICHI   00065

HARVARD UNIVERSITY. LIBRARY. HARVARC-YENCHING
    LIBRARY   11452 11453
HAWAII. UNIVERSITY. EAST-WEST CENTER. LIBRARY
    11656
HAYASHI, TAISUKE   04116 04117
HAZARD, B.H.   CC015
HELLMAN, FLORENCE S.   00138
HENTHORN, WILLIAM E.   01128 11177
HERMANN, VIRGINIA HITCHCOCK   01105
HEWES, GORDON WINAUT   00287
HIROSE, BIN   C0176
HOBBS, CECIL   C1105
HONDA, MINORU   C1081 01C82
HONG, SOON YUNG   00071
HONG, SUN-YONG   00071
HOWE, GEORGE FREDERICK   01037
HUFF, ELIZABETH   11898
HUMAN RELATICNS AREA FILES   11853
HWANG, PYONG-HCN   00061
IKEUCHI, HIROSHI   00390
IMAMURA, TOMOE   04118
IMANISHI, RYU   01083
ITO, HIROBUMI   C0054
IWASAKI, KEISHC   01132
JAPAN. MOMBUSHC. DAIGAKU GAKUJUTSUKYOKU   04170
JAPANESE SOCIETY CF ETHNCLCGY   11447
JONES, HELEN DUDENBOSTEL   C0025 0107C
KAMEDA, JIRO   C1135
KANAZAWA, SHOZABURC   01011 C1051
KANNO, HIROOMI   01010
KAWACHI, YOSHIHIRO   00424
KEIJO FURITSU TOSHCKAN   CC068
KEIJO TEIKOKU CAIGAKU. FUZCKU TCSHOKAN,   COMP
    C0181
KEIJO TEIKOKU CAIGAKU. FUZCKU TCSHCKAN,   EC
    C0182
KEIJO TENSHU-KCKYCKAI, ED   01015
KERNER, ROBERT JCSEPH   CC108
KIM, C. I. EUGENE   01126
KIM, CHONG-IK EUGENE   01126
KIM, CHONG-UK   C1084
KIM, G. F   11917
KIM, KUN-SU   C1C52 01053 11448 11899
KIM, SU-GYONG   C1036
KIM, UN-SOK   C0052
KIM, WCN-YCNG   C1085
KIM, YAK-SIL   1C754
KIM, YANG-SON   04083
KIM, YCNG-DOK   C1114
KIM, YOUN SOO   C1122
KIM, YUN-SU   C1122
KISHI, YUZURU   04119
KNEZ, EUGENE I   C1138

KO, HE-SONG CHON   11852
KO, HCO SUK   CC071
KO, HU-SOK   CCC71
KOH, HESUNG CHUN   11852
KOKURITSU KOKKAI TOSHOKAN,   ED   10570
KOKURITSU KOKKAI TOSHOKAN. SANKO SHCSHIBU   10560
KOKUSAI BUNKA SHINKOKAI   00121
KONDO, KEN'ICHI   01026
KONTSEVICH, L. P   11760
KOREA (GOVERNMENT-GENERAL OF CHOSEN, 1910-1945)
      CCC22 001C7 CO164 00192
KOREA (GOVERNMENT-GENERAL CF CHOSEN, 1910-1945)
      RINJI TOCHI CHCSAKYOKU   01C42
KOREA (GOVERNMENT-GENERAL OF CHOSEN, 1910-1945)
      TOSHOKAN   CC053
KOREA (REPUBLIC) KCNGBOBU   003CC
KOREA (REPUBLIC) KONGBOBU. KONGBOGUK   CO346
      11569
KOREA (REPUBLIC) MUN'GYOBU   01C54 10223
KOREA UNIVERSITY. ASIATIC RESEARCH CENTER   COCO2
      CCCO3
KOREAN CONFLICT RESEARCH FOUNDATICN   11573
KOREAN RESEARCH CENTER   11787
KORYO TAEHAKKYO. ASEA MUNJE YCN'GUSO   COGO2
      CCCO3
KORYO TAEHAKKYO. SEOUL, KCREA. ASEA MUNJE YCN'GUSO
      CC379 C1049
KOYAMA, FUJIO   C1115
KUJI, HANJIRO   01088 04120
KUKHAK YON'GU NONJC CH'ONGNAM KANHAENGHOE   CCO10
KUKHOE TOSOGWAN   04095 04096 04C97 041C0 04111
      11427
KUKHOE TOSOGWAN. SEOUL, KOREA   11849
KUKHOE TOSOGWAN. SEOUL, KOREA. SASCGUK   10269
      11448
KUKHOE TOSOGWAN. SEOUL, KOREA. SASCGUK. CH'AMGC
      SOJIKWA   1C592
KUKKA CHAEGON CH'OEGO HOEUI TCSCGWAN   CCO75
KUNGNIP CHUNGANG TOSOGWAN   CCO68 11445
KUNGNIP CHUNGANG TCSOGWAN. P'YCNGYANG, KCREA.
      00058
KUNGNIP CHUNGANG TCSOGWAN. SECUL, KOREA   COC73
      11441 11442
KUNGNIP TOSOGWAN   00079 C0080 C9105 10576
KUO-LI CHUNG-YANG T'U-SHU-KUAN, EC   01044 01123
      01139
KUROCA, RYO   CC165
KUSUDA, ONOSABURC   11856 11857
KYONGBUK TAEHAKKYO   11654
KYOTO DAIGAKU. BUNGAKUBU TCSHOSHITSU,   ED
      C0175
KYRIAK, THEODORE E.   11590
LAUTENSACH, HERMANN   01C89 010S0
LAYARO, R. DE B   04183

```
LEE, CHONG-SIK      11761
LEE, HONG-JIK       11726
LEE, HYOUN-JONG       11291
LEE, JAI CHUL       00019
LEE, MAHN-SOO       11291
LEE, SOON HI        00050
LEE, YONG-HEE       11292
LEW, YOUNG ICK      10207
LICHTENWANGER, WILLIAM      01105
MAEMA, KYOSAKU        00067 01058
MARCH, ARTHUR CHARLES       01116
MARCUS, RICHARD       00015
MCCUNE, SHANNON BOYD-BAILEY      00024 00110 00123
    00124 01090 01117
MIKI, SAKAE         01016 01020 01024 01141
MISHINA, SHOEI      00131
MIURA, HIRAYUKI      04136
MORI, Y     01023
MORITA, TAUSON      01140
MORITA, YOSHIO      01023
MOSCOW. GOSUDARSTVENNAIA BIBLIOTEKA SSSR. IM. V. I.
    LENINA    11978
MURAKAMI, YOSHIO      00131
MURPHEY, SUNNY      11424
MUSHA, RENZO        04130
MUSIC LIBRARY ASSOCIATION       01105
MYONG, CHAE-HUI      00019
NACHOD, OSKAR       00125 00140 00141 00145 00146
NAGOSHI, NAKAJIRO      01093
NAHM, ANDREW C.      00128
NAITO, SHUNPO      01059
NAKA, MICHIYO      04131
NAKAMURA, EIKO        00187 06021
NAM, CH'ANG-U      00128
NATIONAL CENTRAL LIBRARY       01044 01123 01139
NATIONAL DIET LIBRARY. REFERENCE AND BIBLIOGRAPHY
    DIVISION, ED     10560
NIHON MINZOKUGAKU KYOKAI, ED      11447
NISHIYOSHI, REINSENSAI       04132
NITCHO KYOKAI      00166
NITCHO KYOKAI OSAKAFU RENGOKAI, ED      00179
NO, SUN-MYONG KIM      11559
NOBLE, HAROLD J      04184
NUNN, GODFREY RAYMOND       11656
O'LEARY, TIMOTHY J      11853
O'QUINLIVAN, MICHAEL      00115
ODA, SHOGO        01017 01022 01060 01094
OGIYAMA, HIDEO       01109
OGURA, CHIKAO        01095
OGURA, SHIMPEI      01019
OKAMOTO, YOSHIJI      06766
OKUDA, NAOGI      01018
OKUDA, TAKEHIKO      04122
OKUDAIRA, TAKEHIKO      04121 04122
OMURA, MASUO      00185
```

```
OTA, AKIRA        11858
PAEK, IN        00019 04076 04077
PAGES, LEON        C0157
PAIGE, GLENN D        04167 04168 04169
PAK, SONG-BONG        01096 01097 04084
PAK, TONG-SO        10206 11451
PAK, YONG-JA        11558
PALMGREN, VALFRID        11891
PARK, YUNG-JA        11558
PARRY, ALBERT        00012
PETROVA, OL'GA PETROVNA        11788
POLEMAN, HORACE I        01105
POLICE BUREAU        C0164
PRAESENT, HANS        00141 C0145 00146
PRAGUE. NARODNI A UNIVERSITNI KNIHCVNA        11977
PUTIGNANO, ANDREW        11946
QUAN, L. KING        C0132
REKISHIGAKU KENKYUKAI, ED        CCC63
REKISHIGAKU KENKYUKAI, TOKYO        C1107
RHEE, BYUNG MOCK        11885
RIOSHOKU. SHOMUKA        00168
ROGERS, MICHAEL C.        00016
ROW, SOON MYONG KIM        11559
ROYAL EMPIRE SOCIETY. LONDON. LIBRARY        00158
ROYDS, MRS. W. MASSY        01034
SAKURAGI, AKIRA        01004
SAKURAI, YOSHIYUKI        00062 C1005 01099 011C0
        C1119 04134
SCHROEDER, PETER BRETT        00129
SEIKYU GAKKAI        C1002
SEKINO, SHINKICHI        00389 04135
SEO, KYUNG-BO        11860
SEOK, D. M        0C0C1
SEOUL NATIONAL UNIVERSITY        1145C
SEOUL NATIONAL UNIVERSITY. GRADUATE SCHOCL OF PUBLIC
        ADMINISTRATICN        10206
SHIDEHARA, TAIRA        01003
SHIGAKKAI, ED        C1006
SHIKATA, HIROSHI        11572
SHIMA, GORO        C0184
SHIMAMOTO, HIKOJIRO        06449
SHIMOMURA, FUJIO        01046
SHOSEKI BUNBUTSU RYUTSUKAI        00C65
SHULMAN, FRANK J        11976
SILBERMAN, BERNARD S        CCC08
SIN, SOK-HO        1C582
SO, CHIN-CHOL        04085
SO, KO-JONG        C0091
SO, KYONG-BO        11860
SO, MYONG-UNG        11948 11950
SO, YU-GU        C1C27
SOK, CHU-MYONG        CC001
SONG, TAE-GYUNG        04094
SOUL TAEHAKKYO        11450
```

SOUL TAEHAKKYO. MULLIKWA TAEHAK. TCNGA MUNHWA
    YON'GUSO   0C106
SOUL TAEHAKKYO. PUSOK TOSOGWAN   C0069 00076
    C4078
SOUL TAEHAKKYO. TOSOGWAN   01062 01121 11290
    11293
STEELE, MARION   11425
STEFFENS, JOAN   11853
STREIT, P. ROBERT   01064
STUCKI, CURTIS W   00023 00109
SUDA, AKIYOSHI   00183
SUEMATSU, YASUKAZU   00177 CC393
SURVEYS AND RESEARCH CORPORATION. WASHINGTCN, C.C
    00144
SWANSON, CHANG-SU   01138
TABORN, PAUL   11946
TADA, MASATOMO   01101
TAEHAN MIN'GUK KUKHOE TOSOGWAN   11448
TAEHAN MIN'GUK KUKHOE TOSOGWAN SASOGUK   10269
TALBOT, PHILLIPS   C0142
TAMWON   10334
TAYLOR, LOUISE MARION   11935
TENG, SSU-YU   01065
TEWKSBURY, DONALD G.   11832
TOHO GAKKAI   C0172
TOKIO, SHUNJO   11440
TOKYO GAIKOKUGO GAKKO. KANKOKU KCYUKAI,   EC
    C0C88
TOKYO JINRUI GAKKAI, ED   00197
TOKYO, UNIVERSITY. INSTITUTION OF HISTCRICAL SCIENCE
    01C06
TONG, CH'ON   11787
TONGGUK TAEHAKKYO. SEOUL, KOREA   01066 C1C67
    C1C68
TONGGUK TAEHAKKYO. SEOUL, KOREA. PULGYO MUNHWA
    YON'GUSO   01067 01069
TONGGUK TAEHAKKYC. SEOUL, KCREA. TCSOGWAN   11566
TONGGYCNG OEGUGO HAKKYO HAN'GUK KYCUHOE P'YON, EC
    C0C88
TOYO BUNKO, ED   00170 00171
TOYOGAKU BUNKEN SENTA RENRAKU KYCGIKAI,   ED
    C0189
TOYOTA, SHIRO   C1125
TROLLOPE, MARK NAPIER   00130 03066
UNDERWOOD, HORACE H   00117 00118 00120 03723
    03724
UNITED STATES OPERATIONS MISSICN TC KCREA   10206
U.S. BUREAU OF THE CENSUS   0C0C4 C0C05
U.S. DEPT. OF STATE. DIVISION CF PUBLICATICNS
    00143
U.S. JCINT PUBLICATIONS RESEARCH SERVICE   11590
U.S. LIBRARY OF CONGRESS   11943
U.S. LIBRARY OF CONGRESS. DIVISICN OF BIBLIOGRAPHY
    00138

U.S. LIBRARY OF CONGRESS. GENERAL REFERENCE AND
    BIBLIOGRAPHY DIVISION   00133 00139
U.S. LIBRARY OF CONGRESS. REFERENCE DEPARTMENT
    CC011 00012 CC025 01C70
U.S. NATIONAL AGRICULTURAL LIBRARY   0C129
U.S. NATIONAL ARCHIVES   11946
UYEHARA, CECIL H.   00134
VOS, FRITS   01137
WADA, KIYOSHI   C4123
WATANABE, AKIRA   04124
WATERMAN, RICHARD I   01105
WENCKSTERN, FRIEDRICH VON   C0157 11891
WINKLER, ROBIN L.   00011 0C025
YANG, KEY P   01126
YANG, KEY PAIK   C0020 06763
YANG, KI-BAEK   C0020 01126 06763 11448
YI, CHAE-CH'OL   00019
YI, CHAE-UK   C4125
YI, CHONG-MAN   01027
YI, CHONG-SIK   11761
YI, HONG-JIK   04166 11726
YI, HYON-JONG   11291
YI, KI-BAEK   11436
YI, KYOM-NO   C4098
YI, MAN-SU   11291
YI, MUN-YONG   01127
YI, PYONG-GI   01103 04087
YI, PYONG-MOK   11885
YI, SONG-UI   10754
YI, SUN-HUI   CCC50
YI WANGJIK. SOMUKWA   00168
YI, WON-SIK   01C72
YI, YONG-HUI   11292
YONSE TAEHAKKYO. KUGO KUKMUNHAKHCE   01112
YONSE TAEHAKKYO. SANGGYONG TAEHAK. SANOP KYONGYONG
    YON'GUSO   CC070
YONSE TAEHAKKYO. SEOUL, KOREA. MUNKWA TAEHAK
    C1112
YONSEI UNIVERSITY. COLLEGE OF BUSINESS
    ADMINISTRATION. INDUSTRIAL RESEARCH CENTER
    00C70
YONSEI UNIVERSITY. LIBRARY SCHOOL   C0C19
YOO, YOUNG HYUN   11446
YOON, JAI-POONG   10206 11451
YOSHINO, SAKUZO   00194
YOUNG, JOHN   CC116
YU, HYON-SUK   11560
YU, T'AEG-IL   01104
YU, YONG-HYON   11446
YU, YONG-IK   10207
YUHO KYOKAI. CHOSEN SHIRYO KENKYUKAI   01026
YUN, CHAE-P'UNG   10206 11451
YUN, PYONG-T'AE   C0019
YUNESUKO HIGASHI AJIA BUNKA KENKYU SENTA, TCKYO
    01021

```
Chosŏn tosŏ mongnok                                        11899
Chūgoku yaku Chōsen bungaku sakuhin no
   mokuroku                                                00185
Ch'ulp'um tosŏ haesŏl                                      11450
Ch'ulp'um tosŏ mongnok                                     09105
Chung Han wen-hua lun-chi.                                 01044
Chung Han wen-hua lun-chi.                                 01123
Chung Han wen-hua lun-chi.                                 01139
Chung-kuo k'an-hsing Han-kuo chu-shu mu-lu                 01044
Chung-kuo kuan-yü Han-kuo chu-shu mu-lu                    01139
Chungang Inmin Wiwŏnhoe chemunhŏn                          01043
A classified catalog of Korean books in the
   Harvard-Yenching Institute Library at
   Harvard University                                      11452
A classified catalog of Korean books in the
   Harvard-Yenching Library Harvard
   University                                              11453
Classified catalog of oriented and occidental
   books in the National Assembly Library as
   of Oct. 15, 1961.                                       00075
Climate of Korea: a selected bibliography                  00124
Corean books and their authors                             00130
The development of the studies of Korean
   history and culture in Japan                            00131
Dokutoru Rīsu no Chōsen ni kansuru Ōshu kinkan
   shomokuroku                                             01140
East Asia: a bibliography of bibliographies                11656
Fujita Ryōsaku Sensei chosaku mokuroku                     01133
Futatabi Tokugawa jidai ni okeru Chōsen no
   shoseki ni tsuite                                       04115
Fuzan Wakan Kō.                                            01060
Gakujutsu chikuji kankōbutsu mokuroku.                     04170
General index to the first twenty volumes of
   the Geographical Journal: 1893-1902                     11939
General index to the second twenty volumes of
   the Geographical Journal 1903-1912                      11940
Geographic publications of Hermann Lautensach
   on Korea                                                01090
Geomorphology of Korea: a selected
   bibliography                                            00123
God, Mammon and the Japanese [discussion].                 00110
Guide to historical literature                             01037
A guide to reference and research materials on
   Korean history                                          01128
Haebang chŏn Han'guk kwan'gye munhŏn mongnok:
   pon'gwan sojangbon                                      04096
Haebang chŏn kanhaeng Han'guk chapchi mongnok
   (pongwan sojang)                                        04097
Haengjŏnghak sŏksa hagwi nomun chemok                      11904
Hafou ta hsueh Ha Yen hsüeh shē t'u shu kuan
```

Meiji jidai Nis-Sen ryogo hikaku ron rombun
    hyo   01135
Meiji nenkan Chōsen kenkyū bunken shi   00062
Meiji shoki no Chōsen kenkyū   04134
Microfilm mongnok   04078
Miguk esŏ suyŏdoen Han'gugin paksarok   11427
Minjok munhwa kwan'gye munhŏn mongnok   01092
Minzokugaku kankei zasshi ronbun sōmokuroku,
    1925-1959   11447
Modern Korea by Grajdanzev [critique].   00110
Na-Ryŏ yemunji--Silla, Paekche, Koguryŏ   10754
Naikaku Bunko Kanseki bunrui mokuroku   11913
Nihon de shuppan sareta Chōsen ni kansuru
    tosho mokuroku   00179
Nihon sōsho sakuin   00176
Nihonbun, Chūgokubun, Chōsenbun tō chikuji
    kankōbutsu mokuroku   00189
Ninjin bunseki kaidai   04118
Nipponjin no Chōsen hikiage ni kansuru bunken
    shiryō   01023
Non-self-governing areas with special emphasis
    on mandates and trusteeships: a selected
    list of references   00139
North Korea 1957-1961: a bibliography and
    guide to contents of a collection of
    United States Joint Publications Research
    Service translations on microfilm   11590
Northeastern Asia, a selected bibliography;
    contributions to the bibliography of the
    relations of China, Russia, and Japan,
    with special reference to Korea,
    Manchuria, Mongolia, and eastern Siberia,
    in Oriental and European languages   00108
Nup'anko   01027
O-beijin no Chōsengo kenkyū no shiryō to natta
    wakanjo   01019
Obun Chōsen kankei bunken mokuroku--1940-nen
    igo kankō shomoku   00389
Occidental literature on Korea   03724
Odaesan sago mongnok   11949
Oho Terauchi Bunkō tosho mokuroku   00169
Old Korean geographical works: a bibliography   01117
Opisanie pis'mennykh pamiatnikov koreĭskoĭ
    kultury   11788
Osaka Furitsu Toshokan kanpon mokuroku   00163
Partial bibliography of occidental literature
    on Korea.   00117
Partial bibliography of occidental literature
    on Korea.   00118
A partial bibliography of occidental

141

ADDITIONAL CITATIONS   (see Appendix)

PERIODICALS INDEX

```
ACTA ASIATICA        C0131                                      (1)
ASEA HAKPO       04092                                          (1)
ASIA MAJOR. N.S.        01082                                   (1)
ASIA MINOR. N.S.        01081                                   (1)
ASIATIC RESEARCH BULLETIN        04066 04169                    (2)
ASIATIC SOCIETY OF JAPAN. TRANSACTICNS        04183
                                                                (1)
BUKKYO SHIGAKU       01083                                      (1)
BUNBUTSU SANSEI SHIRYO        04123                             (1)
BUNKEN HOKOKU        C0199 04122 04125 04128                    (4)
CHAYU KONGNON        04082                                      (1)
CHINDAN HAKPO        C1129                                      (1)
CHOSEN       01073 04118 04127                                  (3)
CHOSEN GAKUHO        00187 00389 C039C 00393 00424
    C1C05 C1016 C1C23 01133 01134 C1141 C4073 06449
                                                                (13)
CHOSEN GYOSEI        04120                                      (1)
CHOSEN IHO       04124                                          (1)
CHOSEN KENKYU GEPPC        00180 C0185 00186 01007
    C1C08 C1CC9 C1010                                           (7)
CHOSEN KENKYU SHIRYO        04136                               (1)
CHOSEN KOSEI        01088 01099 04134                           (3)
CHOSEN NO TOSHOKAN        01101                                 (1)
CHOSEN RODO       C1100                                         (1)
CHOSENSHI KOZA       01109                                      (1)
COWA SURVEYS AND BIBLIOGRAPHIES        01077                    (1)
DOKUSHO        01079 01095                                      (2)
DOLMEN       C0184 C1132                                        (2)
FAR EASTERN QUARTERLY        01090                              (1)
GAKUTO       01C13 C1140 04115                                  (3)
GEOGRAPHICAL REVIEW        CC110                                (1)
GEOGRAPHISCHES JAHRBUCH        01089                            (1)
HAN'GUK SAHOEHAK        06761 06762                             (2)
HSIEN-TAI KUO-MIN CHI-PEN CHIH-SHIH TS'UNG-SHU
    C1044 01123 C1139                                           (3)
INMUN KWAHAK        01112                                       (1)
JINRUIGAKU ZASSHI        00183                                  (1)
JOURNAL OF ASIAN STUDIES        04167                           (1)
KAHEI       04132                                               (1)
KEIIGAKU       C1078                                            (1)
KINYU KUMIAI        04121                                       (1)
KOKKA GAKKAI ZASSHI        00194                                (1)
KOKOGAKU       C1076                                            (1)
KOKUGAKUIN ZASSHI        01CC4 04117                            (2)
KONGSANJUUI MUNJE YON'GU        01086 04085                     (2)
KOREAN RESEARCH CENTER BULLETIN        04168                    (1)
KUGO KUNGMUNHAK        01104                                    (1)
KUKHOE TOSOGWANBO        04094 04095 04096 C4097 04098
    C4100 04111                                                 (7)
MANTETSU CHOSA GEPPO        01012                               (1)
MIN'JOK MUNHWA YCN'GU        01092                              (1)
```

```
MINZOKU      C1019                                      (1)
MONUMENTA SERICA      06766                             (1)
MULLI HAKCH'ONG (KYONGHUI TAEHAKKYO)      01096
    04084                                               (2)
MUNJANG      01103                                      (1)
MUSIC LIBRARY ASSOCIATION NOTES      01105             (1)
NARODY AZII I AFRIKI      11760                         (1)
NIPPON KOSHO TOSHIN      01119                          (1)
POMNYUL HAENGJONG NONJIP      01127                     (1)
REKISHI TO CHIRI      01093                             (1)
REKISHIGAKU KENKYU      01074                           (1)
ROYAL ASIATIC SOCIETY. KOREA BRANCH. TRANSACTIONS
    00118 00120 00130 01034 03066 03723 03724 04182
    04184                                               (9)
RYOSHO      01075                                       (1)
SAHAK YON'GU      01097                                 (1)
SEIKYU GAKUSO      00177 01017 01022 01135             (4)
SEN-MAN KENKYU      01094                               (1)
SHIGAKU ZASSHI      04116 04131                         (2)
SHISEN      01120                                       (1)
SHOKO      00198                                        (1)
SHOMOTSU DOKOKAI KAIHO      04119 04130 04135         (3)

SOCIETE ROYAL BELGE DE GEOGRAPHIE (BRUSSELS).
    BULLETIN      01110                                 (1)
SOJI      01080 01085 04074 04075                       (4)
SOJIHAK      04076 04077                                (2)
SOUL TAEHAKKYO TOSOGWANBO      01062 01121 04078      (3)
SUNGDAE      04083                                      (1)
T'OUNG-PAO      01137                                   (1)
TOA NO HIKARI      01003                                (1)
TOHYOP WOLBO      04090                                 (1)
TOKI KOZA      01115                                    (1)
TOKSA YOJOK      04166                                  (1)
TONGA MUNHWA      04093                                 (1)
TONGBANG HAKCHI      04087                              (1)
TONGGUK SAHAK      01084                                (1)
TOSO      04086                                         (1)
YOKSA HAKPO      01114                                  (1)
ZENSHU      01014                                       (1)
```

SERIES INDEX

AJIA KENKYU SOSHO.   01051

CALIFORNIA. UNIVERSITY. NORTHEAST ASIA SEMINAR.
  PUBLICATIONS.   00108

CENTRE FOR EAST ASIAN CULTURAL STUDIES.
  BIBLIOGRAPHY.   01021

CHOSEN GUNSHO TAIKEI ZOKU.   00091

CHOSEN SOTOKUFU TOCHI CHOSA JIGYO HOKOKUSHO,
  BESSATSU.   01042

CHOSON KOSO KANHAENGHOE.   00091

CORNELL UNIVERSITY. SOUTHEAST ASIA PROGRAM.
  DATA PAPER.   00023 00109

ECOLE DES LANGUES ORIENTALES VIVANTES.
  PUBLICATIONS. 3. SER.   1032 1033 1045

HAN'GUK MUNHWA CH'ONGSO.   11726

HAN'GUK TAEJANGHOE, CH'ONGWAN MONGNOK.
  01068 01069

HAWAII. UNIVERSITY. EAST-WEST CENTER.
  INSTITUTE OF ADVANCED PROJECTS.
  ANNOTATED BIBLIOGRAPHY SERIES.   01128

HAWAII. UNIVERSITY. EAST-WEST CENTER.
  LIBRARY. OCCASIONAL PAPERS.   11656

HISHO RUISAN.   00054

HOOVER INSTITUTION BIBLIOGRAPHICAL SERIES.
  00128

INTERNATIONAL INSTITUT FUR
  MISSIONSWISSENSCHAFTLICHE FORSCHUNG.
  VEROFFENTLICHUNGEN.   01064

KOREA RESEARCH AND PUBLICATION, INC.
  MONOGRAPHIC SERIES ON KOREA.   11437

KUGO KUNGMUNHAK CHARYO CH'ONGSO.
  01053

KYUJANGGAK TOSO YON'GU CH'ONGSO.   10204
  10205

150

MARINE CORPS HISTORICAL BIBLIOGRAPHIES,
    NO. 6   00115

PRAGUE. NARODNI A UNIVERSITNI KNIHOVNA.
    CTEME A STUDUJEME, 1956, SES.2.   11977

RESEARCH MONOGRAPHS ON KOREA. SER. B.   00124

RESEARCH MONOGRAPHS ON KOREA. SER. C.   00123

RESEARCH MONOGRAPHS ON KOREA. SER. F.   00287

ROYAL ASIATIC SOCIETY. KOREA BRANCH.
    TRANSACTIONS'.   00117

SOURCE BOOKS ON FAR EASTERN POLITICAL
    IDEOLOGIES.   11832

TOYO BUNKO SOKAN.   00067

TOYOSHI KENKYU SOKAN.   01059

U.S. BUREAU OF THE CENSUS. FOREIGN SOCIAL
    SCIENCE BIBLIOGRAPHIES. SERIES P-92.
    00004 00005

U.S. NATIONAL AGRICULTURAL LIBRARY LIST.
    00129

U.S. NATIONAL ARCHIVES. PUBLICATION, 61-2.
    PRELIMINARY INVENTORIES.   11946

1840
Kakto ch'aekp'an mongnok   11903

1893
Tosho sōmokuroku   00167

1894
Bibliographie coréenne by Courant, Maurice
    [Auguste Louis Marie], 1865-1939   01032

1895
A bibliography of the Japanese empire by
    Wenckstern, Friedrich von, comp   00157

1896
Chōsen shiseki-kō by Hayashi, Taisuke   04116

1899
Taiwan, Chōsen, Manshū shi kenkyū no shiori
    by Naka, Michiyo   04131

1900
Bibliografiia Koreĭ   07114

1901
Bibliographie coréenne Supplement (jusqu'en
    1899)   by Courant, Maurice [Auguste
    Louis Marie], 1865-1939   01033

1902
Catalogue des livres chinois, coréens,
    japonais   by Courant, Maurice (Auguste
    Louis Marie), 1865-1939   11928

1903
Catalog of the Landis Library   04182

1904
Bibliotheca Sinica: dictionnaire
    bibliographique des ouvrages relatifs à
    l'émpire chinois   by Cordier, Henri   00156
Books in the Brooklyn Public Library on the
    Far East, China, Japan, Korea, Manchuria,
    Russia and Siberia   11933
Select list of books (with reference to
    periodicals) relating to the Far East
    by U S Library of Congress   11943

1906
Catalog of the War Office Library   by Great

Britain War Office Library 01028
General index to the first twenty volumes of
the Geographical Journal: 1893-1902 11939

1907

Bibliography of the Japanese empire by
Wenckstern, Friedrich von, comp 11891
Tokugawa jidai ni okeru Chōsen no shoseki
by Furuya, Kiyoshi 01013

1908

Chōsen kenkyū no shiori by Sakuragi, Akira
01004
Futatabi Tokugawa jidai ni okeru Chōsen no
shoseki ni tsuite by Furutani, Kiyoshi
04115
Hanjŏk mongnok kobon by Tokyo Gaikokugo
Gakkō Kankoku Kōyūkai, ed 00088
Kanseki mokuroku kōhon 11243

1909

Chōsen no shiseki by Hayashi, Taisuke 04117
Chōsen shi no sankō shomoku ni tsuite by
Shidehara, Taira 01003
Kankoku kenkyū no bunken by Fukuda, Tokuzō,
comp 01078
La Corée: bibliographie by Cammaerts,
Emile, comp 01110
Teishitsu tosho mokuroku 11242

1911

Chōsen kosho mokuroku by Tokio, Shunjo,
comp 11440
Chōsen no geibun-shi by Asami, Rintarō 11859
Chōsen shoseki mokuroku by Kanazawa,
Shozaburō 01011
Dokutoru Rīsu no Chōsen ni kansuru Ōshu
kinkan shomokuroku by Morita, Tauson 01140
Odaesan sago mongnok 11949

1912

Bibliotheca Japonica by Cordier, Henri,
1849-1925, comp 01045
Chōsen Bukkyō kankei shoseki kaidai by
Imanishi, Ryū, comp 01083
Chōsen geibunshi 11241
Sŏsŏ sŏmok ch'obon by Sŏ, Myŏng-ŭng, 1716-
1787 11950
Tongguk T'onggam by Sŏ, Kŏ-jŏng, 1420-
1488, ed 00091

1913
Chōsen Sōtokufu tosho mokuroku   by Korea
(Government-General of Chōsen, 1910-
1945), ed   00192

1917
Osaka Furitsu Toshokan kanpon mokuroku   00163

1919
Chōsen chishi shiryō   by Korea (Government-
General of Chōsen, 1910-1945) Rinji Tochi
Chōsakyoku   01042
Shiragi jidai no bungei shiryō by Watanabe,
Akira   04124
Tendōkyō kenkyū shiryō by Yoshino, Sakuzō
                                                            00194

1920
Chōsen chishi shiryō ni tsuite by Nagoshi,
Nakajirō   01093

1921
Chōsen Sōtokufu ko tosho mokuroku by Korea
(Government-General of Chōsen, 1910-
1945), ed   00107

1922
Oho Terauchi Bunkō tosho mokuroku   00169

1923
Chōsenshi kankei tosho kaidai by Ogiyama,
Hideo   01109

1924
Catalog of the Asiatic library of Dr G E
Morrison (now a part of the Oriental
Library, Tokyo, Japan)   11936
Riōke Zoshokaku kotosho mokuroku by
Riōshoku Shomuka   00168

1925
Chōsen kokuhō shōkai by Okuda, Naogi   01018
General index to the second twenty volumes
of the Geographical Journal 1903-1912   11940

1926
Catalog of books on China in the Essex
Institute, Salem, Mass , U S A   by

Taylor, Louise Marion   11935

1927
  Catalog of the foreign books in the
    Government-General Library, Seoul, Korea   11937
  Chōsen iyaku shiryō   01073
  Ō-beijin no Chōsengo kenkyū no shiryō to
    natta wakanjo by Ogura, Shimpei   01019
  Richō no hōten by Asō, Takekame   04127
  Transactions of Korea Branch of the Royal
    Asiatic Society Index to transactions 1-
    16   by Noble, Harold J   04184

1928
  Bibliographie von Japan, 1906-1926 by
    Nachod, Oskar   00125
  Kan-kan shiseki ni arawaretaru Nik-Kan
    kōdaishi shiryō by Ōta, Akira, 1884-   11858
  Transactions of the Asiatic Society of Japan
    index First series, Vols 1-50   by
    Layard, R de B   04183

1931
  Bibliographie von Japan, 1927-1929 by
    Nachod, Oskar   00140
  Chōsen Tenshukyō shiryō tenran mokuroku by
    Keijo Tenshu-kokyokai, ed   01015
  Chōsen tōjiki ni kansuru jakkan no bunken ni
    tsuite by Oda, Shōgo   01017
  Chōsen tōkei sōran by Chōsen Keizai
    Kenkyūjo   11572
  Kōrai bunken shōroku by Suematsu, Yasukazu
                                                    00177
  Meiji jidai Nis-Sen ryogo hikaku ron rombun
    hyo by Kameda, Jirō   01135
  Occidental literature on Korea by
    Underwood, Horace H   03724
  A partial bibliography of occidental
    literature on Korea from early times to
    1930   by Underwood, Horace H   00120

1932
  Chōsen bungaku oboegaki by Tada, Masatomo,
    comp   01101
  Chōsen kochizu tenkan mokuroku by Keijō
    Teikoku Daigaku Fuzoku Toshokan, ed   00182
  Chōsen ni okeru shuppanbutsu gaiyō by Korea
    (Government-General of Chōsen, 1910-1945)
                                                    00164
  Chōsen tosho kaidai by Korea (Government-

155

General of Chōsen, 1910-1945)   00022
Corean books and their authors   by
Trollope, Mark Napier   00130
Hōbun rekishi-gaku kankei shō-zasshi Tōyō-
shi rombun yomoku   01131
Short list of Korean books [in the Chosen
Christian College Library]   by Trollope,
Mark Napier   03066

1933
Chōsen minzoku gakkai e no tembo   by
Iwasaki, Keishō   01132
Chōsen Tenshukyō shi ni kansuru omonaru
sankō shoseki oyobi rombun   by Kusuda,
Onosaburō   11856
Chōsenjin taishitsu jinruigaku ni kansuru
bunken mokuroku by Shima, Gorō   00184
Ninjin bunseki kaidai   by Imamura, Tomoe   04118

1934
Chōsen Bukkyō tenseki tenran mokuroku   by
Fujii, Sōju   01014
Chōsen Tenshukyō shi ni kansuru omonaru
sankō chosho oyobi rombun   by Kusuda,
Onosaburō   11857
Tosho mokuroku   by Keijō Furitsu Toshokan   00068

1935
Bibliographie von Japan, 1930-1932   by
Nachod, Oskar   00141
A Buddhist bibliography   by March, Arthur
Charles, 1880-   01116
Chōsen kankei ōbun bunken mokuroku   01074
Chōsen kosho no ichibetsu   by Oda, Shōgo,
comp   01094
Chōsen kosho shōkai   by Chōsen Sōtokufu
Tosho-kan, ed   11854
Chōsen no chizu ni tsuite   by Toyota, Shirō
                                                       01125
Chōsen saikō no chiri-sho ni tsuite   by
Miura, Hirayuki   04136
Chōsen shiryō shūshin oyobi kaisetsu   by
Chōsenshi Henshūkai, ed   11855
Sen-Man kankei jūyō zasshi kiji mokuroku   00199
Sōkan irai no sō-mokuji benran   by Chōsen
Sōtokufu Kambō Bunshoka,   ed   01130
Supplement to 'A partial bibliography of
occidental literature on Korea' by H H
Underwood, 1931   by Gompertz, E   00118

1936

Bibliographie coréenne   The introduction
  by Courant, Maurice [Auguste Louis
  Marie], 1865-1939   01034
Chōsen kosho shiryō by Ito, Hirobumi 00054
Chōsen shiseki kaidai kōgi by Oda, Shōgo 01022
Chōsen tōji bunken mokuroku by Koyama,
  Fujio, comp   01115
Chōsen tōjishi bunken kō by Oda, Shōgo,
  1871-, comp   01060
Index to titles and authors of papers by
  Underwood, Horace H   03723
Keijō Teikoku Daigaku Fuzoku Toshokan, Wakan
  shomei mokuroku by Keijō Teikoku Daigaku
  Fuzoku Toshokan, comp   00181
Sangoku jidai no tenseki by En'ō-sei 04128
Sensatsu meidai by Maema, Kyōsaku, comp 01058

1937

Bibliographie von Japan, 1933-1935 by
  Nachod, Oskar   00145
Chōsen no kyōdoshi, chihōshi by Sakurai,
  Yoshiyuki, comp   01119
Chōsen no shoseki by Furukawa, Kanehide,
  comp   01079
Kankoku heisei kankei bunken rokushu by
  Nishiyoshi, Reinsensai   04132
K B S bibliographical register of important
  works written in Japanese on Japan and
  the Far East, published during the year
  1932-1937   by Kokusai Bunka Shinkōkai 00121
Korai-Chō no tenseki ni tsuite by Okuda,
  Takehiko   04122
Shinshobu bunrui mokuroku by Korea
  (Government-General of Chōsen, 1910-1945)
  Toshokan   00053
Subject catalog   by Royal Empire Society
  London Library   00158

1938

Bibliotheca missionum   by Streit, P
  Robert, 1875-1930   01064
Chōsen no tenseki by Okudaira, Takehiko 04121
Chōsen shoshi joron by Courant, Maurice
  [Auguste Louis Marie], 1865-1939   01095
Jinruigaku zasshi sōsakuin   00197
Korea (1926-1936) mit Nachträgen aus älterer
  Zeit by Lautensach, Hermann, comp 01089
Meiji shoki no Chōsen kenkyū by Sakurai,
  Yoshiyuki   04134

1939
Chōsen kankei ōbun tosho kaidai   01075
Chōsen no shōsetsu   by Yi, Chae-uk   04125
Nihon sōsho sakuin   by Hirose, Bin   00176
Northeastern Asia, a selected bibliography;
   contributions to the bibliography of the
   relations of China, Russia, and Japan,
   with special reference to Korea,
   Manchuria, Mongolia, and eastern Siberia,
   in Oriental and European languages   by
   Kerner, Robert Joseph   00108
Seikyū gakusō ronbun choshabetsu sakuin   01002
Tōyō Bunko Chōsenbon bunrui mokuroku, fu,
   annanbon mokuroku   by Tōyō Bunko, ed   00170

1940
Bibliographie von Japan, 1936-1937   by
   Nachod, Oskar   00146
[Chōsen fūzoku-shū] Shosai no tōka kankei
   bunken   by Musha, Renzō   04130
Chōsen kankei kōkogaku bunken mokuroku   01076
Chōsen koten mokuroku   01041
Chōsen kyūsho kō   by Kuroda, Ryō, 1890-   00165
Chōsen no tōka kankei shiryō tō   by Kishi,
   Yuzuru   04119
Chosŏn munhak myŏngjŏ haeje   by Yi, Pyŏng-gi
                                                                 01103
Taishō nenkan Chōsen kankei bunken kaidai
   by Sakurai, Yoshiyuki,   comp   01099

1941
Chihō bunka no kiroku: Chōsen no kyōdoshi
   chihō shishi   by Kuji, Hanjirō,   comp   01088
Climate of Korea: a selected bibliography
   by McCune, Shannon Boyd-Bailey, 1913-   00124
Geomorphology of Korea: a selected
   bibliography   by McCune, Shannon Boyd-
   Bailey   00123
Meiji nenkan Chōsen kenkyū bunken shi   by
   Sakurai, Yoshiyuki,   ed   00062
Nup'anko   by Sŏ, Yu-gu,   1764-1845   01027

1942
Chōsen kenkyū no seika   by Kuji, Hanjirō   04120
Chōsen-nai hakkō shinbunshi ichiranhyō   11914
Mantetsu chōsa geppō sōmokuroku   01012

1943
Chōsen jinkō rōdō kankei bunken shiryo   by

Sakurai, Yoshiyuki, comp   01100
Chōsen kindai toshokan shiryo   by Sekino,
  Shinkichi   04135
Chōsenban koshomoku   01039
The Japanese empire: industries and
  transportation, a selected list of
  references   by U S Library of Congress
  Division of Bibliography   00138
'Shokō' shuyō kiji mokuroku   00198

1944
Annotated bibliography of the Southwest
  Pacific and adjacent areas   by Allied
  Forces Southwest Pacific Area   00155
Kosen sappu by Maema, Kyōsaku, 1868-1942,
  ed   00067

1945
Biographical sources for foreign countries
  IV The Japanese Empire by U S Library
  of Congress General Reference and
  Bibliography Division   00133
Hokusen Manshū Karafuto oyobi Chishima ni
  okeru hōjin no hogo oyobi hikiage ni
  kansuru kōshō kankei bunken   01050

1946
Chosŏn munhwasa sŏsŏl by Courant, Maurice
  [Auguste Louis Marie], 1865-1939   01036
Chungang Inmin Wiwŏnhoe chemunhŏn   01043
Geographic publications of Hermann
  Lautensach on Korea by McCune, Shannon
  Boyd-Bailey   01090
Recent books on Korea by McCune, Shannon
  Boyd-Bailey   00110

1947
Archaeology of Korea by Hewes, Gordon
  Winaut, 1918-   00287
Chōsen kosho mokuroku by Chosŏn Kosŏ
  Kanhaenghoe Seoul, Korea   01108
Non-self-governing areas with special
  emphasis on mandates and trusteeships: a
  selected list of references by U S
  Library of Congress General Reference
  and Bibliography Division   00139

1948
Ajia kenkyū ni kansuru bunken by Kanazawa,
  Shozaburo, 1872-   01051

1949
Chejudo kwan'gye munhŏnjip by Sŏk, Chu-
    myŏng   00001
Chōsen no zasshi   04170
Chōsenjin jinruigaku ni kansuru bunken by
    Suda, Akiyoshi, 1900-   00183
Old Korean geographical works: a
    bibliography   by McCune, Shannon Boyd-
    Bailey, comp   01117

195?
Kungnip Tosŏgwan kwijungbon kosŏ mongnok by
    Kungnip Tosŏgwan   10576

1950
Bibliography of Asiatic musics; tenth
    installment   01105
Bibliography of Western language materials
    on Korea Rev , enl ed   by McCune,
    Shannon Boyd-Bailey   00024
Chōsen shiryō by Wada, Kiyoshi   04123
Korea: a preliminary bibliography   by U S
    Library of Congress Reference Department
                                                     01070
Korea: an annotated bibliography of
    publications in Far Eastern languages
    by U S Library of Congress Reference
    Department   00011
Korea: an annotated bibliography of
    publications in the Russian language   by
    U S Library of Congress Reference
    Department   00012
Korea: an annotated bibliography of
    publications in Western languages   by U
    S Library of Congress Reference
    Department   00025
Korea, published material, July 2, 1944 to
    July 3, 1950   by U S Dept of State
    Division of Publications   00143
Kŭmsu kangsan by Columbia University   00100
Source materials on Korean politics and
    ideologies   by Tewksbury, Donald G ,
    comp and ed   11832
Za edinuiu nezavisi muiu demokraticheskuiu
    Koreiu Kratkiĭ rekomendatel'nyĭ
    ukazatel' literatury   by Moscow
    Gosudarstvennaia biblioteka SSSR   im V
    I Lenina   11978

1951
Chōsen kanhoku no yon chishi   by Ikeuchi,
    Hiroshi   00390
Ūbun Chōsen kankei bunken mokuroku--1940-nen
    igo kankō shomoku   by Sekino, Shinkichi
                                                   00389
Sambōshū henkan ko   by Suematsu, Yasukazu   00393
Yōan-in zoshochū no Chōsen isho   by Miki,
    Sakae   01016

1952
Publications in Japanese on Korean
    anthropology   by Gerow, Bert A   00007
Shigaku bunken mokuroku, 1946-1950   by
    Shigakkai, ed   01006

1953
Chōsen iseki ko   by Miki, Sakae   01020
Chōsen kankei shigaku ronbun mokuroku   00063
Chōsen-shi no henshū to Chōsen shiryō no
    shūshū   by Nakamura, Eikō   06021

1954
Checklist of archives in the Japanese
    Ministry of Foreign Affairs, Tōkyō Japan,
    1868-1945   by Uyehara, Cecil H , comp   00134
Han'guk ko-munhwa non'go   by Yi, Hong-jik,
    1909-   11726
Kŏm injŏng kyokwayong illamp'yo   by Korea
    (Republic) Mun'gyobu   10223
Korean studies guide   by California
    University   Institute of East Asiatic
    Studies   00015
Post-war Japanese research on the Far East
    (excluding Japan)   by Honda, Minoru,
    comp   01082

1955
Akiba Takashi Hakushi no shōgai to gyōseki
    by Shimamoto, Hikojirō   06449
Chosŏn sŏjihak kaegwan   by Kungnip Chungang
    Tosŏgwan   P'yŏngyang, Korea   Sŏjihak pu
                                                   00058
Chung-kuo k'an-hsing Han-kuo chu-shu mu-lu
    by Kuo-li Chung-yang t'u-shu-kuan, ed   01044
Chung-kuo kuan-yü Han-kuo chu-shu mu-lu   by
    Kuo-li Chung-yang t'u-shu-kuan, ed   01139
Introduction to Asia; a selective guide to
    background reading   by Quan, L King   00132
The literature of Japanese education, 1945-

1954   by Eells, Walter Crosby, comp   11443
[Review of] Korean studies guide   by Vos,
Frits   01137
A survey of Japanese contributions to
Manchurian studies   by Honda, Minoru   01081
T'ai-wan kung-ts'ang Kao-li-pen lien-ho mu-
lu   by Kuo-li Chung-yang t'u-shu-kuan, ed
01123
Tamwŏn kukhak san'go   by Chŏng, In-bo   10334
Tōhōgaku kankei zasshi mokuroku   by Tōhō
Gakkai   00172

1956
Chōsen igakushi oyobi shippeishi no kankō ni
tsuite   by Miki, Sakae, comp   01141
Chōsen isho shi   by Miki, Sakae   01024
Ch'ulp'um tosŏ haesŏl   by Sŏul Taehakkyo   11450
Hōseko Shigekatsu no Chōsen gogaku sho ni
tsuite, fu Chōsen gogaku shomoku   by
Sakurai, Yoshiyuki   01005
Ko-tosŏ chŏnsihoe ch'ulp'um tosŏ haesŏl   11907
Kosŏbu pullyu mongnok   by Kungnip Tosŏgwan
00080
Lidové demokratické zeme Asie: Korea,
Vietnam, Mongolsko; [výberový seznam
literatury]   by Prague   Národní a
universitní knihovna   11977
Sŏul Taehakkyo kaegyo sipchunyŏn Kinyŏm Ko
Tosŏ Chŏnsihoe ch'ulp'um tosŏ haesŏl
Tan'gi 4289 nyŏn 10 wŏl 13-17-il   by Sŏul
Taehakkyo   Pusok Tosŏgwan   00069

1957
Chŏn'guk tosŏgwan illam   11901
Han'guk sŏji ŭi yŏn'gu   by Yi, Pyŏng-gi   04087
Kokushi bunken kaisetsu   by Endō, Motoo,
1908-   01046
Pukhan koejip chŏnsul munhŏn-chip   by Kim,
Un-sŏk, ed   00052

1958
Chōsen kankei bunken tenji mokuroku   by Tōyō
Bunko, ed   00171
Han'guk ch'amgo tosŏ haeje, 1910-1958   by
Yi, Chae-ch'ŏl, ed   00019
Hōsa Bunko Chōsenbon tenkansho kaisetsu   by
Nakamura, Eikō   00187
The Korean collection of the Division of
Oriental Manuscripts, Institute of
Oriental Studies, Academy of Sciences of

the USSR   A bibliographical note   by
Paige, Glenn D   04169
Kuksa kwan'gye chŏsŏ nonmun mongnok   by Kim,
Yong-dŏk, comp   01114
Naikaku Bunko Kanseki bunrui mokuroku   11913
Nipponjin no Chōsen hikiage ni kansuru
bunken shiryō   by Morita, Yoshio   01023
Russian supplement to the Korean studies
guide   by California University East
Asiatic Studies   00016
Shigaku kankei shuyō zasshi rombun mokuroku   01120
A survey of Soviet publications on Korea,
1950-1956   by Paige, Glenn D   04167
Tosŏl kotosŏ kosŏhwa haeje   by Yi, Wŏn-sik,
comp   01072

1959
American doctoral dissertations on Asia,
1933-1958   by Stucki, Curtis W   00109
Checklist of microfilm reproductions of
selected archives of the Japanese Army,
Navy and other government agencies, 1868-
1945   by Young, John, comp   00116
Ch'ulp'um tosŏ mongnok   by Kungnip Tosŏgwan
                                                           09105
Han'guksa yŏn'gu munhŏn mongnok: Chŏnhu
Ilbon hakkye   by Pak, Sŏng-bong   01097
Imanishi Bunko mokuroku   by Kyōtō Daigaku
Bungakubu Toshoshitsu, ed   00175
Japanese penetration of Korea, 1894-1910: a
checklist of Japanese archives in the
Hoover Institution   by Nahm, Andrew C ,
comp   00128
Korea: a selected bibliography in Western
languages, 1950-1958   by Lee, Soon Hi,
1926-   00050
Korea: Far East--Area 17   by Council for
Old World Archaeology   01077
Takahashi Tōru Sensei chosaku nempyō   01134

1960
Bunken shōkai   by Kawachi, Yoshihiro   00424
Chijŏng munhwajae mongnok   by Korea
(Republic) Mun'gyobu   01054
Chōsen ni kansuru Nihongo-han tosho mokuroku
by Nitchō Kyōkai   00166
Han'guk kojŏn munhak yŏn'gu munhŏn haeje   by
Yŏnse Taehakkyo Kugŏ Kukmunhakhoe   01112
Han'guk sŏji munhŏn illam 1941-1942   01080
Han'guk sŏji munhŏn illam 1937-1940   04074

Han'guk Sŏk Paksa hagwi nonmun mongnok 1945-
    1960   by Han'guk Yŏn'guwŏn   00087
An index to English language periodical
    literature published in Korea, 1890-1940
    by Elrod, Jefferson McRee   00006
Korea studies in the Soviet Union   by
    Paige, Glenn D   04168
Kukhak yŏn'gu nonjŏ ch'ongnam by Kukhak
    Yŏn'gu Nonjŏ Ch'ongnam Kanhaenghoe   00010
Nihon de shuppan sareta Chōsen ni kansuru
    tosho mokuroku   by Nitchō Kyōkai Ūsakafu
    Rengōkai, ed   00179
Preliminary inventory of the records of the
    Headquarters, United Nations Command
    (Record Group)   by U S National
    Archives   11946
Reference guide to Korean materials, 1945-
    1959   by Yang, Key Paik   00020
A select bibliography: Asia, Africa, Eastern
    Europe, Latin America   by Talbot,
    Phillips, ed   00142
Toil han Han'guk ŭi munhŏn by Yi, Hong-jik
                                                         04166
The war in Korea, 1950-1953: a list of
    selected references   by Great Britain
    Imperial War Museum Library   11795

1961
Bibliography of Korean studies: a
    bibliographical guide to Korean
    publications on Korean studies appearing
    from 1945 to 1958   by Koryŏ Taehakkyo
    Asea Munje Yŏn'guso   00002
Bibliography on Buddhism   by Hanayama,
    Shinshō, comp   01048
Changsŏ mongnok--Tongyangsŏ, Sŏyangsŏ pullyu
    mongnok 4294 nyŏn siwŏl siboil hyŏnjae-
    by Kukka Chaegŏn Ch'oego Hoeŭi Tosŏgwan
                                                         00075
Changsŏ pullyu mongnok--Haebang ijŏn ilsŏbu
    by Kungnip Tosŏgwan   00079
Chŏngbu kanhaengmul mongnok   by Korea
    (Republic) Kongbobu   00300
Chōsen kankei bunken shiryō sōmokuroku   by
    Yūhō Kyōkai Chōsen Shiryō Kenkyūkai   01026
Chōsenshi kenkyū   by Naitō, Shunpo   01059
Fujita Ryōsaku Sensei chosaku mokuroku   01133
Guide to historical literature   by American
    Historical Association, comp   01037
Han'guk chiryu munhŏn illam 1905-1938   04075

Han'guksa yŏn'gu munhŏn mongnok   by Pak,
    Sŏng-bong, comp   01096
Imanishi Hakushi shūshū Chōsen kankei bunken
    mokuroku by Hara, Sanshichi, ed   00065
An interim report to the government of the
    Republic of Korea   by Surveys and
    Research Corporation   Washington, D C   00144
Japanese studies on Japan and the Far East
    by Teng, Ssu-yü, 1906-, comp   01065
Kosŏ chŏnsi mongnok   11900
Minzokugaku kankei zasshi ronbun sōmokuroku,
    1925-1959 by Nihon Minzokugaku Kyokai,
    ed   11447
Sanŏp kyŏngje munhŏn mongnok (1945-1960) by
    Yŏnse Taehakkyo Sanggyŏng Taehak Sanŏp
    Kyŏngyŏng Yŏn'guso   00070
Yugan'gi pulsŏ mongnok ch'ogo by Kim, Wŏn-
    yong, comp   01085

1962
An annotated bibliography of the United
    States Marines in the Korean war   by
    O'Quinlivan, Michael   00115
Bibliography of social science periodicals
    and monograph series: North Korea, 1945-
    1961   by U S Bureau of the Census   00004
Bibliography of social science periodicals
    and monograph series: Republic of Korea,
    1945-1961   by U S Bureau of the Census
                                                    00005
Chŏnggi kanhaengmul silt'ae illam by Korea
    (Republic) Kongbobu Kongboguk   11569
Chŏnggi kanhaengmul, sahoe tanch'e,
    yŏnghwaŏpchi mit kongyŏnja illamp'yo by
    Korea (Republic) Kongbobu Kongboguk   00346
Chōsen Kagakuin kizō tosho mokuroku   01008
Chōsen Kagakuin kizō zasshi mokuroku   01009
A classified catalog of Korean books in the
    Harvard-Yenching Institute Library at
    Harvard University   by Harvard
    University Library Harvard-Yenching
    Library   11452
Japan and Korea: a critical bibliography
    by Silberman, Bernard S   00008
Koryŏ sagyŏng chŏn'gŭn mongnok by Tongguk
    Taehakkyo Seoul, Korea   01067
Kosŏ mongnok chipsŏng by Tongguk Taehakkyo
    Seoul, Korea Tosogwan   11566
Kugŏ kungmunhak kosŏ chimnok by Kim, Kŭn-su
                                                    01053

List of the Korean Research Center Koreana
collection: in commemoration of sixth
anniversary   by Han'guk Yŏn'gu Tosŏgwan
Seoul, Korea   11787
Sorenpō hakkō Chōsen kankei tosho mokuroku
by Kanno, Hiroomi   01010

1963
American doctoral dissertations on Asia,
1933-1962 by Stucki, Curtis W   00023
Bibliography of Western literature on Korea
from the earliest time until 1950   by
Gompertz, G St G M   00117
Chōsen hokuhanbu no nōgyō mondai ni kansuru
bunken mokuroku   00186
Chosŏn tosŏ mongnok by Kim, Kŭn-su   11899
Chūgoku yaku Chōsen bungaku sakuhin no
mokuroku by Ōmura, Masuo   00185
Han'guk kŭnsesa yŏn'gu charyo mongnok by
Koryŏ Taehakkyo Seoul, Korea Asea Munje
Yŏn'guso   01049
Han'guk kyŏngje haengjŏng yŏn'gu rŭl wihan
charyo ko by Yi, Mun-yŏng, comp   01127
Han'guksa kwan'gye yŏn'gu nonmun mongnok by
Kim, Chong-uk, comp   01084
Japanese studies on Korean history since
World War II   by Okamoto, Yoshiji   06766
Kichōsho maikurofirumu mokuroku   11915
Kinchaku Geunro-gya sōmokuji   00180
Korean publications in the National
Agricultural Library   by Schróeder,
Peter Brett   00129
Koryŏ pulsŏ chŏn'gwan mongnok by Tongguk
Taehakkyo Seoul, Korea   01066
A list of selected books and materials on
modern and contemporary Korean history
with special emphasis on those on
diplomatic history publication in Korea
by Koryŏ Taehakkyo Seoul, Korea Asea
Munje Yŏn'guso   00379
Opisanie pis'mennykh pamiatnikov koreĭskoĭ
kultury by Petrova, Ol'ga Petrovna   11788
Saikin Chōsen kankei zasshi ronbun mokuroku 01007
Title index to the descriptive catalog of
Chinese manuscripts from Tunhuang in the
British Museum   by British Museum
London [Department of Oriental Printed
Books and Manuscripts]   11945

1964
Bibliography of bibliographies of East Asian
    studies in Japan   by Yunesuko Higashi
    Ajia Bunka Kenkyū Senta, Tokyo   01021
Chindan hakpo ch'ong mokch'a   01129
Han'guk hyŏndaeshi ch'ongnam   by Kim, Kŭn-
    su, comp   01052
Han'guk saryo haesŏlchip   by Sin, Sŏk-ho,
    1904-   10582
Han'guk sŏmok, 1945-1962   by Kungnip
    Chungang Tosŏgwan   Seoul, Korea, ed   00073
Han'guk ŭi taehak chŏnggi kanhaengmul pu-
    kodŭng kyoyuk kigwan myonggam   by Yi,
    Pyŏng-mok   11885
Kongsanjuŭi munje yŏn'gu munhŏn mongnok   01086
Korean War bibliography and maps of Korea
    by Blanchard, Carroll Henry, Jr   11573
Kyujanggak tosŏ mongnok--Han'guk   by Sŏul
    Taehakkyo   Pusok Tosŏgwan   00076
Minjok munhwa kwan'gye munhŏn mongnok   01092
Na-Ryŏ yemunji--Silla, Paekche, Koguryŏ   by
    Yi, Sŏng-ŭi, ed   10754
Nihonbun, Chūgokubun, Chōsenbun tō chikuji
    kankōbutsu mokuroku   by Tōyōgaku Bunken
    Sentā Renraku Kyōgikai, ed   00189
North Korea 1957-1961: a bibliography and
    guide to contents of a collection of
    United States Joint Publications Research
    Service translations on microfilm   by
    Kyriak, Theodore E , comp and ed   11590
Sahoehak kwan'gye munhŏn mongnok, 1945-1964
    by Ch'oe, Chae-sŏk   06761
Source materials on Korean political
    developments   by Yang, Key P   01126
Yijo chŏn'gi kugyŏk pulsŏ chŏn'gwan mongnok
    by Tongguk Taehakkyo   Seoul, Korea   01068

1965
Bibliographical note: Korean books on
    tactics   04066
Bibliography of Korean studies: a
    bibliographical guide to Korean
    publications on Korean studies appearing
    from 1959 to 1962   by Koryŏ Taehakkyo
    Asea Munje Yŏn'guso   00003
Chosŏn kojŏn haeje   by Chosŏn Minjujuŭi
    Inmin Konghwaguk Sahoe kwahagwŏn   Kojŏn
    Yŏn'guso P'yŏngyang, Korea Munhŏn
    Yŏn'gusil   00061
The development of the studies of Korean
    history and culture in Japan   by

Mishina, Shōei   00131
Han'guk chapchi mongnok, 1896-1945   by
    Ch'oe, Sun-ja, comp   00072
Han'guk ko-jido yŏn'gu by Kim, Yang-sŏn   04083
Han'guk paksa-rok by Chŏng, Ch'ŏl, ed   10329
Han'guk tosŏgwan kwan'gye munhŏn mongnok,
    1921-1961 by Ko, Hu-sŏk, comp   00071
Korea and the Korean War   by Lee, Chong-sik
                                                       11761
Korean views of America 1954-1964: an
    annotated bibliography   by Henthorn,
    William E   11177
Kyujanggak tosŏ Han'gukpon ch'ongmongnok   by
    Sŏul Taehakkyo Mullikwa Taehak Tonga
    Munhwa Yŏn'guso   00106
Pervyĭ pamiatnik koreĭskoĭ pis'mennosti   by
    Kontsevich, L P   11760
Publications on Korea in the era of
    political revolutions, 1959-1963; a
    selected bibliography   by Chung, Yong-
    Sun   11437
Taehan Min'guk ch'ulp'anmul ch'ong mongnok,
    1963-1964 by Kungnip Chungang Tosŏgwan
    Seoul, Korea, ed   11441
Yijo chŏn'gi pulsŏ chŏn'gwan mongnok   by
    Tongguk Taehakkyo Seoul, Korea Pulgyo
    Munhwa Yŏn'guso   01069
Yŏngnam munhŏnnog (Kyŏngnam-p'yŏn) by Yu,
    T'aeg-il, comp   01104

1966 .
Bibliography of Korean public
    administration, September 1945-April 1966
    by Pak, Tong-sŏ   10206
Chŏngbu kanhaengmul mongnok   by Kukhoe
    Tosŏgwan Seoul, Korea, ed   11849
Chŏnsi tosŏ mongnok   11906
Chōsen kankei shiryō mokuroku   by Kokuritsu
    Kokkai Toshokan, ed   10570
Chosŏn kojido mongnok by Yi, Kyŏm-no   04098
A classified catalog of Korean books in the
    Harvard-Yenching Library Harvard
    University   by Harvard University
    Library Harvard-Yenching Library   11453
Haengjŏnghak sŏksa hagwi nomun chemok   11904
Han'guk haengjŏng munhŏnjip, 1945-1966 by
    Pak, Tong-sŏ   11451
Han'guk kajok kwan'ge munhŏn mongnok 1900-
    1965 by Ch'oe, Chae-sŏk   07055
Han'guk kŭnse taeoe kwan'gye munhŏn piyo by

Chŏn, Hae-jong   10204
Han'guk kwan'gye munhŏn mongnok: Stanford
    Taehakkyo sojang by Kukhoe Tosŏgwan   04095
Han'guk kyŏngje kwan'gye munhŏn chipsŏng by
    Han, U-gŭn, 1915-   10205
Han'guk sinmun chapchi ch'ongmongnok 1883-
    1945 by Kukhoe Tosŏgwan Seoul, Korea
    Sasŏguk, ed   11448
Han'guk sŏji kwan'gye munhŏn mongnok by
    Sŏul Taehakkyo Tosŏgwan   01062
Han'guk sŏji ŭi sŏji by Sŏng, Tae-gyung   04094
Ilsa Karam Mun'go kosŏ chŏja mongnok by
    Sŏul Taehakkyo Tosŏgwan   11293
Kaebyŏkchi ch'ongmokch'a, 1920-1949 by
    Kukhoe Tosŏgwan Seoul, Korea Sasŏguk   10269
Koryŏ munjip mongnok by Sŏul Taehakkyo
    Tosŏgwan   01121
Kŭnse Han'guk oegyo munsŏ ch'ongmok
    oegukp'yŏn by Yi, Yong-hŭi, 1917-, ed   11292
Kyoyuk charyo mongnok   01057
Microfilm mongnok by Sŏul Taehakkyo Pusok
    Tosŏgwan   04078
Sahoehak kwan'gye munhŏn mongnok, 1964 9
    21--1965 12 31 by Ch'oe, Chae-sŏk   06762
A selected bibliography of materials on
    Korean economy by Yoo, Young Hyun   11446
Sŏk Paksa hagwi nonmun chemok chip   11905
Sŏul Taehakkyo kaegyo isipchunyŏn kinyŏm
    kwijung tosŏ chŏnsihoe chŏnsi tosŏ
    mongnok 1966-nyŏn 10-wŏl 13-18-il by
    Sŏul Taehakkyo Tosŏgwan   11290
Taehan Min'guk ch'ulp'anmul ch'ong mongnok,
    1965 by Kungnip Chungang Tosŏgwan
    Seoul, Korea, ed   11442

1967
Catalog of materials on Korea in the
    National Diet Library by National Diet
    Library Reference and Bibliography
    Division, ed   10560
Chŏngch'i kwan'gye munhŏn mongnok by Kukhoe
    Tosŏgwan   04111
Chosŏn ch'ongdokpu Kŭp sosok kwansŏ palgan
    tosŏ mongnok by Kukhoe Tosŏgwan   04100
East Asia: a bibliography of bibliographies
    by Nunn, Godfrey Raymond, 1918-   11656
Haebang chŏn Han'guk kwan'gye munhŏn
    mongnok: pon'gwan sojangbon by Kukhoe
    Tosŏgwan   04096
Han'guksa sillon by Yi, Ki-baek, 1924-   11436

170

Han'guk sŏji kwan'gye munhŏn mongnok   by
   Paek, In   04076
Kyujanggak tosŏ chosŏn ŭpchisojae sŏrhwa
   pullyu   by Chang, Tŏk-sun   04093
A selected and annotated bibliography of
   Korean anthropology   by Knez, Eugene I   01138
Social science resources on Korea: a
   preliminary computerized bibliography
   by Koh, Hesung Chun   11852

1969
A checklist of Korean periodicals, 1945-1966
   by Row, Soon Myong Kim   11559
Chōsen gakuhō no daiisshū kara dai gojisshū
   made no sōmokuji   by Chōsen Gakkai   04073
Han'guk sŏji kwan'gye munhŏn mongnok   by
   Paek, In   04077
HRAF source bibliography   by Human
   Relations Area Files   11853
Korean publications in series: a subject
   bibliography   by Park, Yung-ja   11558
A study of Korean Zen Buddhism approached
   through the Chodangjip   by Seo, Kyung-bo
                                  11860

1970
The Asami Library: a descriptive catalog
   by Fang, Chao-ying   11898
Japan and Korea: an annotated bibliography
   of doctoral dissertations in Western
   languages, 1877-1969   by Shulman, Frank J
                                  11976

SECTION III
CITATIONS WITH COMPLETE ANALYSIS AND ANNOTATION

GUIDE TO SECTION III

CONTENTS

INTRODUCTION

In order to explain what makes up a citation in
this section, it is necessary to discuss briefly the
structure and the function of our input data standardization worksheet, which is called the "cataloging
worksheet." There are two major information fields
on this worksheet: (1) the leader area, which was
designed primarily to sort all of the information
for a single bibliographic reference, and (2) the
text area, which was designed primarily for storage
and printing, and only secondarily for sorting.
The leader area is composed of an identification
number for each bibliographic entry, plus seven additional categories of information: material type;
language of the title; country of publication; topical, geographical, and temporal coverage; and publication year. The alphanumeric codes for this information appears at the top of each entry. These
codes were originally designed only for purposes of
machine sorting or selecting and not for the reader's
use, but they have been included here as a source of
additional information.
The text area contains three major information
subfields: (a) descriptive information (author, title,
imprint, collation, etc.) (b) analytical information
(subject classification and cross-referencing data),
and (c) annotative information. The descriptive information has been standardized, following the Anglo-
American cataloging rules (American Library Association, 1967), with necessary modifications for journal
articles and other types of documents. The analytical
information field contains categories for subject indexes and cross-reference data. The third information field, the annotation section, is designed in
such a way that either our own annotation or any other
published or unpublished annotation can be recorded,
together with the name of the annotator and the year
the annotation was done.

GUIDE TO INFORMATION IN COMPLETE CITATION

MONOGRAPH

00005 aeng   usa   b 1 n   19620231
U.S. Bureau of the Census. Bibliography of
social science periodicals and monograph series:
Republic of Korea, 1945-1961. By Foreign Manpower
Research Office, Bureau of the Census, under grant
from Office of Science Information Service,
National Science Foundation. Washington, D.C.,
U.S. Government Printing Office, 1962. 48 p. 26
cm. (Foreign social science bibliographies.
Series P-92, no. 9)
English. CtY,DLC.
                                                S.
Bibliography. 110.00   450.00   546.00   773.00
190.00   170.00   647.00   648.00   369.00   423.00
183.00   457.00   764.15   163.00   538.00   217.00
536.00   527.00   228.00   288.00   313.00   207.00
652.00   481.00   240.00   312.00   212.00   130.00
582.00   646.00   428.00   430.00   185.00   590.00
173.00   647.04   870.00   175.00   670.00   377.00
460.00 Polity. Religion. Economy.
Christianity--Roman Catholicism. Buddhism.
Confucianism. Tobacco. Salt. Cement. Kites.
Social sciences. Statistics. Tonghak. Kut.
Sirhak. Kwagŏ. Social sciences--Bibliography.
Catalogs, Book. Bibliography--1945-1961.

LEADER AREA

	Code	Explanation
Identification number	00005	
Material type	a	monographs
Language of title	eng	English
Country of publication	usa	United States
Topical codes		
Subject	b	bibliography
Unit focus		
Geographical codes		
General	l	South Korea
Specific		
Temporal codes		
Dynasty	n	undifferentiated
Nature of information		
Beginning year		
Ending year		
Publication year	1962	

TEXT AREA

DESCRIPTIVE AREA
  Author
        U.S. Bureau of the Census.
  Title paragraph
     Title
        Bibliography of social science periodicals
        and monograph series: Republic of Korea,
        1945-1961.
     Author statement
        By Foreign Manpower Research Office, Bureau
        of the Census, etc.
  Imprint
        Washington, D.C., U.S. Government Printing
        Office, 1962.
  Collation
        48 p. 26 cm.
  Series statement
        (Foreign social science bibliographies.
        Series P-92, no. 9)
  Notes
     Language of the document
        English.
     Library location
        CtY,DLC.
     Other notes
  Cataloging source
        S.

ANALYTICAL AREA
  Major subject headings
        Bibliography.
  Personal and corporate subjects
  Geographical subjects
  OCM categories and subdivisions
        110.00   450.00   546.00   773.00 etc.
  Key words, general
        Polity. Religion. Economy. Christianity--
        Roman Catholicism. Buddhism. Confucianism.
        Tobacco. Salt. Cement. Kites. Social
        science. Statistics.
  Key words specific to Korean culture
        Tonghak. Kut. Sirhak. Kwagŏ.
  Library of Congress subject headings
        Social sciences--Bibliography.
        Catalogs, Book.
  Publication years covered by bibliography
        Bibliography--1945-1961.

ANNOTATION

JOURNAL ARTICLE

01022 zjap   kor   b 0 yc   1936
     Oda, Shōgo.   Chōsen shiseki kaidai kōgi
[Lectures on Korean historical sources]. <u>In</u> Seikyū
gakusō, 23 (1936): 145-161.
Japanese. DLC,MH-HY.
                              CEACS'64,UC'54.
Bibliography--bibliographic essay. History--
Bibliography. Kyujanggak. 113.02 175.01 814.01
217.00 Historiography.

"Lists and evaluates six Japanese works which
describe Korean historical works and which can be
used as guides in studying them; summarizes the
history of the Kyujanggak, the royal library
founded in the last years of the Yi dynasty, which
became part of the Keijō Imperial University
library in 1930; and briefly describes the
traditional Chinese methods of writing history,
methods which the Koreans followed." UC'54.

LEADER AREA

	Code	Explanation
Identification number	01022	
Material type	z	journal articles
Language of title	jap	Japanese
Country of publication	kor	Korea (to 1945)
Topical codes		
Subject	b	bibliography
Unit focus		
Geographical codes		
General	0	total Korea
Specific		
Temporal codes		
Dynasty	y	Yi dynasty
Nature of information	c	circa
Beginning year		
Ending year		
Publication year	1936	

TEXT AREA

DESCRIPTIVE AREA
  Author
      Oda, Shōgo.
    Title paragraph
      Romanized title
        Chōsen shiseki kaidai kōgi
      English translation*
        [Lectures on Korean historical sources].
    Journal citation
      <u>In</u> Seikyū gakusō, 23 (1936): 145-161.
  Notes
    Language of the document
      Japanese.
    Library location
      DLC,MH-HY.
    Other notes
  Cataloging source
      CEACS'64, UC'54.

ANALYTICAL AREA
  Major subject headings
      Bibliography -- bibliographic essay.
      History -- Bibliography.
  Personal and corporate subjects
      Kyujanggak.
  Geographical subjects
  OCM categories and subdivisions
      113.02   175.01   814.01   217.00
  Key words, general
      Historiography.
  Key words specific to Korean culture
  Library of Congress subject headings
  Publication years covered by bibliography

ANNOTATION
  Annotation source code
      UC'54.

---

* *An English translation appearing in parentheses
is quoted from the title page of the source. A
translation appearing in brackets has been supplied by HRAF Korea Project staff for this bibliography.*

MATERIAL TYPE CODE

Code

A   Monographs (including monographs in series)

B   Serials (serials, newspapers)

E   Maps (all maps including printed and photographed reproductions)

F   Manuscripts (theses, field notes, dissertations, mimeographed)

W   Newspaper Articles

X   Chapter Titles (a chapter in a monograph or series)

Z   Journal Articles

LANGUAGE OF TITLE CODE

Code

CHIN	Chinese
CZE	Czech
ENG	English
FREN	French
GERM	German
JAP	Japanese
KOR	Korean
RUS	Russian

COUNTRY OF PUBLICATION CODE

Code

BELG	Belgium
CZECH	Czechoslovakia
FRAN	France
GER	Germany (to 1945)
GERE	Germany (Democratic Republic)
GTBR	Great Britain
HONG	Hongkong
JAPAN	Japan
KOR	Korea (to 1945)
NETH	Netherlands
NOKOR	North Korea (Democratic People's Republic of Korea)
SOKOR	South Korea (Republic of Korea)
TAIW	Taiwan
USA	United States
USSR	Union of Soviet Socialist Republics

TOPICAL CODE

Major Subject Classification

Code

0.0

  0.1 Bibliography (including catalogs and B
       index)
  0.2 Series 8
  0.3 Reference work (e.g. Dictionary, 9
       Encyclopedia, Directory, etc.)

1.0 General Works (including traveller's Z
     accounts)

  1.1 History (including both general and H
       specific historical accounts.
       All those which cannot be in-
       cluded in any other functional
       category. e.g. geography of
       Three Kingdoms is not history,
       but geography.)
  1.2 Archeology (Pre-history) A
  1.3 Conflict (Individual conflict, I
       warfare, etc.)
  1.4 Sociocultural Change C
  1.5 Sociocultural pattern (System, J
       Cultural Summary, Orientation)

2.0 Intercultural relations (Korea- I
     China, Korea-Japan, Korea-U.S.S.R.,
     Korea-U.S.A., etc.)

3.0 Land and People (Ecology)

  3.1 Physical setting--geography X
       (including flora, fauna, climate,
       topography, soils) settlement 2
       pattern (national)
       transportation network (physical)
  3.2 Population (demography, minority Y
       groups, physical anthropology)

4.0 Language and Literature

  4.1 Language (including printing and G
       writing)
  4.2 Literature (including novels, T
       poetry, songs, etc.)

		Code
5.0	Community studies (only those based on field work)	6
6.0	Values (Ethos, Themes, Foci, etc.)	V
7.0	Religion and philosophy	R
8.0	Law	L
9.0	Polity	P
10.0	Military	M
11.0	Economy (including technology)	E
12.0	Education	D
13.0	Family and kinship	F
14.0	Social groupings	K
15.0	Social stratification	S
16.0	Psychocultural data (e.g. national character, personality)	Q
17.0	Life cycle (e.g. life history, biography, etc.)	5
18.0	Welfare (health, sickness, medicine, etc.)	W
19.0	Material culture	7
20.0	Artistic and intellectual expression (symbols and activities)	
20.1	Visual arts	U
20.2	Performing arts	N
20.3	Recreation (festivals, etc.)	O
20.4	Ethnoscience (knowledge)	4
20.5	Communications (mass media, press, news and information, public opinion)	3

TOPICAL CODE

Unit Focus, Nature of

		Code
1.	Not applicable	0 or a
2.	Material objects (things)	1 or b
3.	Individuals	2 or c
4.	Groups (e.g. social strata, cliques, etc.)	3 or d
5.	Organizations and associations	4 or e
6.	Family or kin groups	5 or f
7.	Territorial units (community level and also units larger than the community such as kun, up, etc.)	6 or g
8.	State or nation	7 or h
9.	Interstate or international (world)	8 or i
10.	Unknown	9 or j
		k
		l
		m, etc.
11.	Other (e.g. animals)	– or z

General Location

		Code
1.	Total Korea or undifferentiated	0 or a
2.	South Korea (Republic of Korea, ROK)	1 or b
3.	North Korea (Democratic People's Republic of Korea, DPRK)	2 or c
4.	Border (e.g. 38th parallel)	3 or d
5.	Cheju Island	4 or e
6.	Japan (Korean settlements in)	5 or f
7.	China (" " ")	6 or g
8.	U.S.S.R. (" " ")	7 or h
9.	U.S.A (" " ")	8 or i
10.	Unknown	9 or j
11.	(Comparison of) North and South	k
		l
		m, etc.

Specific Location

Codes

Col. 46	Col. 47	
0		Total Korea or undifferentiated
1	0	Undifferentiated South Korea
1	1	Kyŏnggi do
1	2	Ch'ungch'ong Namdo
1	3	Ch'ungch'ong Pukto
1	4	Chŏlla Namdo
1	5	Chŏlla Pukto
1	6	Kyŏngsang Namdo
1	7	Kyŏngsang Pukto
1	8	
1	9	Unknown
2	0	Undifferentiated North Korea
2	1	Hwanghae do
2	2	Kangwŏn do
2	3	Hamgyŏng Namdo
2	4	Hamgyŏng Pukto
2	5	P'yŏng'an Namdo
2	6	P'yŏng'an Pukto
2	7	
2	8	
2	9	Unknown
3	0	Border
3	8	38th parallel
4	0	Chejudo

Dynasties

		Code
1.	Not applicable, undifferentiated (e.g. History, General work)	N
2.	Modern Korea (From 1945- to date)	M
3.	Japanese Occupation (1910-1945)	J
4.	Yi dynasty (1392-1910)	Y
5.	Koryŏ (918-1392)	K
6.	United Silla (110-935 AD)	S
7.	Three Kingdoms (Koguryo 37BC - 668AD) (Paekche 18BC - 660AD) (Karak 42BC - 563AD) (Old Silla 57BC - 660AD).	T
8.	Chinese Colonies (108BC - 313AD)	C
9.	Ancient Korea (up to 108BC) Prehistory	A
10.	Unknown	U

187

Nature of Information

This code modifies either the "Dynasties" code or the "Beginning year and ending year" information.

Codes

E - Exact information

C - Circa

U - Unknown

I - Incomplele

Beginning year and ending year

1. Recorded as precisely as possible when the exact information on beginning and ending years are available. The "nature of information" code = E

2. When the source covers only a one year period it is recorded in the space for "beginning year", and the "nature of information" code = E

3. When only approximate years are available these are recorded and the "nature of information" code = C

4. When the information is incomplete, either the "beginning year" or "ending year" are given and the "nature of information" code = I

188

LIBRARY LOCATION CODE

NUC Symbol	HRAF Code	Name of Library
Azu		University of Arizona
CLSU	CLS	University of Southern California
CLU		University of California, Los Angeles
CSt-H	CSH	Hoover Library, Stanford University
CtU		University of Connecticut, Storrs
	CtY	Sterling Memorial Library, Yale University
CU		University of California, Berkeley
CU-E	CUE	East Asiatic Library, University of California, Berkeley
DLC		Library of Congress
DNAL	DNA	U.S. National Agricultural Library
	HRAF, HRF	Human Relations Area Files
HU-E	EWC, HUE	East-West Center Library, University of Hawaii
IaU		University of Iowa
ICU		University of Chicago
InU		Indiana University
	KEU	Ewha Womans University (Korea)
	KJK	Kyujanggak, Seoul National Library (Korea)
	KNC	National Central Library (Korea)

NUC Symbol	HRAF Code	Name of Library
	KSN	Seoul National University Library (Korea)
	KYU	Yonsei University Library (Korea)
MH		Harvard University, Cambridge
MH-HY	MHY	Harvard-Yenching Library
MH-P	MHP	Peabody Museum, Harvard University
	MH-W, MHW	Widener Library, Harvard University
MiU		University of Michigan, Ann Arbor
NcD		Duke University, Durham
NjP		Princeton University
NN	NNP	New York Public Library, New York
NNC		Columbia University, New York
NNR		Russell Sage Foundation, College of the City of New York, New York
TxU		University of Texas
ViU		University of Virginia
WaU		University of Washington, Seattle
WaU-FE		Far Eastern Library, University of Washington

It was necessary to devise a three digit code for our project when the NUC symbol was in more than three digits or when there was no standardized code (e.g. libraries in Korea and Japan).

CATALOGING SOURCE CODE

Code	Source	ID Number
BAS'62 - '67	Korea: bibliography of Asian studies, 1962-1967. 1963-1968.	6764
CEACS'64	Yunesuko Higashi Ajia Bunka Kenkyū Senta, Tokyo. 1964	1021
Chŏng'66	Chung, Yong-Sun. 1965	11437
Courant'01	Courant, Maurice. 1901	1032 1033
CTK'32	Korea (Government-General of Chosen, 1910-1945). 1932	22
Elrod'60	Elrod, J. McRee. 1960	6
Fang'70	Fang, Chao-ying. 1970	11898
Gerow'52	Gerow, Bert A. 1952	7
Gompertz'63	Gompertz, G. St., G. M. 1963	117
Knez'68	Knez, Eugene I. 1968	1138
KU'65	Koryŏ Taehakkyo. 1965	3
LCF'50	U.S. Library of Congress. 1950	11
LCW'50	U.S. Library of Congress. 1950	25
MH-HY or MHY	Harvard University. 1962 1966	11452 11453
Nunn'67	Nunn, Godfrey Raymond. 1967	11656
Okamoto'62	Okamoto, Yoshiji. 1963	6766
Paek'68	Paek, In. 1968	4076
Paek'69	Paek, In. 1969	4077
S	(Cataloged from original source)	

Code	Source	ID Number
Sakurai'41	Sakurai, Yoshiyuki. 1941	62
Silberman'62	Silberman, Bernard S. 1962	8
SNU'65	Sŏul Taehakkyo. 1965	11450
Stucki'63	Stucki, Curtis W. 1963	23
UC'54	California. University. 1954	15
WH'68	Henthorn, Wm. E. 1968	1128
Yang'60	Yang, Key Paik. 1960	20
Yang'67	Yang, Key P. 1967	6763
YiHj'65	Yi, Hong-jik. 1965	11255

When cataloging source was a library card then the code used is the same as Library Location Code.

ANNOTATION SOURCE CODE

This code is based on the name of the annotator, or source of annotation, and the year the annotation was done.

It is the same as the "cataloging source code" given above. Full citations for sources are given under "References".

00001 akor   kor   b 0 n   1949
    Sŏk, Chu-myŏng.   Chejudo kwan'gye munhŏnjip
[A list of literature on Cheju Island]. By D. M.
Seok. Seoul, Sŏul Sinmunsa, 1949. 252 p. 22 cm.
Korean. CtY,DLC,HU-E,MH-HY,NNC.
                                              S.
Bibliography. Sociocultural pattern--
Bibliography. Chejudo. 113.02 190.00 175.00
538.00 Bibliographies. Ethnology. Agriculture.
Polity. Health. Religion. Ecology. Method.
Chejudo--Bibliography.

00002 aeng   sokor   b 0 n   1961
    Koryŏ Taehakkyo. Asea Munje Yŏn'guso.
Bibliography of Korean studies: a bibliographical
guide to Korean publications on Korean studies
appearing from 1945 to 1958. [V.1]. Seoul,
Asiatic Research Center, Korea University, 1961.
7, 410 p. 24 cm.
English. CtY,DLC,HU-E,MH-HY.
                              S,DLC,Nunn'67.
Sociocultural pattern--Bibliography. 113.02
670.00 190.00 538.00 175.00 870.00 Polity.
Ethnology. Philosophy. Economy. Bibliography--
1945-1958.

00003 aeng   sokor   b 0 n   1965
    Koryŏ Taehakkyo. Asea Munje Yŏn'guso.
Bibliography of Korean studies: a bibliographical
guide to Korean publications on Korean studies
appearing from 1959 to 1962. [V.2]. Seoul,
Asiatic Research Center, Korea University, 1965.
6, 432 p. 24 cm.
English. CtY,DLC,HU-E,MH-HY.
                                              S.
Sociocultural pattern--Bibliography. 113.02
870.00 Religion. Philosophy. Bibliography--
1959-1962.

00004 aeng   usa   b 2 mc   1962
    U.S. Bureau of the Census. Bibliography of
social science periodicals and monograph series:
North Korea, 1945-1961. By Foreign Manpower
Research Office, Bureau of the Census, under grant
from Office of Science Information Service,
National Science Foundation. Washington, D.C.,
U.S. Government Printing Office, 1962. 4, 12 p.
(Foreign social science bibliographies. Series P-
92, no. 8)
English. CtY,DLC,HU-E,MH-P,MH-HY.
                                              S.

Bibliography. 110.00 204.00 190.00 423.00
178.00 369.00 538.00 593.00 580.00 173.00
174.00 183.00 792.00 172.00 531.00 290.00
474.00 240.00 451.00 453.00 651.00 460.00
648.00 181.00 744.00 870.00 175.00 670.00
Industry. Statistics. Community studies.
Buddhism. Communications. Economy. Commerce.
Polity. Social sciences. Social sciences--
Bibliography. Bibliography--1945-1961.

00005 aeng   usa   b 1 n   19620231
       U.S. Bureau of the Census. Bibliography of
social science periodicals and monograph series:
Republic of Korea, 1945-1961. By Foreign Manpower
Research Office, Bureau of the Census, under grant
from Office of Science Information Service,
National Science Foundation. Washington, D.C.,
U.S. Government Printing Office, 1962. 48 p. 26
cm. (Foreign social science bibliographies.
Series P-92, no. 9)
English. CtY,DLC.
                                                   S.
Bibliography. 110.00 450.00 546.00 773.00
190.00 170.00 647.00 648.00 369.00 423.00
183.00 457.00 764.15 163.00 538.00 217.00
536.00 527.00 228.00 288.00 313.00 207.00
652.00 481.00 240.00 312.00 212.00 130.00
582.00 646.00 428.00 430.00 185.00 590.00
173.00 647.04 870.00 175.00 670.00 377.00
460.00 Polity. Religion. Economy.
Christianity--Roman Catholicism. Buddhism.
Confucianism. Tobacco. Salt. Cement. Kites.
Social sciences. Statistics. Tonghak. Kut.
Sirhak. Kwagŏ. Social sciences--Bibliography.
Catalogs, Book. Bibliography--1945-1961.

00006 feng   usa   b 0 n   1960
       Elrod, Jefferson McRee. An index to English
language periodical literature published in Korea,
1890-1940. [Seoul] 1960. 214 p.
English. CtY-D,DLC,HU-E,MH-W. Thesis (Library
Science) -- George Peabody College for Teachers.
"Available on microfilm from the Yonsei University
Library, Seoul, Korea, after March, 1961."
                                                   S.
Bibliography--index. 110.00 175.00 797.00
Christianity. Bibliography--1890-1940.

00007 feng   usa   b 0 n   1952
       Gerow, Bert A. Publications in Japanese on
Korean anthropology: a bibliography of uncataloged
materials in the Kanaseki Collection, Stanford
University Library. [Stanford, Stanford
University, Department of Sociology and
Anthropology, 1952]. 4, 18 l. 28 cm.
English. DLC,HU-E,MH-P,MH-W. Mimeographed.
                                         S,MH-P.
Archeology--Bibliography. Sociocultural pattern--
Bibliography. Bibliography--catalogs--U.S.A.
Kanaseki Collection, Stanford University Library.
113.02 Ethnology. Linguistics. Physical
anthropology. Sociocultural change.
Bibliography--1916-1945.

00008 aeng   usa   b 0 n   1962
       Silberman, Bernard S. Japan and Korea: a
critical bibliography. Tucson, University of
Arizona, 1962. 14, 120 p. 26 cm.
English. CtY,DLC,MH-P. Korea: p. 92-120.
                                              S.
Bibliography. Sociocultural pattern--
Bibliography. Polity--Bibliography.
Intercultural relations--Bibliography. Economy--
Bibliography. 113.02 102.00 870.00 175.00
226.00 190.00 131.00 132.00 135.00 144.00
212.00 648.00 177.00 532.00 533.00 538.00
764.15 654.00 564.00 Confucianism. Buddhism.
Christianity. Government. Agriculture.
Industry. Ecology. Butchers. Japanese
Occupation. Korean War.

00010 akor   sokor   b 0 n   1960
       Kukhak Yŏn'gu Nonjŏ Ch"ongnam Kanhaenghoe.
Kukhak yŏn'gu nonjŏ ch"ongnam [A general survey
of articles and books on Korean studies]. Seoul,
Ŭryu Munhwasa, 1960. 12, 422, 24 p. 21 cm.
Korean. CtY,DLC,MH-HY,MiU,WaU-FE. Separate
section for special reference materials in each
subject area. Title and author indexes.
                                      S,DLC,KU'65.
Language--Bibliography. Literature--Bibliography.
Sociocultural pattern--Bibliography. 533.00
538.00 175.00 190.00 113.02 Ethnology. Korean
studies. Folklore--Bibliography. Bibliography--
1945-1959.

00011 aeng   usa   b 0 n   1950
       U.S. Library of Congress. Reference
Department. Korea: an annotated bibliography of

195

publications in Far Eastern languages. Compiled
under the direction of Edwin G. Beal, Jr., with
the assistance of Robin L. Winkler. Washington,
D.C., 1950. 8, 167 p. 27 cm.
English. CtY,DLC,MH-HY,MH-W.
                                                    S.
Sociocultural pattern--Bibliography. History--
Bibliography. Polity--Bibliography. Economy--
Bibliography. 113.02 870.00 190.00 538.00
172.00 130.00 Bibliographies. Medicine.
Religion. Arts. Periodicals. Travelers'
accounts.

00012 aeng   usa   b 0 n   1950
        U.S. Library of Congress. Reference
Department. Korea: an annotated bibliography of
publications in the Russian language. Compiled by
Albert Parry, John T. Dorosh, and Elizabeth
Gardner Dorosh. Washington, D.C., 1950. 11, 84
p.
English. DLC,HRAF,HU-E,MH.
                                            S,MH-HY.
Bibliography. History--Bibliography. Economy--
Bibliography. 113.02 648.00 576.00 527.00
670.00 530.00 290.00 260.00 369.00 186.00
804.00 160.00 361.00 668.00 439.00 200.00
450.00 659.00 240.00 167.00 496.00 797.00
132.00 504.00 133.00 137.00 102.00 870.00
590.00 130.00 190.00 538.00 105.00 Science.
Military. Polity. Ethnography. Communism.
Travelers' accounts. Christianity. Statistics.
Commerce. Industry. Assassination of the Queen.
Independence Movement. Overseas Koreans.

00015 aeng   usa   b 0 n   1954
        California. University. Institute of East
Asiatic Studies. Korean studies guide. Comp. by
B.H. Hazard, Jr. et al. Ed. by Richard Marcus.
Berkeley, California, 1954. 12, 220 p. maps. 23
cm.
English. CtY,DLC,HRAF,HU-E,MH-HY,MH-W. On spine
and t.p.: 槿域攷. Supplemented by: Fritz Vos,
T'oung Pao, 43 (1955): 408-431. Chronological
list of rulers and dynasties: p. 177-185. Indexes
of titles and authors.
                                            S,DLC.
Bibliography. History. Visual arts. Performing
arts. Sociocultural pattern. 173.02 102.00
113.02 214.00 Maps. Dynastic lists.
Archeology. Buddhism. Confucianism.

Christianity. Shamanism. Reference works.
"An annotated listing of the major works on Korea
in Western as well as Oriental languages.
Arrangement is by topic and each topic has a short
introduction. Also includes chronological tables
and historical maps." Silberman'62.

00016 aeng   usa   b 0 n   1958
        California. University. East Asiatic Studies.
Russian supplement to the Korean studies guide.
Comp. by Robert L. Beckus and Michael C. Rogers.
Berkeley, California, 1958. 12, 211 p. 23 cm.
English. DLC,HU-E,MH-HY. "Intended to supplement
the Korean studies guide, published by the
Institute of East Asiatic Studies and University
of California Press in 1954."
                                        S,DLC.
Bibliography. Yi, Sunsin. 113.02 648.00 700.00
132.00   439.00   504.00   453.00   651.00   135.00
668.00   185.00   669.00   720.00   530.00   870.00
190.00   217.02   815.00   204.00   423.00   797.00
744.00   130.00   175.00   105.00   Polity.
Intercultural relations. Travelers' accounts.
Ethnography. Economy. Sociocultural change.
Industry. Agriculture. Communism. Reference
works. Korean War. Independence Movement.
Democratic People's Republic of Korea. Overseas
Koreans. Bibliography--1850-1956.

00019 akor   sokor   b 0 n   1958
        Yi, Chae-ch°ŏl, ed. Han'guk ch´amgo tosŏ
haeje, 1910-1958 (Guide to Korean reference
books, 1910-June 1958). Edited by Lee Jai-chul;
compiled by Paik In, Myung Chae-hui and Yun Pyong-
tai. Seoul, Yŏnse Taehakkyo Tosŏgwan Hakkyo [and]
Miguk Joji P´ibodi Sabŏm Taehak, 1958. 7, 92 p.
26 cm.
Korean. CSt-H,CtY,CU-E,DLC,MH-HY,ViU. A joint
project carried out by Yŏnse University Library
School and George Peabody College for Teachers.
                                        S,MHY,ViU.
Bibliography. 113.02 656.00 217.02 183.00
173.00   190.00   538.00   252.00   824.00   136.00
751.00   241.00   533.00   532.00   536.00   159.04
590.00   600.00   489.00   537.00   450.00   105.00
Christianity--Roman Catholicism. Ethnography.
History. Intercultural relations. Confucianism.
Buddhism. Economy. Commerce. Law. Government
administration. Education. Trade. Ethnoscience.

Reference works. Sirhak. Korean War.
Independence Movement. Bibliography--1910-1958.

00020 feng   usa   b 0 n   1960
       Yang, Key Paik. Reference guide to Korean
materials, 1945-1959. [Washington, D.C.] 1960.
8, 4, 131 p. 29 cm.
English. CtY,DLC,MH-HY. Thesis (Library Science)
-- Catholic University of America.
                                                   S.
Bibliography--catalogs--U.S.A. Sociocultural
pattern--Bibliography. Library of Congress.
113.02 771.00 812.00 159.04 190.00 538.00
530.00 175.00 130.00 670.00 870.00 820.00
810.00 Bibliography--1945-1959.

00022 ajap   kor   b 0 n   1932   1
       Korea (Government-General of Chōsen, 1910-
1945). Chōsen tosho kaidai [Annotated
bibliography of Korean books]. Seoul, Chōsen
Tsūshinsha, 1932. [730] p. 24 plates. 26 cm.
Japanese. CtY,DLC,HRAF,HU-E,MH-HY,WaU-FE.
Reprint of Seoul, 1919, 21 cm. 2nd. ed. MH-HY has
also 1919 ed. An author and title index arranged
in kana order is included.
                                          S,MHY,CU'54.
Bibliography--catalogs--Korea. History--
Bibliography. Religion and philosophy--
Bibliography. Government-General Library. 113.02
159.04 172.00 600.00 565.00 821.00 787.00
173.02 723.00 725.00 212.00 538.00 Sutras.
Confucianism. Buddhism. Taoism. Agriculture.
Biography. Economy. Polity. Law. Dictionaries.
Gazetteers. Medicine. Arts. Literature.
Calligraphy. Chronology. Genealogy. Classics.

"A selected collection of old Korean books. It
gives brief annotations of all books listed,
information on their authors, and other data. The
basic information is made readily available
through excellent indices, one listing titles
according to traditional Chinese divisions,
another, by the kana order of the first character
of their titles. There is also a special index of
authors arranged by number of strokes which makes
it possible rapidly to look up all writings of a
particular man included in the catalogue and to
find his biography. The Chōsen Tosho Kaidai is the
best and most inclusive work of its kind
available, an essential tool for a study of Korean

history and literature, not only for
bibliographical purposes, but for identification
of books and authors cited in historical texts."
UC'54. "The Korean collection of the Government-
general was formerly the Library of the King of
Korea. This annotated catalog is the most
extensive descriptive catalog in existence devoted
to these works of traditional Korean literature."
LCF'50. "An annotated list on 2726 of Korean
classical works with useful biographical notes.
Appendix contains samples of old Korean books."
Yang'60.

00023   aeng   usa   b 0 n   1963
      Stucki, Curtis W. American doctoral
dissertations cn Asia, 1933-1962, including
master's theses at Cornell University. Ithaca,
Southeast Asia Program, Department of Asian
Studies, Cornell University, 1963. 204 p.   28 cm.
(Cornell University. Southeast Asia Program. Data
paper, 50)
English. CtY,DLC,HRAF. Korea: p. 72-78, 165.
                            S,Silberman'62.
Bibliography--dissertations. Education--
Bibliography. Polity--Bibliography. Economy--
Bibliography. History--Bibliography.
Intercultural relations--Bibliography. 110.00
797.00 538.00 670.00 190.00 Religion.
Agriculture. Sociology. Anthropology. Oriental
Studies--U.S.--Bibliography. Bibliography--1933-
1962.

00024   aeng   usa   b 0 n   1950
      McCune, Shannon Boyd-Bailey. Bibliography of
Western language materials on Korea. Rev., enl.
ed. New York, International Secretariat,
Institute of Pacific Relations, 1950. 17 p.   28
cm.
English. CtY,DLC,MH-HY,MH-W.
                                        S,DLC.
Bibliography. Intercultural relations--
Bibliography. History--Bibliography. 113.02
175.00 105.00 530.00 204.00 Geography.
Polity. Japanese occupation.

"General coverage of the most recent and
accessible titles, and a commentary on the content
and value of the books listed." UC'54. "Selection
of the principal studies made of various aspects
of Korean histcry and culture with informative

annotations. Born in Korea of missionary parents
and long a resident there, Dr. McCune is the
outstanding American authority on Korean
geography." LCW'50.

00025   aeng   usa   b 0 n   1950
    U.S. Library of Congress. Reference
Department. Korea: an annotated bibliography of
publications in Western languages. Compiled by
Helen Dudenbostel Jones and Robin L. Winkler.
Washington, D.C., 1950. 9, 155 p.
English. CtY,DLC,HU-E,MH,MH-HY.
                                        S,MH-HY.
Sociocultural pattern--Bibliography. History--
Bibliography. Polity--Bibliography. Economy--
Bibliography. 113.02 130.00 870.00 190.00
538.00 102.00 Bibliographies. Medicine.
Religion. Periodicals. Arts. Bibliography--
1930-1949.

00050   feng   usa   b 0 n   1959   1
    Lee, Soon Hi, 1926-. Korea: a selected
bibliography in Western languages, 1950-1958.
[Washington, D.C.] 1959. 7, 55 p. 25 cm.
English. DLC,MiU. Thesis (Library Science) --
Catholic University of America. This is a
continuation of Shannon McCune, Bibliography of
Western language materials on Korea. Rev., enl.
ed. New York, International Secretariat, Institute
of Pacific Relations, 1950.
                                              S.
Polity--Bibliography. Intercultural relations--
Bibliography. Economy--Bibliography. Language--
Bibliography. Literature--Bibliography. 113.02
213.01 102.00 642.00 489.00 744.00 797.00
533.00 159.04 600.00 130.00 175.00 172.00
670.00 870.00 Communications. Government.
Agriculture. Industry. Religion. Welfare.
Travelers' accounts. Commerce. Women.
Ethnography. Germ warfare. Tuberculosis.
Christianity--Roman Catholicism. Christianity--
Methodists. Folklore. Arts. Korean War.
Bibliography--1950-1958.

"A partially annotated bibliography of 500 works
on Korea in western languages, majority of which
are in English." Yang'60.

00052   akor   sokor   b 20 me   1957
    Kim, Un-sŏk, ed. Pukhan koejip chŏnsul

200

munhŏn-chip [Bibliography on the puppet state of
North Korea]. [Seoul], Han'guk Asea Pangong
Yŏnmaeng, 1957.   528 p.   21 cm.
Korean.   DLC,WaU-FE.

WaU,DLC.
Bibliography.   110.00   Democratic People's
Republic of Korea.   North Korea--Politics and
government.

00053   ajap   kor   b 0 n   1937
     Korea (Government-General of Chōsen, 1910-
1945) Toshokan.   Shinshobu bunrui mokuroku
[Classified catalog of new books].   Seoul, Chōsen
Sōtokufu Toshokan, 1937-38.   3 v.   27 cm.
Japanese.   DLC,MH-HY.   V. 3, p. 627-790.
Classification: Korea, including also Manchuria,
Mongolia, and Siberia.

UC'54.
Bibliography.   110.00   175.00   433.00   671.00
660.00   217.05

"Lists holdings in Western bindings of the Library
of the Government General as of July, 1937. Books
on Korea are listed in Vol. III. The books are
arranged according to topics listed in a key at
the front. Some periodicals and reprints of old
Korean books are listed, but the main value of the
volume is for indicating recent studies in such
fields as Korean history, politics, law,
economics, etc." UC'54.

00054   ajap   japan   b 0 n   1936
     Ito, Hirobumi.   Chōsen kosho shiryō [Old
source materials related to negotiations with
Korea].   Tokyo, Hisho Ruisan Kankōkai, 1936.   3 v.
(Hisho ruisan, 21-23)
Japanese--English.   NNC.

Yang'60.
Intercultural relations--Korea-China.
Intercultural relations--Korea-Japan.   648.00
Documents, Diplomatic--Bibliography.

"Contains a study on the tributary of Korea to
China." Yang'60.

00058   akor   nokor   b 0 n   1955 1
     Kungnip Chungang Tosŏgwan. P'yŏngyang, Korea.
Sŏjihak pu.   Chosŏn sŏjihak kaegwan
[Introduction to Korean bibliography].
P'yŏngyang, Kungnip Ch'ulp'ansa, 1955.   319 p.

(on double leaves) 27 cm.
Korean. DLC,HRAF. DLC has photo copy.
                                       Yang'67,S.
Literature--Bibliography. Bibliography--
bibliographic essay. 110.00   814.05   212.00
217.02   803.00   821.00   805.00   240.00   758.00
185.00   700.00   823.00   190.00   538.00   670.00
130.00   102.00 Rare books. Dictionaries.
Economy. Buddhism. Confucianism. Intercultural
relations. Method. Theory. Hunmin Chŏngŭm.
Han'gŭl.

00061 akor   nokor   b 0 n   1965   1
       Chosŏn Minjujuŭi Inmin Konghwaguk Sahoe
kwahagwŏn. Kojŏn Yŏn'guso. P'yŏngyang, Korea.
Munhŏn Yŏn'gusil.   Chosŏn kojŏn haeje [Annotated
bibliography of Korean classics]. V.1. [Ed. by] Ha
Yun-do [and] Hwang Pyŏng-hŏn.   P'yŏngyang, Sahoe
Kwahagwŏn Ch'ulp'ansa, 1965. 713 p. illus. 21
cm.
Korean. DLC,MH-HY.
                                  Yang'67,S,MHY.
Bibliography. 814.05 815.00 113.02 130.00
102.00 750.00 Rare books. Technology.
Medicine. Classics. Geography.

"...contains annotations for 175 items of Korean
classical works on geography, maps, medicine, and
technology. The last three volumes will treat
works entirely in the social sciences." Yang'67.

00062 ajap   kor   b 0 n   1941
       Sakurai, Yoshiyuki, ed. Meiji nenkan Chōsen
kenkyū bunken shi [Annotated bibliography of
Korean studies in the Meiji era]. Seoul, Shomotsu
Dōkōkai, 1941. 6, 421 p. map. 23 cm.
Japanese. CSt-H,CtY,DLC,HRAF,MH-HY. Originally
published under title, Meiji nenkan Chōsen Kankei
bunken Shōroku. In Chōsen, 158 (Nov. 1936), 264
(May 1937), and supplemented later by the articles
in the issues: Chōsen, 285 (Feb. 1939) and 293
(Oct. 1939). Author and title index.
                              MH-HY,S,UC'54.
Sociocultural pattern--Bibliography. 113.02
175.00 159.04 631.00 647.00 648.00 433.00
871.00 538.00 771.00 102.00 744.00
Bibliography--1868-1912. Meiji.

"Contains 579 titles of selected studies on Korea,
almost all in Japanese, written during 1868-1912,

arranged in eight general classifications. Each
entry gives general bibliographical data, a brief
biography of the author, a statement (usually
taken from the book itself) about the book's scope
and aim, and the table of contents. There is an
author index and a title index, both in <u>kana</u>
order. In general, this bibliography is the best
one for the period it covers for individual
studies, reports, and secondary works." UC'54. "It
is divided into eight classifications: general,
history and biography, domestic administration and
foreign relations, economics and industry,
description and travel, education and literature,
religion and sanitation, and maps." LCF'50.

00063 xjap   japan   b 0 n   1953
       Chōsen kankei shigaku ronbun mokuroku [List
of magazines and literature on the history of
Korea]. <u>In</u> Rekishigaku Kenkyūkai, ed. Chōsen-shi
no shomondai, Rekishigaku kenkyū tokushū-gō.
Tokyo, Iwanami Shoten, 1953: 97-117.
Japanese. CtY,DLC,HRAF,MH⇁HY.
                                        S,MH-HY.
History--Bibliography. Religion and philosophy--
Bibliography. Conflict--Bibliography. 110.00
175.00 567.00 172.00 600.00 648.00 Economy.
Biology. Surnames. Christianity. Buddhism.
Confucianism. Shamanism. Intercultural
Relations--Korea-Russia/U.S.S.R. --1884-1904.
Bibliography--1927-1953.

00065 ajap   japan   b 0 n   1961
       Hara, Sanshichi, ed. Imanishi Hakushi
shūshū Chōsen kankei bunken mokuroku (Catalog of
the Korean materials collected by the late Prof.
Dr. R. Imanishi). Tokyo, Shoseki Bunbutsu
Ryūtsūkai, 1961. 374, 84, 5 p. (on double
leaves) facsims. 25 cm.
Sinico-Japanese. CtY,DLC,HU-E,MH-HY. Includes a
bibliography of occidental materials on Korea: p.
1-4 (3rd group). Index.
                                        S,MH-HY.
Bibliography--catalogs--Japan. History--
Bibliography. Archeology--Bibliography.
Imanishi, Ryū (1875-1932). Imanishi Collection.
Tenri University. 110.00 870.00 538.00 130.00
175.00 Religion. Buddhism. Confucianism. Arts.
Ethnology. Biography. Bibliography--Collections.
Catalogs, College. Libraries, Private--
Bibliography.

00067 ajap   japan   b 0 n   1944
       Maema, Kyōsaku,   1868-1942, ed.   Kosen sappu
[Annotated bibliography of old Korean books].
Tokyo, Tōyō Bunko, 1944-1957. 3 v. illus.,
plates. 26 cm. (Tōyō Bunkō sōkan, 11 [i.e. 12])
Japanese. CSt-H,CtY,DLC,HRAF,HU-E,MH-HY, WaU-FE.
                                         S,Yang'60.
Bibliography--catalogs--Japan. Literature--
Bibliography. History--Bibliography. Maema
Collection. 113.02 601.00 159.04 870.00
130.00 173.00 571.00 577.00 Rare books.
Classics. Arts. Sutras. Philosophy. Industry.

"Basically a descriptive catalog of Maema's
collection of old Korean books, but it also
includes references to other bibliographies and
catalogs of Korean classical writings." Yang'60.
"An exhaustive work, which covers all the books
written in Korea through the ages, arranges them
in the order of the Japanese syllabary, and adds
detailed annotations." Okamoto'62.

00068 ajap   kor   b 0 n   1934
       Keijō Furitsu Toshokan.   Tosho mokuroku
[Catalog of Keijō Furitsu Toshokan as of July 31,
1933]. Seoul, 1934. 12, 541 p. 26 cm.
Japanese. MH-HY.
                                         S,MHY.
Bibliography--catalogs--Korea. Kungnip Chungang
Tosŏgwan. Keijō Furitsu Toshokan. 110.00

00069 akor   sokor   b 0 n   1956
       Sŏul Taehakkyo. Pusok Tosŏgwan.   Sŏul
Taehakkyo kaegyo sipchunyŏn Kinyŏm Ko Tosŏ
Chŏnsihoe ch"ulp"um tosŏ haesŏl Tan'gi 4289 nyŏn
10 wŏl 13-17-il   (An annotated list of rare
books exhibited in commemoration of 10th
anniversary of Seoul National University, Oct. 13-
17, 1956). Secul, Sŏul Taehakkyo Pusok Tosogwan,
1956. 95 p. 19 cm.
Korean-English. CU-E,MH-HY. Catalog of 67 Korean
works with annctations in Korean and English and
79 works in European languages with annotations in
Korean.
                                         CUE,MHY.
Literature--Bibliography. 113.02 Rare books.

00070 akor   sokor   b 0 mc   1961
       Yŏnse Taehakkyo. Sanggyŏng Taehak. Sanŏp

Kyŏngyŏng Yŏn'guso. Sanŏp kyŏngje munhŏn mongnok
(1945-1960) (The bibliography in business and
economics, 1945-1960). By Industrial Research
Center, College of Business Administration, Yonsei
University. Seoul, Yŏnse Taehakkyo Ch'ulp'anbu,
1961. 7, 192 p. 26 cm.
Korean. CtY,CUE,DLC,KYU,MH-HY,NNC. Forward also
in English, with added title. L.C. has: Editions,
1945-1960 and 1961-1964.
                              Chŏng'66,CUE,S.
Economy--Bibliography. 110.00   430.00   440.00
450.00   470.00   648.00   652.00   651.00   654.00
369.00   463.00   161.00   166.00   162.00   433.00
456.00   175.00   Social policy.   Biography.
Business policy. Industrial psychology. Economic
policy. Industrial management--Bibliography.
Business--Bibliography.   Industry--Bibliography.
Economics--Bibliography.   Bibliography--1945-1960.

00071 akor   sokor   b 0 n   1965
       Ko, Hu-sŏk, comp. Han'guk tosŏgwan kwan'gye
munhŏn mongnok, 1921-1961   (Korean library
literature). [Ed. by] Ko Hu-sŏk [and] Hong Sun-
yŏng.   Seoul, Ihwa Yŏja Taehakkyo Ch'ulp'anbu,
1965. 148 p. 20 cm.
Korean. DLC. Bound, as issued, with Han'guk
chapchi mongnok, 1896-1945, by Ch'oe Sun-ja, p.
149-208.
                                                S.
Bibliography. 110.00   Bibliography--1921-1961.

00072 akor   sokor   b 0 n   1965
       Ch'oe, Sun-ja, comp. Han'guk chapchi
mongnok, 1896-1945   (Korean magazine index, 1896-
1945). By Soon Ja Choi. Seoul, Ihwa Yŏja
Taehakkyo Ch'ulp'anbu, 1965. 149-208 p. 20 cm.
Korean. DLC,MH-HY. Bound, as issued, with
Han'guk tosŏgwan kwan'gye munhŏn mongnok, 1921-
1961, by Ko Hu-sŏk and Hong Sun-yŏng.
                                           S,MHY.
Bibliography--index. Law--Bibliography. Religion
and philosophy--Bibliography. History--
Bibliography. 110.00   341.00   870.00   538.00
190.00   625.00   368.01   450.00   496.00   648.00
186.00   213.00   747.00   204.00   369.00   185.00
533.00   183.00   590.00   278.00   744.00   217.02
Industry. Economy. Agriculture. Christianity.
Buddhism. Ethnography. Polity. Women.
Recreation. Ethnoscience. Ch'ondo kyo. Overseas
Koreans. Bibliography--1896-1945.

00073 akor   sokor   b 0 n   1964
        Kungnip Chungang Tosŏgwan. Seoul, Korea, ed.
Han'guk sŏmok, 1945-1962 (Korean national
bibliography, 1945-1962). Seoul, Kungnip Chungang
Tosŏgwan, 1964. 2, 722 p. 26 cm.
Korean. CU-E,DLC,HRAF,HU-E,MH-HY. Superseded by
Taehan Minguk ch˝ulp˝anmul ch˝ong mongnok,
1963/1964 (1965)--published by Kungnip Chungang
Tosŏgwan (the National Central library).
                                         CUE,S.
Bibliography--catalogs--Korea. Kungnip Chungang
Tosŏgwan. National Central Library. 110.00
533.00   102.00   204.00   175.00   130.00   190.00
538.00   870.00   489.00   670.00   842.00   460.00
523.00   700.00   160.00   586.00   562.00   290.00
576.00 Religicn. Philosophy. Arts. Polity.
Economy. Ethnoscience. Medicine. Industry.
Technology. Christianity. Biography. Buddhism.
Agriculture. Medicine. Communism. Commerce.
Ethnography. Bibliography--1945-1962.

00075 akor   sokor   b 0 n   1961
        Kukka Chaegŏn Ch˝oego Hoeŭi Tosŏgwan.
Changsŏ mongnok--Tongyangsŏ, Sŏyangsŏ pullyu
mongnok 4294 nyŏn siwŏl siboil hyŏnjae-
(Classified catalog of books in the National
Assembly Library of Korea). Seoul, 1961. 10, 900
p. 27 cm.
Korean. DLC,MH-HY.
                              S,Chŏng'66,MHY.
Bibliography--catalogs--Korea. Kukka Chaegŏn
Ch˝oego Hoeŭi Tosŏgwan. National Assembly
Library. 110.00   204.00   369.00   183.00   436.00
652.00   453.00   212.00   523.00   671.00   646.00
204.00   450.00   489.00   533.00   538.00   175.00
Christianity. Buddhism. Marriage. Statistics.
Population. Polity. Industry. Travelers'
accounts. Biography. Bibliography-- up to 1961.

00076 akor   sokor   b 0 ni   19101964
        Sŏul Taehakkyo. Pusok Tosŏgwan   Kyujanggak
tosŏ mongnok--Han'guk [Catalog of the Kyujanggak
collection of Korean books]. Seoul, 1964-1966. 6
v. 26 cm.
Sinico-Korean. CtY,CU-E,HU-E,MH-HY. CONTENTS.-
Han'gukpon. Chippu. 1964.- Han'gukpon. Sabu.
1965 3v.- Han'gukpon. Kyŏngjabu [mit] poyu.
1965.- Sŏmyŏng Saegin. 1966.
                                       S,MHY.

Bibliography--catalogs--Korea. Literature--
bibliography. Kyujanggak. 110.00 538.00 175.00
Royal Library of Yi dynasty.

00079 akor   sokor   b 0 n   1961
    Kungnip Tosŏgwan. Changsŏ pullyu mongnok--
Haebang ijŏn ilsŏbu [Classified catalog of
Japanese books published before 1945 in the
National Library]. Seoul, Kungnip Tosŏgwan, 1961-
1963. 5 v. 27 cm.
Korean-Japanese. CU-E,DLC,MH-HY,WaU-FE. Includes
the catalog of books added to the collection until
1945. V. 5 includes books on Korea.
                            WaU,Chŏng'66.
Bibliography--catalogs--Korea. Kungnip Tosŏgwan.
National Central Library. 110.00

00080 akor   sokor   b 0 n   1956
    Kungnip Tosŏgwan. Kosŏbu pullyu mongnok
[Classified catalog of old books]. Seoul, Kungnip
Tosŏgwan, 1956. 20, 473 p. 26 cm.
Korean. CU-E,DLC,MH-HY,NNC,WaU-FE.
                            DLC,MHY,Yang'60.
Bibliography. 110.00 Rare books.

"Lists 11,987 titles of Korean classics in the
collection of the National Library of Korea as of
August 1945." Yang'60.

00087 akor   sokor   b 0 n   1960
    Han'guk Yŏn'guwŏn. Han'guk Sŏk Paksa hagwi
nonmun mongnok 1945-1960 (List of master's and
doctor's degrees offered in Korea, 1945-1960).
Seoul, 1960. 107, 16 p. 26 cm.
Korean. CtY,CU-E,DLC,HU-E,MH-HY,WaU. Social
science: p. 1, 8-65.
                            S,CUE,Chŏng'66.
Intercultural relations--Bibliography.
Bibliography--dissertations. 538.00   532.00
190.00   369.00   647.00   185.00   665.00   110.00
873.10   870.00   450.00   670.00   771.00   812.00
175.00   130.00   160.00   Economy. Polity. Kye.
Bibliography--1945-1960.

00088 akor   japan   b 0 n   1908
    Tokyo Gaikokugo Gakkō. Kankoku Kōyūkai, ed.
Hanjŏk mongnok kobon [A list of Korean
manuscripts]. Tokyo, 1908. 57, 10 p. 23 cm.
Korean. MH-HY.
                                    MHY,S.

Bibliography. 110.00 175.00 538.00 130.00
700.00 190.00 771.00 590.00 600.00 Rare
books. Buddhism. Medicine. Agriculture.

00091 akor   kor   h 0 ne   1912
Sŏ, Kŏ-jŏng, 1420-1488, ed. Tongguk
T´onggam [Complete mirror of the Eastern
Country]. Seoul, Chōsen Kosho Kankōkai, 1912. 3
v. 23 cm. (Chōsen gunsho taikei zoku, no. 3-5)
Korean. CU-E,MH-HY,WaU. Originally published in
1484. V. 1 contains citations of old books
existing before the author's time.
                                       WaU,UC'54.
Bibliography. History. 110.00 Rare books.
Classics.

00095 fkor   kor   b 0 n
Tŏksindang sŏmok [Catalog of Tŏksindang
books]. [n.p.] ca. 18--. 54 double l. 26 cm.
Korean. MH-HY. Manuscript owned by Yu Sŏng-jong.

                                              MHY.
Bibliography--catalogs--Korea. Religion and
philosophy. Tŏksindang. Buddhism. Rare books.
Catalogs, Private Library.

00100 akor   sokor   b 0 n   1950
Columbia University. Kŭmsu kangsan (Works
on Korea). New York, 1950. 22 p. 28 cm.
Korean and English. DLC,HU-E,MH-HY,WaU-FE. 535
titles from the collections of the East Asiatic
library at Columbia University.
                                       WaU,LCF'50.
Bibliography--catalogs--U.S.A. Columbia
University. East Asiatic Library. 110.00

"This is a classified list of books and
periodicals on Korea in the Korean, Japanese, and
Chinese languages. The romanizations and Chinese
characters are given for each citation. No
annotations." LCF'50.

00106 akor   sokor   b 0 n   1965
Sŏul Taehakkyo. Mullikwa Taehak. Tonga Munhwa
Yŏn'guso. Kyujanggak tosŏ Han'gukpon
ch´ongmongnok (Catalog of Korean books and
manuscripts in the Kyujanggak Collection, Seoul
National University Library). Seoul, 1965.
[704], 105, 115 p. 26 cm.
Sinico-Korean. HRAF,MH-HY. This was previously

issued in 1964/1965 in 5 volumes under title of
Kyujanggak tosč mongnok by Sŏul Taehakkyo, Pusok
Tosŏgwan.
S.
Bibliography--catalogs--Korea. Kyujanggak.

00107 ajap   kor   b 0 n   1921
       Korea (Government-General of Chōsen, 1910-
1945), ed. Chōsen Sōtokufu ko tosho mokuroku
[General catalog of old books in the Library of
Government-General of Korea]. Seoul, 1921. 316
p. 27 cm.
Japanese. CtY,DLC. Supplement, ed. by Keijo
Imperial University. Seoul, 1935. 59 p.   27 cm.
                              S,UC'54,LCF'50.
Bibliography--catalogs--Korea. History--
Bibliography. Religion and philosophy--
Bibliography. Literature--Bibliography.
Government-General Library. 110.00   172.00
130.00 821.00 Classics. Law. Genealogy.
Military. Agriculture.

"Essentially a catalogue of old Korean and Chinese
books possessed by the Government General in 1921,
classified as classics, history, philosophy, and
collected works. There are separate sections for
Chinese and Korean books. While it is probably one
of the most comprehensive lists of old Korean
books available, including many titles not found
in Courant's bibliography, the work omits some
important titles and lacks a satisfactory index.
Despite these defects, the book is one of the
essential reference books for the study of Korea
before 1910." UC'54.

00108 aeng   usa   b 0 n   1939
       Kerner, Robert Joseph. Northeastern Asia, a
selected biblicgraphy; contributions to the
bibliography of the relations of China, Russia,
and Japan, with special reference to Korea,
Manchuria, Mongolia, and eastern Siberia, in
Oriental and European languages. Berkeley,
University of California Press, 1939. 2 v. (39,
675, 31, 621 p.) (Publications of the
Northeastern Asia seminar of the University of
California)
English. DLC. Korea: v. 2, p. 230-270.
                              Chŏng'66,LCW'50.
Intercultural relations--Bibliography. 110.00
648.00 Asia--Bibliography.

"Lists in Vol. II primary and secondary source
materials on Korea in Western (including Russian)
and Oriental languages, some 450 entries arranged
topically." LCW'50.

00109   aeng   usa   b 0 n   1959
        Stucki, Curtis W. American doctoral
dissertations on Asia, 1933-1958, including
appendix of Master's theses at Cornell University.
Ithaca, Southeast Asia Program, Department of Far
Eastern Studies, Cornell University, 1959. 131 p.
28 cm. (Cornell University. Southeast Asia
Program. Data paper, 37)
English. CtY,DLC,MH-HY,TxU,WaU-FE. Dissertations
(all)- Cornell University. Thesis (all)- Cornell
University. Dissertations on Korea; p. 105.
                                    Silberman'62.
Bibliography--dissertations. 110.00 Oriental
Studies--U.S.--Bibliography. Bibliography--1933-
1958.

"An invaluable guide to the great mass of
otherwise unavailable material to be found in
unpublished dissertations." Silberman'62.

00110   zeng   usa   b 0 n   1946
        McCune, Shannon Boyd-Bailey. Recent books on
Korea. In Geographical review, 36 (Apr. 1946):
327-329.
English. DLC.
                                    LCW'50.
Bibliography--bibliographic essay. 102.00

"Critique of Grajdanzev's Modern Korea with some
discussion of Harrington's God, Mammon and the
Japanese, Nelson's Korea and the Old Orders in
Eastern Asia and some mention of maps and
periodical literature." LCW'50.

00115   aeng   usa   b 0 me195019531962
        O'Quinlivan, Michael. An annotated
bibliography of the United States Marines in the
Korean war. Washington, D.C., Historical Branch,
G-3 Division, Headquarters, U.S. Marine Corps,
1962. 31 p. 26 cm. (Marine Corps historical
bibliographies, no. 6)
English. DLC.
                              DLC,Chŏng'66,S.
Intercultural relations--Korea-U.S.A. --

Bibliography. Conflict--Bibliography. 720.00
113.02 Korean War. U.S. Marines. U.S. Marine
Corps--History--Sources --Bibliography.

00116   aeng   usa   b   0   ne186819451959
        Young, John, comp. Checklist of microfilm
reproductions of selected archives of the Japanese
Army, Navy and other government agencies, 1868-
1945. Washington, D.C., Georgetown University
Press, 1959. 144 p.
English. CtY,DLC. For materials on Korea see
index.
                              S,Chŏng'66.
Bibliography--catalogs--Japan. Intercultural
relations--Korea-Japan--Bibliography. Japanese
Army and Navy archives. 110.00 669.00 185.00
648.00 665.00 668.00 217.00 Overseas Koreans.
Japanese army. Japanese navy. Japan--Archives--
Catalogs. Japan--History, Military--Sources. Yi
dynasty. Japanese occupation.

00117   aeng   sokor   b   0   n   1963
        Gompertz, G. St.G. M. Bibliography of
Western literature on Korea from the earliest time
until 1950. Seoul, Dong-a Publishing Co., 1963.
263 p. (Transactions of the Korea Branch of the
Royal Asiatic Society, 40)
English. DLC,MH-HY. Based on Horace Underwood's
'Partial bibliography of occidental literature on
Korea'.
                              S,Gerow'52,MHY.
Sociocultural pattern--Bibliography. Diamond
Mountains. Kŭmgang-san. Quelpart. Dagelet.
Ullŭngdo. Chejudo. 113.02 648.00 369.00
565.00 530.00 651.00 341.00 323.00 130.00
177.00 764.15 436.05 821.00 567.00 527.00
181.00 773.00 769.05 172.00 167.02 797.00
644.00 870.00 590.00 160.00 744.00 670.00
576.00 Intercultural relations. Women.
Children. Sociology. Ethnology. Society.
Travelers' accounts. Marriage. Costumes.
Etiquette. Rites. Recreation. Folklore. Arts.
Peddlers. Social change. Buddhism.
Confucianism. Shamanism. Christianity. Jesuit
missions. Material culture. Ginseng.
Bibliographies. Overseas Koreans. Hideyoshi's
invasions. Catalogs, Book. Indexes.
Bibliography--1588-1950.

"The first sections of a revised and annotated

211

bibliography based on Horace Underwood's 'Partial
bibliography of occidental literature on Korea'."
Chŏng'66.

00118 zeng   kor   b 0 n   1935
     Gompertz, E. Supplement to 'A partial
bibliography of occidental literature on Korea' by
H. H. Underwood, 1931. By E. Gompertz and G.
Gompertz. In Transactions of the Korea Branch of
the Royal Asiatic Society, 24 (1935): 21-48.
English. CtY,DLC. Not indexed.
                                    S,LCW'50.
Bibliography. Religion and philosophy--
Bibliography. 110.00   190.00   530.00   764.15
815.00   204.00   175.00   797.00 Polity.
Travelers' acccunts. Health. Commerce.
Industry. Christianity--Protestants.
Intercultural relations. Christianity--Roman
Catholicism. Catalogs, Book. Bibliography--1818-
1935.

"Lists 369 additional titles. A second supplement,
containing 1740 further titles up to 1940 had been
printed at the time war broke out in the Pacific."
Gompertz'63.

00120 zeng   kor   b 0 n   1931
     Underwood, Horace H. A partial bibliography
of occidental literature on Korea from early times
to 1930. In Transactions of the Korea Branch of
the Royal Asiatic Society, 20 (1931): 17-185 and
1-17.
English. CtY. Author index: p. 1-17 (2d group).
Japanese translation by Hashimoto Tokumatsu,
Bunken hōkoku, 6, no. 2-3 (1940).
                              S,UC'54,LCW'50.
Bibliography. Religion and philosophy--
Bibliography. 110.00   190.00   530.00   764.15
815.00   204.00   175.00   728.00   496.00   312.00
316.00   750.00   797.00   172.00   450.00   670.00
105.00 Polity. Sociocultural change.
Intercultural relations. Travelers' accounts.
Ethnology. Christianity--Roman Catholicism.
Christianity--Protestants. Agriculture. Ecology.
Commerce. Industry. Health. Catalogs, Book.
Indexes. Bibliography--1594-1930.

"Divides its material into fourteen sections, the
titles in each section arranged by date of
publication. It lists some 2,882 items and has an

author index. It gives quite thorough coverage and
is one of the basic bibliographies of Western
books and articles on Korea before 1931. The
listing was expanded and brought down to 1935 in a
supplement which follows Underwood's method of
classification: Gompertz, E. and G. 'Supplement to
'A Partial Bibliography. . . on Korea' by H.H.
Underwood, 1931,' TAKBRAS, 24 (1935), 21-48."
UC'54. "It is preceded by an interesting paper on
'Occidental Literature on Korea', describing the
scope of the Literature on Korea', describing the
scope of the Bibliography and some of the
difficulties encountered in compiling it."
Gompertz'63.

00121   aeng   japan   b   0   n   1937
         Kokusai Bunka Shinkōkai. K.B.S.
bibliographical register of important works
written in Japanese on Japan and the Far East,
published during the year 1932-1937. Tōkyō, 1937-
1943. 6 v.
English. AzU,CiU,CtY,CUE,DLC,NcD,NjP,WaU. Korea:
1932 (1937) p. 104-110; 1933 (1938) p. 108-113;
1934 (1940) p. 132-140; 1935 (1942) p. 125-130;
1936 (1942) p. 111-117; 1937 (1943) p. 119-127.
                                        S,UC'54.
Bibliography. 110.00   170.00   530.00   159.04
590.00   217.02   776.00   551.00   183.00   173.00
648.00   511.00   647.00   601.00   567.00   212.00
670.00   771.00   812.00   190.00   Travelers'
accounts. Women. Shamanism. Tombs. Buddhism.
Confucianism. Clans. Material culture. Trade.
Bibliography--1932-1937.

"Has a special section for books and articles on
Korea, usually listed with brief annotations. The
Registers are highly selective, so that anyone
using them should refer also to other sources."
UC'54.

00123   aeng   usa   b   0   j   1941
         McCune, Shannon Boyd-Bailey. Geomorphology
of Korea: a selected bibliography. November 1,
1941. [Cambridge, Mass., Korean Research
Associates... 1941]. 7, 3 p. illus., [map].
(Research monographs on Korea. Ser. C, 1)
English. DLC,HRAF.
                                        LCW'50.
Physical setting--geography--Bibliography. 110.00
133.00 Geomorphology. Geology--Bibliography.

Geomorphology--Bibliography.

"The basic sources dealing with the geology and geomorphology of Korea." LCW'50.

00124 aeng   usa   b 0 j   1941
    McCune, Shannon Boyd-Bailey, 1913-. Climate
of Korea: a selected bibliography. March 1, 1941.
[Ypsilanti, Mich., University Lithoprinters,
1941]. [12] p. illus., (maps)., diagrs. 23 cm.
(Research monographs on Korea. Ser. B, 2)
English. DLC.
                                           LCW'50.
Physical setting--geography--Bibliography. 110.00
132.00 Climatclogy--Bibliography. Weather--
Bibliography.

00125 agerm   ger   b 0 n   1928
    Nachod, Oskar. Bibliographie von Japan,
1906-1926; [containing a detailed listing of books
and essays on Japan which have appeared since the
publication of the second volume of Wenckstern
"Bibliography of the Japanese Empire" up to 1926
in European languages]. Leipzig, K. W.
Hiersemann, 1928. 2 v. (15, 832) p. (9575 nos.)
German. CtY,DLC. Korea: p. 662-691, 757-759;
comprising Nos. 8427-8910 and 9553-9574. Issued
also in English edition: London, Goldston, 1928.
Also, supplements: Bibliographie von Japan, 1927-
1929, Leipzig, 1931; and Bibliographie von Japan,
1930-1932, Leipzig, 1935.
                                           LCW'50.
Bibliography. 110.00 Bibliography--1906-1926.

"This important Bibliography continues the work of
Wenckstern and contains a lengthy section on
Korea. Many other titles dealing with Korea are
found in the general subject classifications."
Gompertz'63.

00128 aeng   usa   b 0 ye189419101959
    Nahm, Andrew C., comp. Japanese penetration
of Korea, 1894-1910: a checklist of Japanese
archives in the Hoover Institution. Compiled by
Andrew C. Nahm under the direction of Peter A.
Berton. [Stanford University, Calif.], Hoover
Institution on War, Revolution, and Peace,
Stanford University, 1959. 5, 103 p. 28 cm.
(Hoover Institution bibliographical series, 5)
English. CtY,DLC,MH-W.

S,DLC,Chŏng'66.
Polity--Bibliography. Economy--Bibliography.
Intercultural relations--Korea-Japan--
Bibliography. An, Chung-gŭn. Pak, Yŏng-hyo.
Itō, Hirobumi. 113.02 217.00 503.00 578.00
579.00 640.00 650.00 660.00 700.00 504.00
316.00 204.00 175.00 648.00 489.00
Christianity. Intercultural Relations--Korea-
Russia/U.S.S.R. Intercultural Relations--Korea-
U.S.A. Intercultural Relations--Korea-Great
Britain. Intercultural Relations--Korea-France.
Tonghak Revolt. Overseas Koreans. Harbin
Incident. Japanese Legation (Seoul). Japanese
Residency-General in Korea. Japan--Archives--
Catalogs. Documents, Diplomatic--Bibliography.

00129 aeng   usa   b 0 n   1963
       Schroeder, Peter Brett. Korean publications
in the National Agricultural Library. Washington,
D.C., National Agricultural Library, U.S.
Department of Agriculture, 1963. 25 p. (U.S.
National Agricultural Library list, 79)
English. DLC,HU-E.
                         DLC,Chŏng'66,S.
Bibliography--catalogs--U.S.A. Economy--
Bibliography. National Agricultural Library.
110.00 241.00 313.00 314.00 137.00 230.00
240.00 433.00 204.00 311.00 312.00 369.00
474.00 136.00 162.00 262.00 Agriculture.
Periodicals. Agriculture--Bibliography. Forests
and forestry--Eibliography.

00130 zeng   kor   b 0 n   1932
       Trollope, Mark Napier. Corean books and
their authors. In Transactions of the Korea Branch
of the Royal Asiatic Society, 21 (1932): 1-58.
English. CtY,DLC,HU-E.
                         UC'54,LCW'50,S.
Bibliography--bibliographic essay. 113.02
Ethnoscience.

"A historical treatment of Korean literature
classified as classics, history, philosophy, and
collected works. The article is one of the best
introductions in a Western language to Korean
intellectual and literary activities. During his
stay in Korea Bishop Trollope collected some 10,
000 Korean books, and his article is based upon
lecture notes he had intended to expand into a
book before his sudden death in Seoul in 1933."
UC'54.

00131   zeng   japan   h 0   n   1965
      Mishina, Shōei. The development of the
studies of Korean history and culture in Japan. By
Mishina Shōei and Murakami Yoshio. In Acta
Asiatica: bulletin of the Institute of Eastern
Culture, 9 (1965): 83-110.
English. HRAF.
                                                    S.
Bibliography--bibliographic essay. 110.00 172.00
173.00 217.02 814.00 829.00 185.00 650.00
369.00 190.00 613.00 144.00 130.00 227.00
313.00 316.00 436.00 440.00 450.00 644.00
538.00 183.00 428.00 496.00 205.00 420.00
670.00 Economy. Agriculture. Commerce.
Ethnology. Korean studies. History.
Intercultural relations. Myŏn. Korean studies in
Japan--Bibliography.

00132   aeng   usa   b 0   n   1955
      Quan, L. King. Introduction to Asia; a
selective guide to background reading.
Washington, D.C., Reference Department, Library of
Congress, 1955. 214 p.
English. DLC.
                                        DLC,Chŏng'66.
Bibliography. 110.00

00133   aeng   usa   b 0   je   1945
      **U.S. Library of Congress. General Reference
and Bibliography Division.** Biographical sources
for foreign countries. IV. The Japanese Empire.
Comp. by Nelson R. Burr. Washington, 1945.   114
p.
English. CtY,DLC.
                                        LCW'50.
Intercultural relations--Korea-Japan--
Bibliography. 159.04 110.00 Biography.
Japanese in Korea. History--Bibliography.
Japanese in Korea--Bibliography. Japan--History--
Meiji Period--Bibliography. Japan--Colonies--
Administration--Bibliography.

"See Index under Korea. Emphasis is on Japanese in
Korea." LCW'50.

00134   aeng   usa   b 0   ne186819451954
      Uyehara, Cecil H., comp. Checklist of
archives in the Japanese Ministry of Foreign

216

Affairs, Tōkyō Japan, 1868-1945. Compiled by Cecil
H. Uyehara, under the direction of Edwin G. Beal,
Jr. Washington, D.C., Photoduplication Service,
Library of Congress, 1954. 262 p.
English. CtY,DLC. For materials on Korea see
index.
                              S,DLC,Chŏng'66.
Bibliography--catalogs--Japan. Polity--
Bibliography. Intercultural relations--Korea-
Japan--Bibliography. Intercultural Relations--
Korea-Russia/U.S.S.R. --Bibliography. Japanese
Ministry of Foreign Affairs. 110.00 643.00
648.00 175.00 496.00 217.00 668.00 489.00
Overseas Koreans. Japanese Ministry of Foreign
Affairs. Documents, Diplomatic--Bibliography.
Japan--Archives--Catalogs. Yi dynasty. Japanese
occupation.

00138   aeng   usa   b 0 je   1943
         U.S. Library of Congress. Division of
Bibliography. The Japanese empire: industries and
transportation, a selected list of references.
Compiled by Florence S. Hellman, chief
bibliographer. Washington, D.C., 1943. 56 p.
English. DLC. See Subject index under Korea.
                              LCW'50.
Economy--Bibliography. 110.00 489.00 Industry.
Japan--Economic conditions--Bibliography.
Manchuria--Economic conditions--Bibliography.

"Includes wide coverage of western language
periodical material." LCW'50.

00139   aeng   usa   b 0 n   1947
         U.S. Library of Congress. General Reference
and Bibliography Division. Non-self-governing
areas with special emphasis on mandates and
trusteeships: a selected list of references. Comp.
by Helen F. Conover. Washington, D.C., 1947. 2
v. (9, 467 p.) 27 cm.
English. DLC. Korea: v. 2, p. 269-279.
                              LCW'50.
Bibliography. 110.00

"87 titles listed including bibliographies,
pamphlets, monographic and periodical literature."
LCW'50.

00140   agerm   ger   b 0 n   1931
         Nachod, Oskar. Bibliographie von Japan,

                        217

1927-1929, [with supplements for the years 1906-
1926; volume 3 of the collected work, number 9576-
13595]. Leipzig, K. W. Hiersmann, 1931. 2 v.
(13, 410 p.)
German. CtY,DLC. Korea: p. 355-365. These 2
volumes are supplements to the first 2 volumes by
Nachod.
                                        LCW'50.
Bibliography. 110.00 Bibliography--1906-1929.

00141 agerm   ger   b 0 n   1935
       Nachod, Oskar. Bibliographie von Japan,
1930-1932, [with supplements for the years 1906-
1929; volume 4 of the collected work, number
13596-18398]. [From the unfinished work
supplemented and published by] Hans Praesent.
Leipzig, K. W. Hiersmann, 1935. 14, 351 p.
German. CtY,DLC. Korea: p. 301-325.
                                        LCW'50.
Bibliography. 110.00 Bibliography--1906-1932.

00142 aeng   usa   b 0 n   1960
       Talbot, Phillips, ed. A select bibliography:
Asia, Africa, Eastern Europe, Latin America. New
York, American Universities Field Staff, 1960.
English. Korea: p. 42-45.
                                      Silberman'62.
Bibliography. 113.02

"A short highly selective annotated guide to the
best works on Korea." Silberman'62.

00143 aeng   usa   b 0 n   1950
       **U.S. Dept. of State. Division of
Publications.** Korea, published material, July 2,
1944 to July 3, 1950. Washington, D.C.,
Government Printing Office, 1950. 5 p.
English. DLC,MH-W.
                                    MH-W,LCW'50.
Intercultural relations--Korea-U.S.A. --
Bibliography. Polity--Bibliography. Economy--
Bibliography. 110.00 U.S.--Government
publications--Korea. Bibliography--1944-1950.

"A bibliography of State Department publications
relating to Korea printed since 1944, including
articles on Korea in the Department of State
Bulletin." LCW'50.

00144   aeng   sokor   b   0   n   1961
        Surveys and Research Corporation. Washington,
D.C. An interim report to the government of the
Republic of Korea. [By James S. Fitzgerald].
[Korean translation by Lee Jay Cho]. Seoul,
Statistical Advisory Group, Surveys and Research
Corporation, 1960-1962. 7 v.
Korean-English. CU,DLC,MH-W. V. 2: Statistical
publications in Korea, 1961, 38, 32 p. Added
t.p.: Taehan Min'guk Chŏngbu e taehan Kŏnŭisŏ.
                                MHW,Silberman'62.
Bibliography. Economy. Statistics.

00145   agerm   ger   b   0   n   1937
        Nachod, Oskar. Bibliographie von Japan,
1933-1935, [with supplements for the years 1906-
1932; volume 5 of the collected work begun by
Oskar Nachod, number 18399-25376]. [By] Hans
Praesent and Wolf Haenisch. Leipzig, K. W.
Hiersmann, 1937. 2 v. (11, 452 p.)
German. CtY,DLC. Korea: p. 368-383.
                                LCW'50.
Bibliography. 110.00 Bibliography--1906-1935.

"This work and the two later volumes by Nachod
contain together some 655 references to material
on Korea published from 1930 to 1935." UC'54.

00146   agerm   ger   b   0   n   1940
        Nachod, Oskar. Bibliographie von Japan,
1936-1937, [with supplements for the years 1906-
1935; volume 6 of the collected work, number
25377-33621]. [Revised by] Wolf Haenisch [and]
Hans Praesent]. Leipzig, K. W. Hiersmann, 1940.
11, 569 p.
German. CtY,DLC. Korea: p. 470-479.
                                LCW'50.
Bibliography. 110.00 Bibliography--1906-1937.

00155   aeng   b   0   n   1944
        Allied Forces. Southwest Pacific Area.
Annotated bibliography of the Southwest Pacific
and adjacent areas. [n.p.] 1944-1945. 4 v.
fold. map.
English. DLC. At head of title: Allied
Geographical Section, Southwest Pacific Area.
Korea: v. 3, Malaya, Thailand, Indo-China, the
China Coast and the Japanese Empire, p. 155-167.
Each entry gives description of contents,
photographs, and maps. Also the location of copies
in Australian libraries. Emphasis is on

topographical and geological information.
                                        LCW'50.
Bibliography.   Intercultural relations--Korea-
Japan --Bibliography.   183.00   744.00   186.00
316.00   130.00   102.00   504.00   491.00   489.00
360.00   190.00   160.00   870.00   771.00   113.02
Women.   Communications.   Social conditions.
Polity.   Economy.   Travelers' accounts.
Bibliography--1834-1943.

"120 titles listed alphabetically according to
author." LCW'50.

00156   afren   fran   b   0   yc   1904
        Cordier, Henri.   Bibliotheca Sinica:
dictionnaire bibliographique des ouvrages relatifs
à l'émpire chinois. 2.éd., rev., corr., et
considérablement augm.   Paris, 1904-1924.   4 v. (2
fasc. in each) with suppl. v. (4 fasc.).
Altogether 4428 cols. with 40 p. listing contents.
French.   DLC.   In double cols., numbered
continuously.   Korea: v. 4, cols. 2939-3008; and
suppl. v., cols. 4405-4428; also passim.
Originally published 1878-1895.
                                        UC'54.
Bibliography.   110.00   Bibliography-- up to 1900.

"This invaluable work was first published in 1878-
95, containing 2242 cols., but the enlarged second
edn. shown above is the one in general use. Being
extremely scarce, it has been reproduced by later
facsimile reprints. The Korean sections form a
comparatively small part of the whole work, which,
to quote Prof. Giles, 'is carried out with a
fulness and accuracy which leaves nothing to be
desired, and is essential to all systematic
workers in the Chinese field.' It is no less
essential to students of the literature on Korea;
though the absence of a detailed index makes its
use somewhat laborious. Numerous references to
Korea occur throughout." Gompertz'63. "Lists
sources in western and Oriental languages. The
tables of contents for the Korean Repository and
partial summaries of the contents of the Korea
Review and the Transactions of the Korean Branch
of the Royal Asiatic Society are included.
References to reviews of books and articles are
also listed. Especially helpful for sources before
1900." LCW'50.

00157   aeng   neth   b   0   n   1895
         Wenckstern, Friedrich von, comp.   A
bibliography of the Japanese empire; being a
classified list of all books, essays and maps in
European languages relating to Dai Nihon (Great
Japan) published in Europe, America and in the
East from 1859-1893 A. D. (6th year of Ansei-26th
of Meiji). To which is added a facsimile-reprint
of: Léon Pagès, Bibliographie japonaise depuis le
15 sciècle ['] jusqu'à 1859. Leiden, E. J. Brill,
1895. 14, 338, 67 p.
English-French. DLC. Closely classified; author
and title index. Reprinted in 1910 and 1929.
                                         LCW'50.
Bibliography.   110.00   Bibliography--1859-1893.
Bibliography--1477-1859.

"This is the first vol. of the standard
bibliography on Japan, and the cover is inscribed:
Vol.1: 1477-1893. Vol.2 was published in 1907,
after which the bibliography was continued by
Oskar Nachod in 1928 and later. Wenckstern does
not classify works on Korea separately but gives a
large number of titles dealing with Korea."
Gompertz'63.

00158   aeng   gtbr   b   0   j   1937
         Royal Empire Society. London. Library.
Subject catalog. V.4. Ed. by Lewin Evans. London,
1937. 812 p.
English. DLC. Korea: p. 683.
                                         LCW'50.
Bibliography--catalogs--Great Britain. Royal
Empire Society. London. Library. 110.00
Catalogs, Subject. Libraries--Catalogs--Subject.

00163   ajap   japan   b   0   n   1917
         Osaka Furitsu Toshokan kanpon mokuroku.
[Catalog of Korean books in the Osaka Prefectural
Library, March, 1916]. Osaka, 1917. 32 p.   27
cm.
Japanese.
                                         CEACS'64.
Bibliography--catalogs--Japan. Osaka Prefectural
Library. Osaka Furitsu Toshokan. 110.00

00164   ajap   kor   b   0   j   1932
         Korea (Government-General of Chōsen, 1910-
1945). Chōsen ni okeru shuppanbutsu gaiyō
[Survey of publications in Korea]. [Comp. by]

Chōsen Sōtokufu. Keimukyoku. Seoul, 1932. 149 p.
Japanese. DLC. On cover: [confidential].
LCF'50,DLC.
Bibliography. 214.00 656.00 110.00 Censorship
of the press.

"Surveys the book trade in Korea with an account
of censorship activities for all publications and
pertinent statistics and tables. It is marked
'confidential' ('hi')." LCF'50.

00165 ajap   japan   b 0 y   1940
       Kuroda, Ryō, 1890-. Chōsen kyūsho kō
[Studies of old Korean books]. Tōkyō, Iwanami
Shoten, 1940. [7], 295 p. illus. 22 cm.
Japanese. CtY,DLC,MH-HY,WaU-FE. A collection of
bibliographical studies. Reprinted 1959.
                              MHY,LCF'50.
Bibliography--bibliographic essay. Religion and
philosophy--Bibliography. Printing culture. Rare
books. Buddhism.

00166 ajap   japan   b 0 n   1960
       Nitchō Kyōkai. Chōsen ni kansuru Nihongo-
han tosho mokuroku, 1945-1960 [List of
publications on Korea in Japanese 1945-1960].
Ōsaka, Nitchō Kyōkai Ōsakafu Ronggokai Nitchō
Bōeki Bunka Senta, 1960. 37 p.
Japanese. DLC.
                              Chŏng'66.
Bibliography. 110.00 Catalogs. Bibliography--
1945-1960.

00167 ajap   japan   b 0 n   1893
       Tosho sōmokuroku [General catalog of books].
Tokyo, Tōkyō Shosekishō Kumiai Jimusho, 1893-1940.
9 v.
Japanese.
                              UC'54.
Bibliography. 110.00 Social sciences. Catalog,
Publisher.

"Separate volumes were issued in 1893, 1896, 1906,
1911, 1918, 1923, 1929, 1933, and 1940. Lists
titles published or handled by the Tōkyō
Bookdealers Association in print as of date of
publication of each volume, a coverage of most
books published in the Japanese Empire. Most
volumes have three parts--title catalogue,

publisher catalogue, and classified catalogue, the
last covering in some detail publications in the
social sciences. There is a subject index in each
volume, and indices in the 1911, 1918, 1923, 1929,
and 1933 volumes are especially valuable for books
on Korea." UC'54.

00168 ajap   kor   b 0 y   1924
    Riōshoku. Shomuka. Riōke Zoshokaku kotosho
mokuroku [Catalog of old books kept at the
Library of Yi Royal House]. Seoul, 1924. 90 p.
26 cm.
Japanese. MH-HY. Rev. ed. 1935, 191 p. 27 cm.
                                    CEACS'64.
Bibliography--catalogs--Korea. Yi Wangjik.
Sōmukwa. Riōke Zoshokaku. 110.00 Rare books.
Catalogs, Private library. Libraries, Private--
Bibliography.

00169 ajap   japan   b 0 n   1922
    Ūho Terauchi Bunkō tosho mokuroku [Catalog
of Gen. M. Terauchi's collection, now preserved in
Yamaguchi Women's Junior College]. Yamaguchi,
1922. 107 p. 15 cm.
Japanese.
                                    CEACS'64.
Bibliography--catalogs--Japan. Terauchi
Collection. Yamaguchi Women's Junior College.
110.00 Catalogs, Private library. Libraries,
Private--Bibliography.

00170 ajap   japan   b 0 n   1939
    Tōyō Bunko, ed. Tōyō Bunko Chōsenbon bunrui
mokuroku, fu, annanbon mokuroku [Classified
catalog of Korean books in the Tōyō Bunko with a
catalog of Annamese books appended]. Tōkyō, 1939.
101, 15 p. 27 cm.
Japanese. CSt-H,HU-E. Fu, annanbon mukuroku: p.
93-101.
                                    CEACS'64.
Bibliography--catalogs--Japan. Tōyō Bunkō.
110.00 Libraries, Private--Bibliography.
Catalogs, Classified. Catalogs, Private library.

"A catalogue of all the old books on Korea in the
Oriental Library in Tōkyō in 1939, classified by
the traditional Chinese system, with an index of
titles by number of strokes. The information on
modern editions of old Korean books is one of the
catalogue's most useful features. There is also a

special section on s̲ō̲s̲h̲o̲ (collectanea), and
titles of the individual works in each collected
edition are listed." UC'54.

00171   ajap   japan   b 0 n   1958
    Tōyō Bunko, ed. Chōsen kankei bunken tenji
mokuroku [Annotated catalog of old rare Japanese
and Western publications concerning Korea
preserved in the Tōyō Bunko]. Tokyo, 1958. 29 p.
19 cm.
Japanese. MH-HY,NNC.
                                    CEACS'64.
Bibliography--catalogs--Japan. Tōyō Bunkō.
113.02 Bibliographical exhibitions. Exhibitions-
-Bibliography.

00172   ajap   japan   b 0 n   1955
    Tōhō Gakkai. Tōhōgaku kankei zasshi
mokuroku [Bibliography of Japanese periodicals
relating to Oriental studies]. Tōkyō, 1955. 11
p. 16 cm.
Japanese.
                                    CEACS'64.
Bibliography--periodicals. Periodicals--Oriental
Studies.

00175   ajap   japan   b 0 n   1959
    Kyōtō Daigaku. Bungakubu Toshoshitsu, ed.
Imanishi Bunko mokuroku [Catalog of Dr. R.
Imanishi's collection]. Kyoto, 1959. 128 p.   25
cm.
Japanese. CtY,MH-HY.
                                    CEACS'64.
Bibliography--catalogs--Japan. Imanishi, Ryū
(1875-1932). Imanishi Collection. Tenri
University. 110.00 Libraries, Private--
Bibliography. Catalogs, College. Bibliography--
Collections.

00176   ajap   japan   b 0 n   1939
    Hirose, Bin.   Nihon sōsho sakuin [Index to
Japanese collectanea]. Tōkyō, Musashino Shoin,
1939. [892] p.
Japanese. CtY.
                                  S,CEACS'64.
Bibliography. Classics. History. Indexes.
Bibliography--1900-1931.

"A complete index to all the important modern
collections printed in Japan before 1931. Since

many Korean books and shorter works of Korean
authors were included in collections printed in
Japan from the late Meiji period onward, it is
often possible to find here works listed nowhere
else." UC'54.

00177 zjap   kor   b 0 ke   1931
    Suematsu, Yasukazu.   Kōrai bunken shōroku
[Notes on the historical materials for the study
of the Koryō kingdom]. In Seikyū gakusō, 6, 8, 12
(1931-1932).
Japanese.   DLC,MH-HY.
                                CEACS'64,MHY.
Bibliography--bibliographic essay.

00178 ajap   japan   b 0 n
    Tōhō gakuhō sōmokuji [General index to the
Tōhō gakuhō, v.1-10]. Tōkyō.   4 p.   26 cm.
Japanese.   CU-E.
                            CU-E,CEACS'64.
Bibliography--index.   Periodicals--Indexes.
Indexes.   Oriental Studies--Periodicals.

00179 ajap   japan   b 0 n   1960
    Nitchō Kyōkai Ōsakafu Rengōkai, ed. Nihon
de shuppan sareta Chōsen ni kansuru tosho mokuroku
[Bibliography cf books on Korea published in
Japan, Aug. 15, 1945-Aug. 15, 1960]. Ōsaka, 1960.
38 p.   36 cm.
Japanese.
                                CEACS'64.
Bibliography.   110.00 Catalogs. Korean studies
in Japan--Bibliography.   Bibliography--1945-1960.

00180 zjap   japan   b 2 m   1963
    Kinchaku Geunro-gya sōmokuji   [General index
to the Kŭlloja, a DPRK journal nos. 16, 17]. In
Chōsen kenkyū geppō, 13 (1963): 36.
Japanese.   DLC.
                                CEACS'64,DLC.
Bibliography--index.   204.00   110.00 Democratic
People's Republic of Korea.   Indexes.
Periodicals--Indexes.   Economic Conditions--
Indexes.   Political development--Indexes.

00181 ajap   kor   b 0 n   1936
    Keijō Teikoku Daigaku. Fuzoku Toshokan, comp.
Keijō Teikoku Daigaku Fuzoku Toshokan, Wakan
shomei mokuroku [Keijo Imperial University
Library title catalog of Japanese and Chinese

books]. Seoul, 1933-1936. 3 v.
Japanese. CU.

UC'54.
Bibliography--catalogs--Korea. Keijō Teikoku
Daigaku. Keijc Imperial University Library.
110.00 Libraries, University and College--
Catalogs. Catalogs, University Library.

"Lists all Japanese and Chinese books at Keijō
Imperial University in 1936, omitting old Korean
books of the fcrmer Royal Library, medical books,
and miscellanecus Korean books published before
1900. Books on Korea are scattered throughout the
sections of this listing." UC'54.

00182 ajap   kor   b 0 n   1932
      Keijō Teikoku Daigaku. Fuzoku Toshokan, ed.
Chōsen kochizu tenkan mokuroku   [Exhibition
catalog of old maps of Korea]. Seoul, 1932. 1 v.
Japanese. Includes 120 items.
                                   CEACS'64.
Bibliography--catalogs--Korea. Physical setting--
geography--Bibliography. Keijō Teikoku Daigaku.
110.00 102.00 Maps. Maps--Exhibitions.
Bibliographical exhibitions. Exhibitions--Maps--
Bibliography.

00183 zjap   japan   b 0 n   1949
      Suda, Akiyoshi, 1900-. Chōsenjin jinruigaku
ni kansuru bunken [Bibliography on physical
anthropology of the Koreans]. In Jinruigaku
zasshi, 60, no.3 (1949): 123-136.
Japanese. CU-E. Lists articles in Japanese,
English and German periodicals.
                                   CEACS'64.
Bibliography. 110.00 140.00 Physical
anthropology. Anthropology--Bibliography.
Somatology--Bibliography. Bibliography--1887-
1948.

00184 zjap   japan   b 0 n   1933
      Shima, Gorō. Chōsenjin taishitsu jinruigaku
ni kansuru bunken mokuroku [Bibliography on
Korean physical anthropology]. In Dolmen, 2, no. 4
(1933): 6-8.
Japanese. CSt-H,CU-E,DLC,MiU,NNC,WaU.
                                   CEACS'64.
Bibliography. 110.00 140.00 Physical
Anthropology.

00185 zjap   japan   b 0 n   1963
     Omura, Masuo.   Chūgoku yaku Chōsen bungaku
sakuhin no mokuroku [A list of Korean literary
works translated into Chinese]. In Chōsen kenkyū
geppō, 23 (1963): 60-65.
Japanese.
                              CEACS'64.
Literature--Bibliography. 110.00 Korean studies.
Catalogs. Korean studies in China--Bibliography.

00186 zjap   japan   b 2 m   1963
     Chōsen hokuhanbu no nōgyō mondai ni kansuru
bunken mokuroku [Bibliography on agricultural
problems of North Korea]. In Chōsen kenkyū geppō,
21 (1963): 39-43.
Japanese.
                              CEACS'64.
Economy--Bibliography. 110.00 241.00
Agriculture--Economic aspects.

00187 zjap   japan   b 0 n   1958
     Nakamura, Eikō.   Hōsa Bunko Chōsenbon
tenkansho kaisetsu (Explanatory notes on the
Korean books collected in the Hōsa Library,
Nagoya). In Chōsen gakuhō, 13 (1958): 203-220.
Japanese. CLU,CSH,DLC,HU-E,MH-HY,MiU,NjP, NNC,
WaU.
                                         S.
Bibliography--catalogs--Japan.   Hōsa Bunko.
113.02

00189 ajap   japan   b 0 n   1964
     Tōyōgaku Bunken Sentā Renraku Kyōgikai, ed.
Nihonbun, Chūgokubun, Chōsenbun tō chikuji
kankōbutsu mokuroku   (Union catalog of the
periodicals in Japanese, Chinese, Korean and other
languages preserved in the Tōyō Bunko, Tōyō Bunka
Kenkyūjo, Tokyo Univ. and Jinbun Kagaku Kenkyūjo,
Kyōto Univ.).   Tokyo, Tōyōgaku Bunken Sentā
Renraku Kyōgikai, 1963 [i.e. 1964]. 178 p.   26
cm.
Japanese. DLC.
                              CEACS'64,DLC.
Bibliography--catalogs--Japan. Bibliography--
periodicals. Tōyō Bunko, Tokyo. Tōkyō Daigaku.
Tōyō Bunka Kenkyūjo. Kyōto Daigaku. Jinbun Kagaku
Kenkyūjo. 110.00 Union lists of periodicals.
Periodicals--Bibliography--Union lists.

00192   ajap   kor   b 0 n   1913
        Korea (Government-General of Chōsen, 1910-
1945), ed.   Chōsen Sōtokufu tosho mokuroku
[Classified catalog of the collections of the
Government-General of Chōsen].   Seoul, 1913, 1927,
1933. 3 v.
Japanese. DLC.
                                    LCF'50,UC'54.
Bibliography--catalogs--Korea. Government-General
Library. 110.00 646.00 Catalogs, classified.
Bibliography--1895-1910.

The 1913 edition is divided into Japanese and
Chinese books; Korean books; publications of the
Government of Korea, 1895-1910; publications of
the Japanese Regency-General of Korea, and the
Japanese Government-General of Chōsen, and of
their subordinate agencies, offices and bureaus;
old Korean books; and books in Western languages.
- LCF'50. The 1927 edition lists the holdings of
the Government-General as of March, 1927, omitting
old Korean books. It is much less extensive than
the Shinshobu Bunrui Mokuroku [1938], but it
includes a few Korean and Chinese titles although
the majority are Japanese. Official government
publications are especially well represented.
There are no annotations. Titles are arranged
alphabetically under topics, and there is an
alphabetical index of all the books. - UC'54.
Another edition was published in 1933.

00194   zjap   japan   b 0 n   1919
        Yoshino, Sakuzō.   Tendōkyō kenkyū shiryō
[Source materials for the study of Ch'ōndo kyo].
In Kokka Gakkai zasshi, 33, no.5, 7-10 (1919): 34,
no. 1 (1920). 104 p.
Japanese. CU-E,DLC.
                                    CEACS'64.
Religion and philosophy--Bibliography. 110.00
794.00 Ch'ōndo kyo.

00197   ajap   japan   b 0 n   1938
        Jinruigaku zasshi sōsakuin [General index to
Jinruigaku zasshi, v.1-50]. Tokyo, Tōkyō
Jinruigakkai, 1938. 1 v. 26 cm.
Japanese. CU-E.
                                    CUE.
Bibliography--index. 110.00 Indexes.
Periodicals--Indexes. Anthropology--Indexes.
Bibliography--1886-1935.

00198 zjap   japan   b 0 n   1943
'Shokō' shuyō kiji mokuroku [Index to major
articles of the Shokō, no.1-142]. In Shokō, 16,
no. 2-3 (1943).
Japanese. MH-HY.
                              CEACS'64.
Bibliography--index.

00199 zjap   japan   b 0 n   1935
Sen-Man kankei jūyō zasshi kiji mokuroku
[Monthly list cf important Japanese articles
concerning Korea and Manchuria]. In Bunken hōkoku,
1, no.1 (1935); 10, no. 11 (1944).
Japanese. DLC,MHY,NNC.
                              CEACS'64.
Bibliography. 110.00

00287 aeng   usa   b 0 n   1947
Hewes, Gordon Winaut, 1918-. Archaeology of
Korea: a selected bibliography. Hamilton, New
York, Korean Research Associates, 1947. 18 p.
map. 23 cm. (Research monographs on Korea. ser.
F, 1)
English. DLC,HU-E,MH-P.
                              S,Silberman'62.
Archeology--Bibliography. 113.02 172.00 764.15
173.00 323.00 530.00

"A short bibliography of the most recent, as of
1947, and important works on the archaeology of
Korea." Silberman'62.

00300 akor   sokor   b 0 n   1961
Korea (Republic) Kongbobu. Chŏngbu
kanhaengmul mongnok [Bibliography of government
publication]. Seoul, Taehan Min'guk Kongbobu,
1961. 93 p.
Korean. DLC.
                                        DLC.
Bibliography. 110.00 Government Publications--
Bibliography. Catalogs. Official Publications--
Bibliography.

00346 akor   sokor   b 1 mc1962   1962
Korea (Republic) Kongbobu. Kongboguk.
Chŏnggi kanhaengmul, sahoe tanch'e, yŏnghwaŏpchi
mit kongyŏnja illamp'yo [Lists of Korean
periodicals, associations, institutions, moving
picture business firms, and theaters]. Seoul,
Kongbobu Kongbcguk, 1962. 78, 42 p. forms.

229

26 cm.
Korean. DLC,MH-HY. Includes legislation.
Appendix: P'yegandoen Chŏnggi Kanhaengmul
illamp'yo [a list of discontinued periodicals].
DLC,Chŏng'66.
Bibliography. Visual arts. 110.00 204.00
575.00 546.00 671.05 Catalogs, Periodical.
Associations, institutions, etc.--Directories.
Societies--Directories. Motion-picture industry--
Directories. Theaters--Directories. Periodicals-
-Bibliography.

00379 aeng   sokor   b 0 n   1963
       Koryŏ Taehakkyo. Seoul, Korea. Asea Munje
Yŏn'guso. A list of selected books and materials
on modern and contemporary Korean history with
special emphasis on those on diplomatic history
publication in Korea. Seoul, Asiatic Research
Center, Korea University, 1963. 20 p.
English. DLC.
                                         Chŏng'66.
History--Biblicgraphy. 175.00 648.00

00389 zjap   japan   b 0 n   1951
       Sekino, Shinkichi. Ōbun Chōsen kankei
bunken mokuroku--1940-nen igo kankō shomoku
[Korea: list of books in European languages, 1940-
50]. In Chōsen gakuhō, 1 (1951): 299-307.
Japanese. CLU,CU-E,DLC,HU-E,MH-HY,NjP,NNC, WaU.
                                        Okamoto'62.
Bibliography. 110.00 Bibliography--1940-1950.

00390 zjap   japan   b k2 y   1951
       Ikeuchi, Hiroshi. Chōsen kanhoku no yon
chishi [Four geographical records of the northern
part of Korea]. In Chōsen gakuhō, 1 (1951): 239-
244.
Japanese. CLU,CU-E,DLC,HU-E,MH-HY,NjP,NNC, WaU.
                                        Okamoto'62.
Physical setting--geography--Bibliography.
Bibliography--bibliographic essay. 110.00 130.00
Gazetteers.

"A bibliographical study of the Pukkwan chi ;
(manuscript copy of the Kyujanggak there is also
a printed edition); the Kwanbuk chi (only known
copy in the Research Institute for Oriental
History of Tokyo University); the Pungno kiryak
(only a manuscript copy); and the Kwanbuk kimun
(the Paeksan Hŭksu Mun'go copy was lost by fire,

but Mr. Ikeuchi himself has a handwritten copy)."
Okamoto'62.

00393 zjap   japan   l   0   ye   1951
    Suematsu, Yasukazu.   Sambōshū henkan ko   [A
critical study of the publication of the Sambong-
jip]. In Chōsen gakuhō, 1 (1951): 55-68.
Japanese.   CLU,CU-E,DLC,HU-E,MH-HY,NjP, NNC,WaU.
                                     Okamoto'62.
Law. Bibliography--bibliographic essay. 110.00
692.00 Yi dynasty, early.

"A bibliographical study of the Sambong-jip of
Chŏng To-jŏn, especially of the copies preserved
in the Naikaku Bunko and the Hōsa Bunko in Nagoya.
This article is very important for the study of
the judicial system of the early Yi period."
Okamoto'62.

00424 zjap   japan   b   0   n   1960
    Kawachi, Yoshihiro.   Bunken shōkai [A
review of publications]. In Chōsen gakuhō, 16
(1960): 167-188.
Japanese.   CSt-H,DLC,HU-E,MH-HY,NjP,NNC,WaU.
                                     Okamoto'62.
Bibliography. 110.00 175.00

"A detailed presentation of books and articles in
the field of Kcrean studies published recently in
Korea. Independent Korea has made great efforts to
study her histcry and is about to surpass Japanese
studies both in quantity and quality." Okamoto'62.

01002 ajap   korea   b   0   n   1939
    Seikyū gakusō ronbun choshabetsu sakuin
[Author index to the Seikyū gakusō, v.1-30].
Seoul, Seikyū Gakkai, 1939. 9 p. 23 cm.
Japanese. DLC. Supplement to Seikyū gakusō, 30.
                                     CEACS'64.
Bibliography--index.   Indexes.   Folklore--
Periodicals--Indexes.   Periodicals--Indexes.
History--Periodicals--Indexes.   Language--
Periodicals--Indexes.   Literature--Periodicals--
Indexes.

01003 zjap   japan   b   0   n   1909
    Shidehara, Taira.   Chōsen shi no sankō
shomoku ni tsuite   [On the reference books of
Korean history]. In Tōa no hikari (Ex Oriente
lux), 3, no.11 (1908); 4, no.2 (1909).

Japanese.
CEACS'64.
History--Biblicgraphy. 175.01 110.00

01004 zjap japan b 0 n 1908
Sakuragi, Akira. Chōsen kenkyū no shiori
[Korean studies guide]. In Kokugakuin zasshi, 14,
no.1 (1908): 65-73; 14, no.2 (1908): 156-165.
Japanese. CtY,CU-E,DLC.
CEACS'64,S.
Bibliography. 110.00 648.00 130.00 175.00
670.00 538.00 190.00 Historiography. Reference
works.

01005 zjap japan b 0 jc 1956
Sakurai, Yoshiyuki. Hōseko Shigekatsu no
Chōsen gogaku sho ni tsuite, fu Chōsen gogaku
shomoku [The writings of Shigekatsu Hōseko on
Korean language; with an appendix, bibliography of
Korean language studies]. In Chōsen gakuhō, 9
(1956): 455-466.
Japanese. DLC.
CEACS'64.
Language--Bibliography. Hōseko, Shigekatsu.
110.00 190.00

01006 ajap japan b 0 n 1952
Shigakkai, ed. Shigaku bunken mokuroku,
1946-1950 [Catalog of historiographical
literature, 1946-1950]. Tōkyō, Yamagawa
Shuppansha, 1952. 1, 2, 204 p.
Japanese. CtY. Korea: p. 120-121.
S,UC'54.
History--Biblicgraphy. 110.00 175.00 172.00
Archeology. Arts. Ethnology. Historiography.
Bibliography--1946-1950.

"A catalogue edited by the Shigakkai (Historical
Studies Society) at Tōkyō University which lists
most books, articles, and other studies on history
and related subjects published in Japan from 1946
to 1950. Forty-three articles and about ten books
on Korea are listed." UC'54.

01007 zjap japan b 0 n 1963
Saikin Chōsen kankei zasshi ronbun mokuroku
[Bibliography of periodical articles concerning
Korea]. In Chōsen kenkyū geppō, 2, 5/6, 8, 11
(1962); 14, 18, 21 (1963).
Japanese. DLC.

CEACS'64.
Bibliography. 110.00 Indexes. Periodicals--
Indexes.

01008 zjap   japan   b 2 m   1962
    Chōsen Kagakuin kizō tosho mokuroku   [List
of books presented by the Academy of Science,
DPRK]. In Chōsen kenkyū geppō, 11 (1962): 56-59.
Japanese. DLC.
                              CEACS'64.
Bibliography. 110.00 815.00 Catalogs.

01009 zjap   japan   b 2 m   1962
    Chōsen Kagakuin kizō zasshi mokuroku   [List
of periodicals presented by the Academy of
Science, DPRK]. In Chōsen kenkyū geppō, 11 (1962):
40.
Japanese. DLC.
                              CEACS'64.
Bibliography. 110.00 815.00 204.00
Periodicals--Bibliography. Catalogs--Periodicals.

01010 zjap   japan   b 2 m   1962
    Kanno, Hiroomi.   Sorenpō hakkō Chōsen kankei
tosho mokuroku [Bibliography of USSR publications
concerning Korea]. In Chōsen kenkyū geppō, 11
(1962): 51-56.
Japanese. DLC.
                              CEACS'64.
Bibliography. 110.00 Korean studies. Catalogs.
Korean Studies in U.S.S.R. --Bibliography.

01011 ajap   japan   b 0 n   1911
    Kanazawa, Shozaburō.   Chōsen shoseki
mokuroku [Annotated catalog of old Korean books].
Tokyo, 1911. 78 p. 23 cm.
Japanese.
                              CEACS'64.
Bibliography. 113.02 175.00 130.00 190.00
538.00 870.00 Rare books. Religion.
Philosophy. Arts. Catalogs, Rare book.

01012 zjap   japan   b 0 n   1942
    Mantetsu chōsa geppō sōmokuroku   [General
index to the Mantetsu chōsa geppō]. In Mantetsu
chōsa geppō, 22, no. 1 (1942): 200-244.
Japanese. MH-HY,NNC.
                              CEACS'64.
Bibliography--index.

233

01013 zjap   japan   b 0 yc   1907
    Furuya, Kiyoshi. Tokugawa jidai ni okeru
Chōsen no shoseki [A study of Korean books
preserved in Japan during the Edo period]. In
Gakutō (The Beacon light of learning), 11, no.10-
11, (1907); 12, no.6 (1908).
Japanese.
                                        CEACS'64.
Bibliography--bibliographic essay. 110.00 213.00
214.00

01014 zjap   japan   b 0 n   1934
    Fujii, Sōju. Chōsen Bukkyō tenseki tenran
mokuroku   [Exhibition catalog of the Korean
Buddhist scriptures]. In Zenshu, 41, no. 7 (1934):
24.
Japanese. MH-HY.
                                        CEACS'64.
Religion and philosophy--Bibliography. 779.04
Buddhism.

01015 ajap   kor   b 0 n   1931
    Keijo Tenshu-kokyokai, ed. Chōsen Tenshukyō
shiryō tenran mokuroku [Catalog of books and
documents on the history of Catholicism in Korea].
Seoul, 1931. 1 v.
Japanese.
                                        CEACS'64.
Religion and philosophy--Bibliography. 110.00
797.00 Christianity--Roman Catholicism.
Exhibitions--Catholic literature. Bibliographical
exhibitions--Bibliography.

01016 zjap   japan   b 0 yc159215981951
    Miki, Sakae. Yōan-in zoshochū no Chōsen
isho [Korean medical books in the Yōan-in
Collection]. In Chōsen gakuhō, 1 (1951): 263-270.
Japanese. CLU,CU-E,DLC,HU-E,MH-HY,NjP,NNC, WaU.
                                        CEACS'64.
Welfare--medicine--Bibliography. Bibliography--
catalogs--Japan. Yōan-in Library. 750.00 110.00

"Catalogue of books on medicine which were brought
back from the Korean expedition and presented to
the physician Manase Shōrin by Hideyoshi."
Okamoto'62.

01017 zjap   japan   b 0 n   1931
    Oda, Shōgo. Chōsen tōjiki ni kansuru jakkan
no bunken ni tsuite [On the books and materials

                        234

on Korean ceramics]. In Seikyū gakusō, 3 (1931):
98-112; 4 (1931): 110-114.
Japanese. DLC,WaU.

CEACS'64.
Visual arts--ceramics--Bibliography. 323.00
172.05 113.02 Koryo. Yi dynasty.

01018 ajap   kor   b 0 n   1925
    Okuda, Naogi. Chōsen kokuhō shōkai [Brief
annotations of Korean classical works]. Seoul,
Chōsen Sōtokufu Toshokan, 1925. 1 v.
Japanese.
                                       Yang'60.
Bibliography. 113.02 Rare books. Classics.

01019 zjap   japan   b 0 n   1927
    Ogura, Shimpei. Ō-beijin no Chōsengo kenkyū
no shiryō to natta wakanjo   [Japanese and Chinese
materials used by Western scholars for the study
of Korean language]. In Minzoku, 3, no. 1 (1927):
75-86.
Japanese.
                                       CEACS'64.
Language--Bibliography. 110.00 190.00

01020 ajap   b 0 n   1953
    Miki, Sakae   Chōsen iseki ko [A study of old
medical books of Korea]. [n.p.] 1953. 152 p. 24
cm.
Japanese.
                                       CEACS'64.
Welfare--medicine--Bibliography. Medicine.

01021 aeng   japan   b 0 n   1964
    Yunesuko Higashi Ajia Bunka Kenkyū Senta,
Tokyo. Bibliography of bibliographies of East
Asian studies in Japan. Comp. by Centre for East
Asian Cultural Studies. [Tokyo] Centre for East
Asian Cultural Studies, 1964. 216 p. 21 cm.
(Centre for East Asian Cultural Studies.
Bibliography, 3)
English. DLC. Korea: p. 31-40. Editor: Kimpei
Goto. A supplement to A survey of Japanese
bibliographies concerning Asian studies.
                                               S.
Bibliography--Bibliographies. 217.00 110.00
Bibliographies.

01022 zjap   kor   b 0 yc   1936
    Oda, Shōgo. Chōsen shiseki kaidai kōgi

[Lectures on Korean historical sources]. In Seikyū gakusō, 23 (1936): 145-161. Japanese. DLC,MH-HY.
                                   CEACS'64,UC'54.
Bibliography--bibliographic essay. History--
Bibliography. Kyujanggak. 113.02 175.01 814.01
217.00 Historiography.

"Lists and evaluates six Japanese works which describe Korean historical works and which can be used as guides in studying them; summarizes the history of the Kyujanggak, the royal library founded in the last years of the Yi dynasty, which became part of the Keijō Imperial University library in 1930; and briefly describes the traditional Chinese methods of writing history, methods which the Koreans followed." UC'54.

01023 zjap   japan   b 0 mc1945   1958
       Morita, Yoshio. Nipponjin no Chōsen hikiage ni kansuru bunken shiryō (Bibliography concerning the Japanese repatriation from Korea). In Chōsen gakuhō, 13 (Oct. 1958): 221-258.
Japanese. CLU,CSt-H,CtY,DLC,HU-E,MH-HY, MiU,NjP, NNC,WaU.
                                      S,CEACS'64.
Intercultural relations--Korea-Japan--
Bibliography. 113.02 648.00 563.01 167.00
720.00 727.05 159.04 700.00 178.00 740.00
Korean War.

"274 items with annotations." Okamoto'62.

01024 ajap   japan   b 0 n   1956
       Miki, Sakae. Chōsen isho shi [Bibliography of Korean books on medicine]. Sakai, Osaka, 1956.
24, 477, 27 p. illus. 27 cm.
Japanese. DLC,HU-E. Mimeographed. 120 copies printed. Added t.p.: The bibliography of Korean medicine, ancient and medieval.
                                      CEACS'64.
Welfare--medicine--Bibliography. 110.00
Medicine.

01026 ajap   japan   b 0 n   1961
       Yūhō Kyōkai. Chōsen Shiryō Kenkyūkai.
Chōsen kankei bunken shiryō sōmokuroku [Catalog of reference materials pertaining to Korea]. [Ed. by] Kondō Ken'ichi. Chigasaki, Yūhō Kyōkai Chōsen Shiryō Hensankai, 1961. 16, 180 p. 25 cm.

Japanese. DLC,HU-E,MH-HY. At head of title:
Zaidan Hōjin Yūhō Kyōkai, Shadan Hōjin Chūō Nikkan
Kyōkai hokan. Limited to 200 copies.
CEACS'64,DLC.
Bibliography. Polity--Bibliography. 110.00
Reference works. Libraries, Private--
Bibliography. Catalogs, Private library.

01027 akor   sokor   b 0 n   1941
      Sŏ, Yu-gu, 1764-1845. Nup'anko [Study on
printed books]. [Ed. and comp. by Yi Chong-man].
Seoul, Taedong Ch'ulp'ansa, 1941. 266 p.
Korean. DLC,HRAF.
                                      S,Yang'60.
Bibliography. 113.02 Rare books. Bibliography--
1392-1941. Yi dynasty. Japanese occupation.

"Contains annotated 634 items of Korean books
published since the founding of Yi dynasty
(1392)." Yang'60.

01028 aeng   gtbr   b 0 n   1906
      Great Britain. War Office. Library. Catalog
of the War Office Library. London, H. M.
Stationery Off., 1906-1912. 3 v.
English. DLC. See also Supplement to War Office
Library catalog. Parts 1 and 2. Comp. by F. J.
Hudleston. London, H. M. Stationery Off., 1916.
744 p. Part 3 (Subject-index) annual supplement.
1st (Jan. 1912) London, 1913- . (See Subject index
under Korea).
                                      LCW'50.
Bibliography--catalogs--Great Britain. Great
Britain. War Office Library. 110.00

01032 afren   fran   b 0 n   1894
      Courant, Maurice [Auguste Louis Marie], 1865-
1939. Bibliographie coréenne: tableau littéraire
de la Corée, contenant la nomenclature des
ouvrages publiés dans ce pays jusqu'en 1890 ainsi
que la description et l'analyse détaillées des
principaux d'entre ces ouvrages. Paris, E.
Leroux, 1894-1896. 3 v. illus., 28 cm.
(Publication de l'Ecole des langues orientales
vivantes, 3. ser., v. 18-20)
French with Korean and Chinese. CtY,DLC,HRAF,HU-
E,MH-HY,MH-P. A selection of geographical works
from this book appears as McCune, Shannon, Old
Korean geographical works: a bibliography.
Hamilton, N.Y. Colgate University, 1948. 13 p.

237

The Introduction has been translated into English,
Korean, and Japanese: Mrs. W. Massy Royds,
Introduction to Courant's "Bibliographie coréenne,
" Transactions of the Korea Branch of the Royal
Asiatic Society, 25 (1936): 1-99; Kim Su-gyŏng,
Chosŏn munhwasa sŏsŏl, Seoul, Pŏmjanggak, 1946;
Ogura Chikao, Chōsen shoshi joron, Dokusho, 2-3
(1938).
                          S,DLC,UC'54,MH.
Bibliography. Literature--Bibliography. History-
-Bibliography. Education--Bibliography. Religion
and philosophy--Bibliography. Intercultural
relations--Bibliography. 113.02 190.00 538.00
217.00 443.00 214.00 130.00 Ethnology.
Military. Arts. Confucianism. Etiquette.
Inscriptions. Biography. Divination. Taoism.
Buddhism. Medicine. Astronomy. Calendar.
Christianity--Roman Catholicism. Bibliography--
up to 1890.

"The best Western compilation of Korean books from
earliest times until 1899, a total of some 3,200
titles. The volumes are arranged topically, and
there are valuable detailed indices giving titles,
authors, and important dates and places mentioned
in the bibliography. Courant gives whenever
possible a complete bibliographical history for
each title, a summary of its contents, and
critical remarks on it. Names and titles are
identified by Chinese characters, and Courant
indicates those European collections, private or
institutional, in which copies of the books may be
found. Care should be used in reading this book,
for Courant had opinions about Korea's
intellectual history which have been shown to be
fallacious. His bibliography remains nevertheless
a monumental and invaluable reference for Korean
studies, the work of a diligent scholar who had
first-hand contact with the materials he treats."
UC'54. The introduction is a valuable essay on
Korean literature, libraries, and book stores in
the late nineteenth century.

01033   afren   fran   b 0 n   1901
        Courant, Maurice [Auguste Louis Marie], 1865-
1939. Bibliographie coréenne. Supplement
(jusqu'en 1899). Paris, Imprimerie rationale, E.
Leroux, 1901. 10, 122 p. 28 cm. (Publications
de l'Ecole des langues orientales vivantes, 3.
ser., v. 21)

French with Korean and Chinese. CtY,DLC,HRAF,HU-
E,MH-HY.
                                           S,DLC.
Bibliography. Literature--Bibliography. History-
-Bibliography. Education--Bibliography. Religion
and philosophy--Bibliography. Intercultural
Relations--Bibliography. 110.00 190.00 130.00
Arts. Confucianism. Ethnology. Science.
Etiquette. Inscriptions. Biography.
Bibliography-- up to 1899.

01034 zeng   kor   b 0 n   1936
       Courant, Maurice [Auguste Louis Marie], 1865-
1939. Bibliographie coréenne. The introduction.
Translated by Mrs. W. Massy Royds. In Transactions
of the Korea Branch of the Royal Asiatic Society,
25 (1936): 1-99.
English. CtY,DLC,HRAF,MH-HY. A partial
translation appeared in the Korean Repository, 4
(1897): 201-206, 258-266.
                                           S.
Bibliography--bibliographic essay. 217.00   538.00
113.02 214.00   190.00 443.00

01036 akor   sokor   b 0 n   1946
       Courant, Maurice [Auguste Louis Marie], 1865-
1939. Chosŏn munhwasa sŏsŏl [Introduction to
Korean cultural history]. [Tr. by] Kim Su-gyŏng.
Seoul, Pŏmjanggak, 1946. 191 p. 18 cm.
Korean. DLC,MH-HY,WaU-FE. Translation of the
Introduction to Bibliographie coréenne by Maurice
Courant.
                              DLC,MHY.
Bibliography--bibliographic essay. 217.00   538.00
113.02 214.00   190.00 443.00

"A translation of Introduction to Bibliographie
Coréenne, tableau littéraire de la Corée, 1894.
One of the most revealing descriptions of Korean
literary activities, such as history of books,
letters, philosophy, and literature." Yang'60.

01037 aeng   usa   b 0 n   1961
       American Historical Association, comp. Guide
to historical literature. Board of Editors; George
Frederick Howe et al. New York, Macmillan, 1961.
35, 942 p. 24 cm.
English. DLC. Korea: p. 241-248.
                              DLC,Chong'66.
History--Bibliography. 110.00

01039   ajap   japan   b 0 n   1943
        Chōsenban koshomoku [A catalog of the old
books published in Korea]. Tokyo, Kunshodō
Shoten, 1943. 1 v.
Sinico-Korean.
                                        WH'68.
Bibliography. 110.00 Classics. Rare books.
Bibliography--Rare books. Rare books--
Bibliography.

01041   ajap   japan   b 0 n   1940
        Chōsen koten mokuroku [A catalog of Korean
classics]. Tokyo, Kunshodō Shoten, 1940.
Japanese-Sinico-Korean.
                                        WH'68.
Bibliography. 110.00 Classics. Rare books.

01042   ajap   kor   b 0 n   1919
        **Korea (Government-General of Chōsen, 1910-
1945) Rinji Tochi Chōsakyoku.** Chōsen chishi
shiryō [Materials on Korean geography]. Seoul,
Chōsen Sōtokufu, 1919. 3, 438 p. col. illus.,
fold. col. map. 19 cm. (Chōsen Sōtokufu Tochi
Chōsa Jigyō hōkokusho, bessatsu)
Japanese. DLC,MH-HY.
                                        MHY,DLC.
Physical setting--geography--Bibliography. 110.00
Land. Markets. Administrative and political
divisions.

01043   akor   sokor   b 0 m   1946
        Chungang Inmin Wiwŏnhoe chemunhŏn
[Documents of the Central People's Committee].
Seoul, Chungang Inmin Wiwŏnhoe, Sŏgiguk, 1946.   66
p.
Korean.
                                        WH'68.
Polity. Political development--Collected works.

01044   xchin   taiw   b 0 n   1955
        Kuo-li Chung-yang t'u-shu-kuan, ed. Chung-
kuo k'an-hsing Han-kuo chu-shu mu-lu
[Bibliography of literature on Korea written by
Koreans and published in China]. In Tung Tso-pin
et al. Chung Han wen-hua lun-chi. Taipei, Chung-
hua wen-hua ch'u-pan shih-yeh wei-yüan-hui, 1955:
1-7. (Hsien-tai kuo-min chi-pen chih-shih ts'ung-
shu, 3)
Chinese. CtY. This bibliography is the second

appendix of the book.
                                              S,CtY.
Bibliography. 110.00   175.00   Gazetteers.
Literature--poetry. Philosophers. Travelers'
accounts.

01045   afren   fran   b 0 n   1912
        Cordier, Henri, 1849-1925, comp. Bibliotheca
Japonica: dictionnaire bibliographique de ouvrages
relatifs à l´empire japonais rangés par ordre
chronologique jusqu´à 1870 suivi d'un appendice
renfermant la liste alphabétique des principaux
ouvrages parus de 1870 à 1912. Paris, 1912. 12,
762 p. (Publications de l'Ecole des Langues
Orientales Vivantes, 5, no. 8 (1912))
French. CU-E,DLC.
                                      Gompertz'63,DLC.
Bibliography. 110.00   Bibliography--1870-1912.
Bibliography-- up to 1870.

"This important bibliography follows the same
method as the compiler's much larger 'Bibliotheca
Sinica'. It is specially valuable for the early
period of Catholic Missions in Japan, early
voyages and travels, etc., and contains a number
of useful references to Korea. A later facsimile
reprint was published." Gompertz'63.

01046   ajap   japan   b 0 n   1957
        Endō, Motoo, 1908-. Kokushi bunken kaisetsu
[Annotated bibliography on history]. [Edited by]
Endō Motoo [and] Shimomura Fujio.   Tokyo, Asakura
Shoten, 1957-1965. 2 v. 22 cm.
Japanese. CtY,DLC. Korea: p. 585-604. Indexed.
                                            S,WH'68.
History--Bibliography. Intercultural relations--
Korea-Japan--Bibliography. 113.02 Polity.
Trade. Classics.

01048   aeng   japan   b 0 n   1961
        Hanayama, Shinshō, comp. Bibliography on
Buddhism. Tokyo, Hokuseidō, 1961. 13, 869 p. 27
cm.
English. DLC. Works published prior to 1928,
includes numerous works on Korea.
                                               DLC.
Religion and philosophy--Bibliography. 110.00
Buddhism.

01049 akor   sokor   b   0   n   1963
Koryŏ Taehakkyo. Seoul, Korea. Asea Munje
Yŏn'guso. Han'guk kŭnsesa yŏn'gu charyo mongnok-
-Oegyosa rŭl chungsimŭro   (A list of selected
books and materials on modern and contemporary
Korean history: with special emphasis on those on
diplomatic history published in Korean). Seoul,
Asiatic Research Center, Korea University, 1963.
20 p. 27 cm.
Korean. DLC.
                                      DLC,S.
Intercultural relations--Korea-Japan--
Bibliography. Polity--Bibliography. Conflict--
Bibliography. History--Bibliography. 648.00
175.00 204.01 665.00 436.00 185.00 798.00
159.04 870.00 669.00 110.00 Economy. Women.
Christianity--Protestants. Christianity--Roman
Catholicism. Diplomatic history. Korean War.
Independence Movement. Tonghak Revolt. Kabo
Kyongjang. Kapsin Chŏngbyŏn. Tongnip Movement.
Tongnip Hyŏphoe. Imo kullan. Bibliography--1886-
1962.

01050 ajap   japan   b   0   n   1945
Hokusen Manshū Karafuto oyobi Chishima ni
okeru hōjin no hogo oyobi hikiage ni kansuru kōshō
kankei bunken   [Source materials on Japan's
negotiations for the protection and repatriation
of its residents in North Korea, Manchuria and
Sakhalin]. Tokyo, Gaimushō, 1945.
Japanese.
                                      WH'68.
Intercultural relations--Bibliography. 648.00
563.00 167.00

01051 ajap   japan   b   0   n   1948
Kanazawa, Shozaburo, 1872-. Ajia kenkyū ni
kansuru bunken [Books and materials on Asian
studies]. Tokyo, Sōgensha, 1948. 116 p. illus.
(Ajia kenkyū sōsho, 5)
Japanese. CtY,DLC.
                          DLC,CEACS'64.
Bibliography. 110.00 Asian Studies.

01052 akor   sokor   b   0   n   1964
Kim, Kŭn-su, comp. Han'guk hyŏndaeshi
ch'ongnam [Bibliography of modern poetry of
Korea]. Seoul, Sudo Yŏja Sabŏm Taehak, Kugŏ
Kungmun Hakhoe, 1964. 40 p. 25 cm.
Korean. CU-E,KNC.
                                      CUE.

Literature--poetry--Bibliography. 110.00 538.00
Poetry, Modern--Bibliography.

01053 akor   sokor   b   0   n   1962
     Kim, Kŭn-su. Kugŏ kungmunhak kosŏ chimnok
[Bibliography on old literature of Korean language
and literature]. Seoul, Tongguk Taehakkyo,
Kungmun Hakhoe, 1962. 412 l. 24 cm. (Kugŏ
kungmunhak charyo ch'ongsŏ, 9)
Sinico-Korean. MH-HY. Chosŏn tosŏ mongnok: 87-
409. Section cn music attached.
                                              MHY.
Language--Bibliography. Literature--Bibliography.
110.00 Music.

01054 akor   sokor   b   0   n   1960
     Korea (Republic) Mun'gyobu. Chijŏng
munhwajae mongnok [List of cultural properties
designated by the government]. Seoul, Mun'gyobu,
1960. 276, 6 p. 26 cm.
Korean. CU-E,DLC,MH-HY. Errata (6 p.) inserted.
                                            CUE,DLC.
Bibliography. Visual arts. 650.00 Monuments.
Antiquities--Catalogs. Catalogs--Cultural
properties. Art treasures--Catalogs. Monuments--
Preservation--Catalogs.

01057 akor   sokor   b   0   n   1966
     Kyoyuk charyo mongnok [Bibliography of
educational materials]. Seoul, Sŏul Tŭkpyŏlsi
Kyoyukch'ŏng, 1966. 1 v.
Korean. KYU.
                                              KYU.
Education--Bibliography. 110.00

01058 ajap   kor   b   0   n   1936
     Maema, Kyōsaku, comp. Sensatsu meidai 12
kwŏn [Annotated bibliography of Korean books].
Seoul, 1936.
Japanese-Korean. KSN. A sister ed. of Kosen
sappu.
                                              KSN.
Bibliography. 113.02 Classics.

01059 ajap   japan   b   0   ye140218021961
     Naitō, Shunpo. Chōsenshi kenkyū (Studies in
history of Korea). Kyōto Tōyōshi Kenkyūkai, 1961.
[646] p. illus. 22 cm. (Tōyōshi kenkyū sōkan,
10)
Japanese. MH-HY,WaU-FE. Table of contents also

in English.
                                    MHY,WaU.
History.   Intercultural relations--Korea-Japan.
113.02 Travelers' accounts.

01060 ajap   japan   b 0 n   1936
       Oda, Shōgo, 1871-, comp. Chōsen tōjishi
bunken kō [Bibliography on the history of Korean
pottery]. Tokyo, Gakugei Shoin, 1936. 6, 170 p.
illus., facsims. 20 cm.
Japanese. DLC,KNC. Appendix: Fuzan Wakan Kō.

                                        DLC.
Visual arts--ceramics--Bibliography. 110.00
323.00 Pottery--History--Bibliography.

01062 zkor   sokor   b 0 n   1966
       Sŏul Taehakkyo. Tosŏgwan. Han'guk sŏji
kwan'gye munhŏn mongnok (An index of Korean
bibliographies). In Sŏul Taehakkyo Tosŏgwanbo, 4
(1966): 27-75.
Korean. DLC,MH-HY.
                                    MHY,DLC,S.
Bibliography--bibliographies. 110.00 213.00
217.00 204.00 159.04 538.00 539.00 175.00
130.00 643.00 648.00 644.00 590.00 Classics.
Medicine. Maps. Shamans. Christianity--Roman
Catholicism. Government. Confucianism. Ch'ŏndo
kyo. Bibliography--1576-1965.

01064 agerm   ger   b 0 n   1938
       Streit, P. Robert, 1875-1930. Bibliotheca
missionum. [Continued by] P. Johannes Dindinger.
Aachen, 1938. 11, 565 p. 26 cm.
(Veröffentlichungen des Internationalen Instituts
für Missionswissenschaftliche Forschung)
German. CtY,DLC. V. 10: Missions-literatur
Japans und Koreas, 1800-1909 [Missions-literature
of Japan and Korea, 1800-1909]. Korea: p. 388-495.
                              Gompertz'63,DLC.
Religion and philosophy--Bibliography. 797.00
113.02 Biography. Christianity--Roman
Catholicism. Religion--Bibliography.
Bibliography--1800-1909.

"This is the tenth volume of Streit's monumental
Bibliography of Catholic Missions and is essential
to any intensive study of the Missions in Korea.
It includes copious references to the life and
works of each individual Missionary, as well as to

the work of the Missions in general." Gompertz'63.

01065　aeng　　　hong　　　b　0　n　　　　1961
　　　Teng, Ssu-yü, 1906-, comp.　Japanese studies
on Japan and the Far East.　[Hong Kong], Hong Kong
University Press, 1961.　10, 485 p.　26 cm.
English.　CLSU,Cst-H,CtY,CU-E,DLC,ICU,InU, MH-HY,
MiU,NNC.　A shcrt bibliographical and biographical
introduction, with the collaboration of Masuda
Kenji and Kaneda Hiromatsu.
　　　　　　　　　　　　　　　　　　　DLC.
Bibliography.　113.02　Bio-bibliography.

01066　akor　　　sokor　　　b　0　k　　　　1963
　　　Tongguk Taehakkyo. Seoul, Korea.　Koryŏ pulsŏ
chŏn'gwan mongnok　[Exhibition catalog of Buddhist
literature of Koryŏ dynasty].　Seoul, Tongguk
University, 1963.　46 p.　21 cm.
Korean.　CU-E,DLC,MH-HY.
　　　　　　　　　　　　　　　　　　　MHY,DLC.
Bibliography--catalogs--Korea.　Religion and
philosophy--Bibliography.　Tongguk Taehakkyo.
779.00　110.00　Buddhism.　Exhibitions--Catalogs.

01067　akor　　　sokor　　　b　0　k　　　　1962
　　　Tongguk Taehakkyo. Seoul, Korea.　Koryŏ
sagyŏng chŏn'gŭn mongnck　[Exhibition catalog of
Koryŏ Buddhist scriptures in manuscript].　Seoul,
Tongguk Taehakkyo, 1962.　18 p.　21 cm.
Korean.　DLC,MH-HY,WaU-FE.　Exhibition held, May
5-7, 1962, in commemoration of founding Tongguk
Taehakkyo, Pulgyo Munhwa Yŏn'guso.
　　　　　　　　　　　　　　　　　　　WaU,MHY.
Bibliography--catalogs--Korea.　Religion and
philosophy--Bibliography.　Tongguk Taehakkyo.
779.00　Buddhism.

01068　akor　　　sokor　　　b　0　yc　　　　1964
　　　Tongguk Taehakkyo. Seoul, Korea.　Yijo
chŏn'gi kugyŏk pulsŏ chŏn'gwan mongnok
[Exhibition catalog of Buddhist scriptures
translated intc Korean during the first half of Yi
dynasty].　Seoul, Tongguk Taehakkyo, 1964.　66 p.
21 cm.　(Han'guk Taejanghce, ch'ongwan mongnok, 3)
Korean.　CU-E.
　　　　　　　　　　　　　　　　　　　CUE.
Bibliography--catalogs--Korea.　Religion and
philosophy--Bibliography.　Tongguk Taehakkyo.
779.00　110.00　Buddhism.　Exhibitions--Catalogs.

01069   akor   sokor   b   0   yc   1965
        Tongguk Taehakkyo. Seoul, Korea. Pulgyo
Munhwa Yŏn'guso.   Yijo chŏn'gi pulsŏ chŏn'gwan
mongnok [Exhibition catalog of Buddhist
literature published during the first half of Yi
dynasty]. Seoul, Tongguk Taehakkyo, 1965. 104 p.
21 cm. (Han'guk Taejanghoe, ch'ongwan mongnok, 4)
Korean. CU-E,DLC,MH-HY. At head of title: Fifty-
ninth commemoration of the opening of the school.
                                        MHY,DLC.
Bibliography--catalogs--Korea. Religion and
philosophy--Bibliography. Tongguk Taehakkyo.
779.00 Buddhism.

01070   aeng   usa   b   0   ne193019501950
        U.S. Library of Congress. Reference
Department. Korea: a preliminary bibliography.
Comp. by Helen Dudenbostel Jones et al.
Washington, D.C., 1950. 3 v.
English. DLC. 1. Publications in Western
languages; 2. Publications in the Russian
language; 3. Publications in Far Eastern
languages.
                                           DLC.
Bibliography. 110.00 Japanese Occupation.
Modern Korea.

"Completed in ten days following the outbreak of
the Korean War. This work contains 743 entries,
chiefly Japanese publications, and covers the
period 1930-1950." Henthorn'68.

01072   akor   sokor   b   0   n   1958
        Yi, Wŏn-sik, comp. Tosŏl kotosŏ kosŏhwa
haeje [Annotated bibliography of old books and
paintings with illustrations]. Taegu, Hyŏndae
Ch'ulp'ansa, 1958. 311 p.
Korean.
                                        Chŏng'66.
Bibliography. Visual arts--painting. 532.00
113.02 Rare books.

01073   zjap   kor   b   0   n   1927
        Chōsen iyaku shiryō [Source materials on
Korean medicine]. In Chōsen, 143 (1927): 8-18.
Japanese. KSN,MH-HY.   .
                                           MHY.
Welfare--medicine--Bibliography. 110.00
Medicine.

01074 zjap   japan   b 0 n   1935
       Chōsen kankei ōbun bunken mokuroku
[Bibliography of Korean studies in European
languages]. In Rekishigaku kenkyū, 4 (1935): 130-
139.
Japanese. DLC,KSN.
                                        DLC.
Bibliography. 110.00

01075 zjap   b 0 n   1939
       Chōsen kankei ōbun tosho kaidai [Annotated
bibliography of Korean studies in European
languages]. In Ryōsho, 5, 6, 8, 10 (1939-1940).
Japanese.
                                        WH'68.
Bibliography. 113.02

01076 zjap   japan   b 0 n   1940
       Chōsen kankei kōkogaku bunken mokuroku
[Bibliography of Korean archeology]. In Kōkogaku,
11 (1940).
Japanese. KNC.
                                        KNC.
Archeology--Bibliography. 110.00

01077 zeng   usa   b 0 n   1959
       Council for Old World Archaeology. Korea:
Far East--Area 17. In COWA surveys and
bibliographies, 1 (1959): 7, 26-27; 2 (1961): 14,
43-45; 3 (1964): 5-6, 25.
English. CU-E,HRAF. Surveys and bibliographies
are separately paginated.
                                        S.
Archeology. 113.02

01078 zjap   b 0 n   1909
       Fukuda, Tokuzō, comp. Kankoku kenkyū no
bunken [Bibliography on Korean studies]. In
Keiigaku, 110 (1909).
Japanese.
                                        WH'68.
Bibliography. 110.00   175.00   Social sciences.

01079 zjap   japan   b 0 n   1937
       Furukawa, Kanehide, comp. Chōsen no shoseki
[Korean publications]. In Dokusho, 1, no.3 (1937):
2-6.
Japanese. DLC,KSN.
                                        DLC.
Bibliography. 110.00   Bibliography--Addresses,
essays, lectures.

01080   zkor   sokor   b   0   n   1960
        Han'guk sŏji munhŏn illam 1941-1942
(Bibliography on Korean bibliography, 1941-1942).
In Sŏji, 1, no.2 (August 1960): 30-32.
Korean.   CU-E,DLC,MH-HY,WaU-FE.
                                            DLC,S.
Bibliography.   110.00   217.00   213.00   648.00
175.00   160.00   620.00   204.00   346.00   341.00
460.00   102.00   Bibliographies.   Medicine.
Buddhism.   Rare books.   Classics.   Bibliography--
1941-1942.

01081   zeng   gere   b   0   n   1955
        Honda, Minoru.   A survey of Japanese
contributions to Manchurian studies. By Honda
Minoru and E. E. Ceadel, comps. In Asia minor,
n.s., 5, no.1 (1955): 59-105.
English-German.   DLC.
                                              DLC.
Intercultural relations--Korea-China--
Bibliography.   Intercultural relations--Korea-
Manchuria --Bibliography.   110.00   648.00   Liao.
Khitan.

01082   zeng   b   0   n   1954
        Honda, Minoru, comp.   Post-war Japanese
research on the Far East (excluding Japan).
Compiled by Honda Minoru and E. B. Ceadel. In
Asia Major, n.s., 4, no.1 (1954).
English-German.   DLC.
                                              DLC.
Bibliography.   110.00

01083   zjap   japan   b   0   n   1912
        Imanishi, Ryū, comp.   Chōsen Bukkyō kankei
shoseki kaidai [An annotated bibliography of
Korean Buddhism]. In Bukkyō shigaku, 1, no.1
(1911): 31-39; 1, no.2 (1911): 121-125; 1, no.3
(1911): 197-202.
Japanese.   DLC,KSN.
                                              DLC.
Religion and philosophy--Bibliography.   113.02
Buddhism.

01084   zkor   sokor   b   0   n   1963
        Kim, Chong-uk, comp.   Han'guksa kwan'gye
yŏn'gu nonmun mongnok   [Bibliography of studies
on Korean history]. In Tongguk sahak, 7 (1963):

248

126-168.
Korean. DLC,MH-HY,WaU.
                                                  DLC.
Archeology--Bibliography. History--Bibliography.
110.00 172.00 175.00

01085 zkor   sokor   b 0 n   1961
       Kim, Wŏn-yong, comp. Yugan'gi pulsŏ mongnok
ch'ogo (First list of dated early Korean
Buddhistic books). In Sŏji, 2, no.1 (Oct. 1961):
15-43.
Korean. CU-E,DLC,MH-HY,WaU-FE.
                                          S,CUE,DLC.
Religion and philosophy--Bibliography. 110.00
217.02 Buddhism. Rare books. Incunabula--
Bibliography.

01086 zkor   sokor   b 0 n   1964
       Kongsanjuŭi munje yŏn'gu munhŏn mongnok
[Bibliography of studies on Communism]. In
Kongsanjuŭi munje yŏn'gu, 1, no.1 (1964): 253-255.
Korean. MH-HY.
                                                  MHY.
Polity--Bibliography. 668.00 Communism.
Democratic People's Republic of Korea.
Bibliography--1957-1963.

01088 zjap   b 0 n   1941
       Kuji, Hanjirō, comp. Chihō bunka no kiroku:
Chōsen no kyōdoshi chihō shishi [Records of local
culture: local history and geography of Korea]. In
Chōsen kōsei, 20, no.8 (1941).
Japanese.
                                                WH'68.
History--Biblicgraphy. Physical setting--
geography--Bibliography.

01089 zgerm   ger   b 0 n   1938
       Lautensach, Hermann, comp. Korea (1926-1936)
mit Nachträgen aus älterer Zeit [Korea (1926-1936)
with addenda from earlier times]. In
Geographisches Jahrbuch, 53, no.1 (1938): 255-274.
German. DLC.
                                          Gompertz'63.
Physical setting--geography--Bibliography. 113.02
Geography--Bibliography. History--Bibliography.
Bibliography--1926-1936.

"A well selected and annotated bibliography,
mainly on the geography of Korea." Gompertz'63.

01090   zeng   usa   b 0 n   1946
        McCune, Shannon Boyd-Bailey. Geographic
publications of Hermann Lautensach on Korea. In
Far Eastern quarterly, 5 (1946): 330-332.
English. DLC.
                                   LCW'50,DLC.
Bibliography--bibliographic essay. Physical
setting--geography--Bibliography. Lautensach,
Hermann. 113.02 130.00 Field date--1933.

"Brief introduction to Lautensach, the geographer
and geopolitician, with 19 articles cited
including two by Lautensach's students and one
review of an article by Lautensach. Lautensach has
made an outstanding contribution in the field of
Korean geography. He has made studies of Portugal
and Korea: the extremes of the Eurasian land
mass." LCW'50. "A useful list and commentary on
the prolific writings of Dr. Lautensach based on
his ten months of field work in the Far East,
especially Korea, in 1933." Gompertz'63.

01092   zkor   sokor   b 0 n   1964
        Minjok munhwa kwan'gye munhŏn mongnok
[Bibliography of source materials on Korean
national culture]. In Minjok munhwa yŏn'gu, 1
(1964): 254-336.
Korean. DLC,KEU. A catalog of pre-1945
publications.
                                         S,DLC.
Bibliography. Bibliography-- up to 1945.

01093   zjap   japan   b 0 n   1920
        Nagoshi, Nakajirō.   Chōsen chishi shiryō ni
tsuite [As to source materials on Korean
geography]. In Rekishi to chiri, 4 (1920).
Japanese. CU-E,DLC,KSN.
                                          DLC.
Physical setting--geography--Bibliography. 110.00

01094   zjap   b 0 n   1935
        Oda, Shōgo, comp. Chōsen kosho no ichibetsu
[A brief study of old Korean books]. In Sen-Man
kenkyū, 8, no.8 (1935).
Japanese.
                                         WH'68.
Bibliography. 110.00 Classics. Rare books.

01095   zjap   japan   b 0 n   1938
        Courant, Maurice [Auguste Louis Marie], 1865-

1939. Chōsen shoshi joron [Introduction to
Korean bibliography]. [Tr. by] Ogura Chikao. In
Dokusho, 2, no.3 (1938): 1-31.
Japanese. DLC. Translation of the Introduction
to Bibliographie coréenne by Maurice Courant.
                                        WH'68.
Bibliography--bibliographic essay. 217.00 538.00
113.02 214.00 190.00 443.00

01096 zkor   sokor   b 0 n   1961
      Pak, Sŏng-bong, comp. Han'guksa yŏn'gu
munhŏn mongnok [Bibliography on the studies of
Korean history]. In Mulli hakch'ong (Kyŏnghŭi
Taehakkyo), 1 (1961): 198-251.
Korean. DLC,KYU. This issue covers materials on
archeology and folklore published before Aug. 15,
1945.
                                        S,DLC.
Archeology--Bibliography. 110.00 530.00 175.00
527.00 369.00 190.00 103.00 601.00 585.00
765.00 576.00 769.05 770.00 780.00 621.00
592.00 823.00 580.00 562.00 428.00 551.00
183.00 291.00 362.00 341.00 262.00 302.01
844.00 764.04 644.00 346.00 141.00 142.00
Women. Surnames. Dolmen. Folklore. Hyangga.
Mudang. Ondol. Bibliography--1832-1944.

01097 zkor   sokor   b 0 n   1959
      Pak, Sŏng-bong. Han'guksa yŏn'gu munhŏn
mongnok: Chŏnhu Ilbon hakkye [Catalog of research
materials on Korean history: postwar Japanese
learned circle]. In Sahak yŏn'gu, 3 (1959): 119-
132; 4 (1959): 143-156.
Korean. CU-E,DLC,MH-HY,MiU,WaU-FE.
                                    DLC,Yang'60.
History--Bibliography. 110.00 Bibliography--
1945-1958.

"An index to articles on Korean history by
Japanese authors, appeared in various Japanese
journals, 1945-1958." Yang'60.

01099 zjap   b 0 n   1940
      Sakurai, Yoshiyuki, comp. Taishō nenkan
Chōsen kankei bunken kaidai [Annotated
bibliography of source materials on Korea
published during Taishō period]. In Chōsen kōsei,
19 (1940): supplement, 20 (1941).
Japanese.

Bibliography.   113.02   Bibliography--1912-1926.

01100   zjap   b   0   n   1943
     Sakurai, Yoshiyuki, comp.   Chōsen jinkō rōdō
kankei bunken shiryo [Source materials on Korean
population and labor problems]. In Chōsen rōdō, 3,
no.1 (1943).
Japanese.
Economy--Bibliography. Population--Bibliography.
160.00   460.00   Labor and laboring classes--
Bibliography.

01101   zjap   kor   b   0   n   1932
     Tada, Masatomo, comp.   Chōsen bungaku
oboegaki [A ncte on Kcrean literature]. In Chōsen
no toshokan, 4 (1932): 1-9.
Japanese.
                                              MHY.
Literature.

01103   zkor   kor   b   0   n   1940
     Yi, Pyŏng-gi.   Chosŏn munhak myŏngjŏ haeje
[Annotations on the masterpieces in Korean
literature]. In Munjang, 2, no.8 (1940): 215-231.
Korean.   DLC,MH-HY.
                                         DLC,S.
Literature--Bibliography.   159.04   175.00   538.00
539.00   190.00   552.00   177.00   213.00   576.00
369.00   560.00   580.00   590.00   113.02   Buddhism.
Classics.   Rare books.   Hunmin Chŏngŭm.

01104   zkor   sokor   b 16   n   1965
     Yu, T°aeg-il, comp.   Yŏngnam munhŏnnog
(Kyŏngnam-p′yŏn) [Bibliography of source
materials on Kyŏngnam Province]. In Kugŏ
kungmunhak, 28 (1965): 127-202.
Korean.   CU-E,DLC,MH-HY.
                                         MHY,DLC.
Literature--Bibliography.   Language--Bibliography.
Kyŏngsang Namdo.   110.00   Local history--
Bibliography.

01105   zeng   b   0   n   1950
     Bibliography of Asiatic musics; tenth
installment. V. Central East Asia: A. General, B.
Japan, C. Korea. Compiled by Richard A. Waterman,
William Lichtenwanger, Virginia Hitchcock Hermann,
Horace I. Poleman, and Cecil Hobbs. In Music

Library Association notes, 2d ser., 7, no.2
(1950): 265-279.
English. CtY,DLC. Korea: p. 279.
                                              S,CtY.
Performing arts--music--Bibliography. 533.00
534.00 536.00 538.00

01107 xjap   japan   b 0 n
       Bunken mokuroku: chōsen [Bibliography of
source materials: Korea]. In Rekishigaku nenpō
furoku. Tokyo, Rekishigaku Kenkyūkai.
Japanese. DLC,MH-HY.
                                                DLC.
History--Biblicgraphy.

01108 ajap   japan   b 0 n   1947
       Chosŏn Kosŏ Kanhaenghoe. Seoul, Korea.
Chōsen kosho mokuroku [A catalog of old Korean
books]. Tokyo, Kunshodō Shoten, 1947.
Japanese.
                                              WH'68.
Bibliography. 110.00 Rare books. Bibliography--
Rare books. Rare books--Bibliography.

01109 zjap   b 0 n   1923
       Ogiyama, Hideo. Chōsenshi kankei tosho
kaidai [Annotated bibliography of books on Korean
history]. In Chōsenshi kōza, 8 (1923).
Japanese-Korean. CSt,DLC,MH-HY.
                                            MHY,DLC.
History--Biblicgraphy. 113.02

01110 zfren   belg   b 0 n   1909
       Cammaerts, Emile, comp. La Corée:
bibliographie. In Bulletin de la Societé Royal
Belge de Géographie, Brussels, 28 (1904): 80-81.
French. CtY,DLC.
                                   DLC,Gompertz'63.
Physical setting--geography--Bibliography. 110.00

01112 zkor   sokor   b 0 n   1960
       Yŏnse Taehakkyo. Kugŏ Kukmunhakhoe. Han'guk
kojŏn munhak yŏn'gu munhŏn haeje [Annotated
bibliography of research on Korean classical
literature]. In Inmun kwahak, 5 (1960): 163-199.
Korean. CU-E,MH-HY.
                                   CUE,MHY,Paek'68.
Literature--Bibliography. 113.02 538.00
Classics.

01114 zkor   sokor   b 0   me194519581958
       Kim, Yong-dŏk, comp. Kuksa kwan'gye chŏsŏ
nonmun mongnok [Bibliography of books and
articles on Korean history]. In Yŏksa hakpo, 10
(1958): 329-340.
Korean. CU-E,DLC,MH-HY,WaU-FE.
                                        MHY,DLC.
History. 110.00

01115 zjap   japan   b 0   n   1936
       Koyama, Fujio, comp. Chōsen tōji bunken
mokuroku [Bibliography of source materials on
Korean pottery]. In Tōki kōza, 13 (1936): 1-24.
Japanese. CtY,MH-HY.
                                        MHY.
Visual arts--pottery--Bibliography. 323.00
110.00

01116 aeng   gtbr   b 0   n   1935
       March, Arthur Charles, 1880-. A Buddhist
bibliography. London, Buddhist Lodge, 1935. 11,
257, [1] p. 23 cm.
English. CtY,DLC. Contains some entries on
Korea. Edition limited to 500 copies.
                                        CtY,DLC.
Religion and philosophy--Bibliography. 110.00
Buddhism.

01117 aeng   usa   b 0   n   1949
       McCune, Shannon Boyd-Bailey, comp. Old
Korean geographical works: a bibliography.
Hamilton, New York, Korean Research Associates,
Colgate University, 1949. 7, 6 p. 28 cm.
English. NNR,MiU,TxU. Caption title. Selection
from Maurice Courant's Bibliographie coréenne.
                                        WH'68,UC'54.
Physical setting--geography--Bibliography.

01119 zjap   b 0   n   1937
       Sakurai, Yoshiyuki, comp. Chōsen no
kyōdoshi, chihōshi [Chronicles of provinces and
local history of Korea]. In Nippon kosho tōshin,
84 (1937).
Japanese.
                                        WH'68.
History--Bibliography. 110.00 175.00

01120 zjap   japan   b 0   n   1958
       Shigaku kankei shuyō zasshi rombun mokuroku
[Bibliography of major journal articles on history

and related subjects]. In Shisen, 10 (1958).
Japanese. CU-E.
                                              CUE.
History--Bibliography. 110.00 175.00

01121 zkor   sokor   b 0 k   1966
    Sŏul Taehakkyo. Tosŏgwan.   Koryŏ munjip
mongnok (A catalog of literary works in the
Goryeo [Koryŏ] dynasty). In Sŏul Taehakkyo
Tosŏgwanbo, 4 (1966): 77-87.
Korean. DLC,KNC,MH-HY.
                                              MHY,S.
Literature--Bibliography. 110.00   530.00   159.04
Classics. Rare books. Bibliography--0918-1392.

01122 fgerm   ger   b 0 n   1967
    Kim, Youn Soo.   Sozialwissenschaftliche
bibliographie über Korea [Social science
bibliography on Korea]. [Freiburg] 1967?
German. Unpublished manuscript.
                                              WH'68.
Bibliography. 110.00 Social sciences--
Bibliography.

01123 xchin   taiw   b 0 n   1955
    Kuo-li Chung-yang t°u-shu-kuan, ed.   T´ai-wan
kung-ts´ang Kac-li-pen lien-ho mu-lu
[Bibliography of Chinese literature published in
Korea and located in Taiwan public libraries and
research institutions]. In Tung Tso-pin et al.
Chung Han wen-hua lun-chi.   Taipei, Chung-hua wen-
hua ch´u-pan shih-yeh wei-yüan-hui, 1955: 1-32.
(Hsien-tai kuo-min chi-pen chih-shih ts´ung-shu,
3)
Chinese. CtY,MH-HY. This bibliography is the
third appendix of the book.
                                       S,CtY,MH-HY.
Bibliography--catalogs--China, Republic of.
110.00 175.00 130.00 797.00 Biography.
Travelers' accounts. Archeology. Buddhism.
Philosophers. Intercultural relations--Korea-
China. Chinese classics.

01125 zjap   b 0 n   1935
    Toyota, Shirō.   Chōsen no chizu ni tsuite
[Concerning maps of Korea]. In Chōsen kenkyū
shiryō (1935).
Japanese. KSN.
                                              KSN.
Physical setting--geography--Bibliography. 110.00
102.00 Maps.

01126 xeng   usa   b 0 n   1964
       Yang, Key P. Source materials on Korean
political developments. In C. I. Eugene Kim, ed. A
pattern of political development: Korea.
Kalamazoo, Korea Research and Publication, 1964:
177-200.
English. DLC,MH-W. Bibliographical footnotes.
                                        S,MHW.
Polity--Bibliography. 648.00 650.00 665.00
159.04 204.00 Political development. Korean
War. Overseas Koreans. April Revolution.
Unification.

01127 zkor   sokor   b 0 n   1963
       Yi, Mun-yŏng, comp. Han'guk kyŏngje
haengjŏng yŏn'gu rŭl wihan charyo ko
(Bibliography cn public administration for the
Korean economy). In Pŏmnyul haengjŏng nonjip, 5
(1963): 225-28S.
Korean. CU-E,DLC.
                                    CUE,DLC,S.
Economy--Biblicgraphy. Polity--Bibliography.
313.00   575.00   423.00   369.00   439.00   647.00
228.00   813.00   134.00   135.00   650.00   378.00
489.00   208.00   648.00   450.00   651.00   460.00
670.00   453.00   Public administration.
Agriculture. Industry. Communications. National
defense.

01128 aeng   usa   b 0 n   1968
       Henthorn, William E., comp. A guide to
reference and research materials on Korean
history: an annotated bibliography. [Honolulu]
Institute of Advanced Projects, East-West Center,
1968. 3, 152 l. 28 cm. (Occasional papers of
Research Publications and Translations, East-West
Center, Honolulu. Annotated bibliography series,
4)
English. DLC,HRAF. Titles also in Korean and
Japanese characters.
                                            S.
History--Biblicgraphy. Bibliography--
Bibliographies. 113.02 Dictionaries. Biography.
Gazetteers. Bibliographies.

01129 zkor   sokor   b 0 n   1964
       Chindan hakpo ch῀ong mokch῀a [Title index to
articles in Chindan hakpo, v.1-24]. In Chindan

256

hakpo, 25/27 (1964): 506-512.
Korean. Index of articles in Chindan hakpo, a bi-
annual "scholarly journal devoted to the studies
of Korea and her neighbouring countries", v. 1-24
(Nov. 1934-Aug. 1963).
Knez'68,S.
Bibliography--index. 538.00 190.00 533.00
536.00 175.00 771.00 130.00 Trade.
Periodicals--Indexes. Indexes. Bibliography--
1934-1963.

01130 ajap kor b 0 n 1935
Chōsen Sōtokufu Kambō Bunshoka, ed. Sōkan
irai no sō-mokuji benran [Index to articles
appearing in Chōsen since the publication of its
first issue]. Seoul, 1935. 77 p.
Japanese. MH-HY. A supplementary issue in
commemoration of the twenty-fifth anniversary of
the publication, Chōsen.
CEACS'64,MHY.
Bibliography--index. Bibliography--1911-1935.

01131 ajap jap b 0 n 1932
Hōbun rekishi-gaku kankei shō-zasshi Tōyō-shi
rombun yomoku [Index of articles and monographs
on Oriental history appearing in Japanese serial
publications and special thesis collections].
Tokyo, Ōtsuka Shigakkai, 1932. 210 p.
Japanese. Korea: p. 120-153.
Knez'68.
History--Bibliography. Bibliography--1868-1931.

01132 zjap japan b 0 n 1933
Iwasaki, Keishō. Chōsen minzoku gakkai e no
tembo [Prospects of Korean ethnology]. In
Dolmen, 2, no.4 (1933): 112-115.
Japanese. MiU.
Knez'68.
Bibliography. 110.00 815.00 Ethnology.

01133 zjap japan b 0 n 1961
Fujita Ryōsaku Sensei chosaku mokuroku
[List of works of the late Professor Fujita
Ryosaku]. In Chōsen gakuhō, 20 (1961): 151-178.
Japanese. CSt-H,DLC,MH-HY.
S,Knez'68,CSH.
Archeology--Bibliography. Fujita, Ryosaku.
110.00 159.04 530.00 175.00 Ethnology.
Sociology. Bibliography--1917-1961.

01134　zjap　　　japan　　b　0　n　　　　1959
　　　Takahashi Tōru Sensei chosaku nempyō
(Bibliography of Prof. Dr. Tōru Takahashi's
writings]. In Chōsen gakuhō, 14 (Oct. 1959): 15-22
(1st section).
Japanese.　CSt-H,CtY,DLC,MH-HY.
　　　　　　　　　　　　　　　　　S,Knez'68,CSH.
History--Bibliography. Sociocultural pattern--
Bibliography.　Takahashi, Toru.　110.00　175.00
172.00　190.00　538.00　812.00　771.00　870.00
757.00　Ethnology.　Sociology.　Bibliography--
1909-1959.

01135　zjap　　　kor　　　b　0　yc　　　　1931
　　　Kameda, Jirō.　Meiji jidai Nis-Sen ryogo
hikaku ron rombun hyo [List of comparative
treatises on Japanese and Korean linguistics that
appeared during the Meiji period]. In Seikyū
gakusō, 6 (1931): 148-156.
Japanese.　DLC,MH-HY.
　　　　　　　　　　　　　　　　Knez'68,MHY.
Language--Bibliography.　110.00　190.00　171.00

01137　zeng　　　neth　　b　0　n　　　　1955
　　　Vos, Frits.　[Review of] Korean studies
guide. In T´oung-pao, 43, no. 5 (1955): 408-431.
English.　CtY.
　　　　　　　　　　　　　　　　　　　　　S.
Bibliography.　113.02　Language.　Literature.
Geography.　History.　Education.　Arts.
Sociology.　Religion.　Reference works.

01138　aeng　　　sokor　　b　0　n　　　　1968
　　　Knez, Eugene I.　A selected and annotated
bibliography of Korean anthropology. By Eugene I.
Knez and Chang-su Swanson.　Seoul, Taehan Min'guk
Kukhoe Tosōgwan, 1968.　10, 235 p.　map.
English-Korean.　Author index: p. 201-204.　Title
index: p. 205-233.
　　　　　　　　　　　　　　　　　　　　　S.
Sociocultural pattern--Bibliography.　172.05
113.02　Physical anthropology.　Linguistics.
Archeology.　Arts.　Handicrafts.　Material
culture.　Sociocultural change.

01139　xchin　　　taiw　　b　0　n　　　　1955
　　　Kuo-li Chung-yang t´u-shu-kuan, ed.　Chung-
kuo kuan-yü Han-kuo chu-shu mu-lu [Bibliography
of Chinese literature on Korea]. In Tung Tso-pin
et al. Chung Han wen-hua lun-chi.　Taipei, Chung-

hua wen-hua ch'u-pan shih-yeh wei-yüan-hui, 1955:
1-62. (Hsien-tai kuo-min chi-pen chih-shih
ts'ung-shu, 3)
Chinese. CtY. This bibliography is the first
appendix of the book.
                                        S,CtY.
Bibliography. 110.00 175.00 130.00 173.02
538.00 764.00 797.00 105.00 Biography.
Travelers' accounts. Gazetteers. Tribute.
Archeology.

01140 zjap   japan   b 0 n   1911
       Morita, Tauson. Dokutoru Rīsu no Chōsen ni
kansuru Ūshu kinkan shomokuroku [Recently
published Western books on Korea]. In Gakuto, 7
(1911): 1-8.
Japanese. CtY.
                                        S,CtY.
Bibliography. Intercultural relations--Korea-
Japan--Bibliography. 175.00 565.00 178.00
159.00 668.00 Conflict.

01141 zjap   kor   b 0 n   1956
       Miki, Sakae, comp. Chōsen igakushi oyobi
shippeishi no kankō ni tsuite [Publications on
the history of Korean medicine and diseases]. In
Chōsen gakuhō, 10 (1956).
Japanese. DLC,MH-HY.
                                        WH'68,MHY.
Welfare--medicine--Bibliography. Welfare--
disease--Bibliography. 110.00 Medicine.
Disease.

03066 zeng   korea   b 0 n   1932
       Trollope, Mark Napier. Short list of Korean
books [in the Chosen Christian College Library].
In Transactions of the Korea Branch of the Royal
Asiatic Society, 21 (1932): 59-104.
English. CtY,DLC.
                                        S,Elrod'60.
Bibliography--catalogs--Korea. Chosen Christian
College Library. Yonsei University Library.
110.00 Classics. History. Philosophy.
Catalogs, Book. Bibliography--0918-1933.

"Korean literature since the Koryo Dynasty (X
cent.)." LCW'50.

03723 zeng   kor   b 0 n   1936
       Underwood, Horace H. Index to titles and

authors of papers published in the Transactions of
the Korea Branch of the R.A.S., volumes 1 to 25.
In Transactions of the Korea Branch of the Royal
Asiatic Society,25 (1936): 109-122.
English. DLC,MH,MH-HY.
                                          Elrod'60.
Bibliography--index. 110.00 Bibliography--1900-
1936.

03724 zeng   kor   b 0 n   1931
       Underwood, Horace H. Occidental literature
on Korea. In Transactions of the Korea Branch of
the Royal Asiatic Society,20 (1931): 1-15.
English. DLC,MH,MH-HY.
                                          Elrod'60.
Bibliography--bibliographic essay. 110.00
Method.

04066 zeng   sokor   b 0 n   1965
       Bibliographical note: Korean books on
tactics. In Asiatic research bulletin, 8, no. 7
(Oct. 1965): 20-25; 8, no. 8 (Nov. 1966): 15-21.
English.
                             BAS'65,BAS'66.
Military--Bibliography. 110.00

04073 zjap   japan   b 0 n   1969
       Chōsen Gakkai. Chōsen gakuhō no daiisshū
kara dai gojisshū made no sōmokuji (Index to
Chōsen gakuhō from no.1 to no.50). In Chōsen
gakuhō, no.50 (1969): 5-77.
Japanese. DLC,HRAF.
                                              S.
Bibliography--Index. Indexes. Periodicals--
Indexes.

04074 zkor   sokor   b 0 n   1960
       Han'guk sŏji munhŏn illam 1937-1940
(Bibliography on Korean bibliography, 1937-1940).
In Sŏji, 1, no.1 (Jan. 1960): 42-46.
Korean. CU-E,DLC,MH-HY,WaU-FE.
                                          MHY,S.
Bibliography. 110.00 217.02 777.00 621.00
170.00 213.00 668.00 648.00 538.00 539.00
373.00 204.00 183.00 590.00 Bibliographies.
Classics. Rare books. Medicine. Maps. Economy.
Law. Language. Bibliography--1937-1940.

04075 zkor   sokor   b 0 n   1961
       Han'guk chiryu munhŏn illam 1905-1938

(Bibliography of Korean paper, 1905-1938). In
Sŏji, 2, no.1 (Oct. 1961): 48-50.
Korean. CU-E,DLC,MH-HY,WaU-FE.
MHY,S.
Economy--Bibliography. 110.00 289.00 369.00
204.00 Paper. Bibliography--1905-1938.

04076 zkor sokor b 0 n 1968
Paek, In. Han'guk sŏji kwan'gye munhŏn
mongnok [A list of books related to Korean
bibliography]. In Sŏjihak, 2 (1969): 62-76.
Korean. DLC,MH-HY.
MHY,S.
Bibliography--Bibliographies. 110.00 217.02
213.00 170.00 538.00 539.00 648.00 346.00
214.00 369.00 472.00 159.04 377.00 630.00
Travelers' accounts. Bibliographies. Classics.
Rare books. Buddhism. Maps. Confucianism.
Medicine. Children. Christianity--Roman
Catholicism. Ch'ondo kyo. Hunmin Chŏngŭm.
Korean War. Bibliography-- up to 1967.

04077 zkor sokor b 0 n 1969
Paek, In. Han'guk sŏji kwan'gye munhŏn
mongnok [A list of books related to Korean
bibliography]. In Sŏjihak, 1 (1968): 34-54.
Korean. DLC,MH-HY.
MHY,S.
Bibliography--Bibliographies. 110.00 648.00
190.00 870.00 217.02 204.00 213.00 214.00
170.00 813.00 159.00 538.00 539.00 601.00
102.00 647.00 183.00 668.00 Classics. Rare
books. Women. Polity. Law. Children.
Buddhism. Christianity--Roman Catholicism.
Travelers' accounts. Bibliographies. Korean War.
Bibliography-- up to 1967.

04078 zkor sokor b 0 n 1966
Sŏul Taehakkyo. Pusok Tosŏgwan. Microfilm
mongnok (A list of microfilm records). In Sŏul
Taehakkyo Tosŏgwanbo, 4 (1966): 19-25.
Korean. MH-HY.
MHY,S.
Bibliography. 110.00 217.02 648.00 170.00
159.04 576.00 700.00 538.00 539.00 647.00
204.00 102.00 Classics. Rare books. Religion.
Travelers' accounts.

04082 zkor sokor b 0 mc19501953
Han'guk pan'gong yŏnmaeng. Yugio kwan'gye

munhŏn kaeryak [Summaries of literature related
to the Korean War]. In Chayu kongnon 1, no.3
(June).
Korean.
                                           Paek'69.
Conflict--Bibliography. 110.00 720.00 Korean
War.

04083 zkor   sokor   b 0 n   1965
      Kim, Yang-sŏn.   Han'guk ko-jido yŏn'gu [A
study of old Kcrean maps]. In Sungdae, 10 (1965).
Korean.
                                           Paek'68.
Physical setting--geography--Bibliography. 102.00
Maps.

04084 zkor   sokor   b 0 n
      Pak, Sŏng-bong.   Han'guk kuksa yŏn'gu munhŏn
mongnok, 4 [List of literature on Korean
history]. In Mulli hakch'ong (Kyŏnghŭi Taehakkyo),
4.
Korean.
                                           Paek'68.
History--Biblicgraphy. 110.00   175.00

04085 zkor   sokor   b 0 m
      So, Chin-chŏl.   Tongnansa kwan'gye charyo
haeje.   [Annotated materials related to the
Korean War]. In Kongsanjuŭi munje yon'gu, 3
(Nov.).
Korean.
                                           Paek'68.
Conflict--Bibliography. 110.00 720.00 Korean
War.

04086 zkor   sokor   b 0 n
      An, Ch°un-gŭn.   Han'guk pakpo (changgi)
sŏjigo [Biblicgraphy on Korean chess-changgi]. In
Tosŏ, 11.
Korean.
                                           Paek'68.
Recreation--Bibliography. 110.00   524.04
Changgi.

04087 zkor   sokor   b 0 n   1957
      Yi, Pyŏng-gi.   Han'guk sŏji ŭi yŏn'gu
[Study of Korean bibliography]. In Tongbang
hakchi, 3 (1957); 5 (1961).
Korean. DLC.
                                           Paek'69.
Bibliography.

04090   zkor   sokor   b 0 n   1967
     Han'guk Tosŏgwan Hyŏphoe.
1967   nyŏndo pun sŏnjŏng tosŏ mongnok [Selected
bibliography for the year of 1967]. In Tohyŏp
wŏlbo, 8, no. 6-10 (July/Aug.-Dec., 1967).
Korean.
                                              Paek'69.
Bibliography. 110.00 Bibliography--1967.

04092 zkor   sokor   b 0 n
     Chang, Ki-gŭn. Han'guk munjip ŭi haeje
[Annotated bibliography of Korean anthology]. In
Asea hakpo, 3 (May).
Korean.
                                              Paek'69.
Literature--Bibliography. 538.00

04093 zkor   sokor   b 0 n   1968
     Chang, Tŏk-sun. Kyujanggak tosŏ chosŏn
ŭpchisojae sŏrhwa pullyu [Classification of
folklore printed in Korean local papers and
located at Kyujanggak Library]. In Tonga munhwa
(Sŏul Tae), 6 (Dec. 1968).
Korean.
                                              Paek'69.
Bibliography. Folklore.

04094 zkor   sokor   b 0 n   1966
     Sŏng, Tae-gyung. Han'guk sŏji ŭi sŏji
[Bibliography of Korean bibliography]. In Kukhoe
Tosŏgwanbo, 3, no. 5-7 (June-Aug. 1966).
Korean.
                                              Paek'68.
Bibliography--Eibliographies. 110.00
Bibliographies.

04095 zkor   sokor   b 0 n   1966
     Kukhoe Tosŏgwan. Han'guk kwan'gye munhŏn
mongnok: Mi Stanford Taehakkyo sojang [List of
literature related to Korea: literature located at
Stanford University, U.S.A.]. In Kukhoe Tosŏgwanbo,
3, no. 9 (Oct. 1966).
Korean.
                                              Paek'68.
Bibliography. 110.00

04096 zkor   sokor   b 0 n   1967
     Kukhoe Tosŏgwan. Haebang chŏn Han'guk

kwan'gye munhŏn mongnok: pon'gwan sojangbon [List
of literature related to Korea before the
liberation of Korea from Japan: publications
located at National Assembly Library]. In Kukhoe
Tosŏgwanbo, 4, no. 11 (Nov. 1967).
Korean.
                                        Paek'68.
Bibliography. 110.00

04097 zkor   sokor   b 0 n   1968
       Kukhoe Tosŏgwan. Haebang chŏn kanhaeng
Han'guk chapchi mongnok (pongwan sojang) [List of
Korean magazine publications before the liberation
of Korea from Japan: publications located at the
National Assembly Library]. In Kukhoe Tŏsogwanbo,
5, no. 1 (1968).
Korean.
                                        Paek'68.
Bibliography. 110.00 204.00

04098 zkor   sokor   b 0 n   1966
       Yi, Kyŏm-no. Chosŏn kojido mongnok [A list
of old Korean maps]. In Kukhoe Tosŏgwanbo, 3, no.
6-8 (July-Sept. 1966).
Korean.
                                        Paek'69.
Physical setting--geography--Bibliography. 102.00
Maps.

04100 zkor   sokor   b 0 n   1967
       Kukhoe Tosŏgwan. Chosŏn ch'ongdokpu Kŭp
sosok kwansŏ palgan tosŏ mongnok [A list of books
published by the Governemt-General of Chōsen and
its related offices]. In Kukhoe Tosŏgwanbo, 4, no.
2 (Feb. 1967); 5, no. 1 (1968).
Korean.
                                        Paek'68.
Bibliography. Intercultural relations--Korea-
Japan. 110.00 648.00 Chōsen Sōtokufu.

04111 zkor   sokor   b 0 n   1967
       Kukhoe Tosŏgwan. Chŏngch'i kwan'gye munhŏn
mongnok [A list of books related to political
science]. In Kukhoe Tosŏgwanbo, 4 (1967).
Korean.
                                        Paek'68.
Polity--Bibliography. 110.00 Political science.

04115 zjap   b 0 n   1908
       Furutani, Kiyoshi. Futatabi Tokugawa jidai

ni okeru Chōsen no shoseki ni tsuite [Korean
books of Tokugawa period]. In Gakutō, 12, no. 6
(1908).
Japanese.
                                        Paek'69.
Bibliography.

04116 zjap   b   0   n   1896
       Hayashi, Taisuke.   Chōsen shiseki-kō
[Studies on Korean historical books]. In Shigaku
zasshi, 7, no. 13 (1896).
Japanese.
                                        Paek'69.
History--Biblicgraphy.

04117 zjap   b   0   n   1909
       Hayashi, Taisuke.   Chōsen no shiseki
[Historical works of Korea]. In Kokugakuin zasshi,
18, no. 5 (1909).
Japanese.
                                        Paek'69.
History--Biblicgraphy.

04118 zjap   b   0   n   1933
       Imamura, Tomoe.   Ninjin bunseki kaidai
[Bibliographical literature on ginseng]. In
Chōsen, 213 (1933): 2-34.
Japanese.
                                        Paek'69.
Bibliography. Ginseng.

04119 zjap   b   0   n   1940
       Kishi, Yuzuru.   Chōsen no tōka kankei shiryō
tō   [Data on Korean lamplights]. In Shomotsu
Dōkōkai kaihō, 7 (1940): 4-6.
Japanese.
                                        Paek'69.
Bibliography. 354.00 373.00 Lamp-lights.

04120 zjap   b   0   n   1942
       Kuji, Hanjirō.   Chōsen kenkyū no seika [The
result of Korean study]. In Chōsen gyōsei, 22,
no.2 (1942): 1S.
Japanese.
                                        Paek'69.
Bibliography.

04121 zjap   b   0   n   1938
       Okudaira, Takehiko.   Chōsen no tenseki
[Korean classics]. In Kinyū Kumiai, 117 (1938).

Japanese.

Bibliography. Classics.

Paek'69.

04122 zjap   b 0 n   1937
    Okuda,   Takehiko.   Korai-Chō no tenseki ni
tsuite [Books in Koryō dynasty]. In Bunken
hōkoku, 2, no.4 (Apr. 1936): 20-23.
Japanese.
                                          Paek'69.
Bibliography. Classics.

04123 zjap   b 0 n   1950
    Wada, Kiyoshi.   Chōsen shiryō [Korean
historical materials]. In Bunbutsu sansei shiryō,
11 (1950).
Japanese.
                                          Paek'69.
History--Biblicgraphy.

04124 zjap   b 0 s   1919
    Watanabe, Akira.   Shiragi jidai no bungei
shiryō [Data on Silla period literature]. In
Chōsen ihō, (Nov. 1919).
Japanese.
                                          Paek'69.
Literature--Bibliography.

04125 zjap   b 0 n   1939
    Yi, Chae-uk.   Chōsen no shōsetsu [Korean
fiction]. In Bunken hōkoku, 5, no.5 (1939): 26.
Japanese.
                                          Paek'69.
Literature--Bibliography. 538.00

04127 zjap   b 0 y   1927
    Asō, Takekame.   Richō no hōten [Yijo code].
In Chōsen, 145 (1927): 81-86.
Japanese.
                                          Paek'68.
Law--Bibliography. 671.05

04128 zjap   kor   b 0 t   1936
    En'ō-sei.   Sangoku jidai no tenseki
[Classics of Three Kingdom period]. In Bunken
hōkoku, 2, no.3 (1936): 16-17.
Japanese.
                                          Paek'69.
Bibliography. Classics.

04130   zjap   b 0 n   1940
    Musha, Renzō.   [Chōsen fūzoku-shū] Shosai no
tōka kankei bunken   [(Korean customs collection)
published literature on lamp-lights]. In Shomotsu
Dōkōkai kaihō, 9 (1940): 25-26.
Japanese.
                                        Paek'68.
Bibliography. 354.00 373.00 Lamp-lights.

04131   zjap   b 0 n   1899
    Naka, Michiyo.   Taiwan, Chōsen, Manshū shi
kenkyū no shiori   [A guide to the study of Taiwan,
Korea, Manchuria]. In Shigaku zasshi, 11, no.1
(1899): 57-66.
Japanese.
                                        Paek'68.
Bibliography.

04132   zjap   b 0 n   1937
    Nishiyoshi, Reinsensai.   Kankoku heisei
kankei bunken rokushu   [Six kinds of literature
on Korean monetary system]. In Kahei, 224 (1937).
Japanese.
                                        Paek'68.
Economy--Bibliography. 436.00

04134   zjap   b 0 n   1938
    Sakurai, Yoshiyuki.   Meiji shoki no Chōsen
kenkyū   [Study on Korea in the early Meiji
period]. In Chōsen kōsei, 2, no.8 (1938).
Japanese.
                                        Paek'68.
Bibliography.

04135   zjap   b 0 n   1943
    Sekino, Shinkichi.   Chōsen kindai toshokan
shiryo   [Sources on modern Korean library
history]. In Shomotsu Dōkōkai kaihō, 18 (1943):
14.
Japanese.
                                        Paek'68.
Education--Bibliography. 217.00

04136   zjap   b 0 n   1935
    Miura, Hirayuki.   Chōsen saikō no chiri-sho
ni tsuite   [Korean geographical books]. In Chōsen
kenkyū shiryō, 59 (1935).
Japanese. See also Chōsen ihō (Dec. 1916).
                                        Paek'68.
Physical setting--geography--Bibliography.

04166 zkor   sokor   b 0 n   1960
     Yi, Hong-jik.   Toil han Han'guk ŭi munhŏn
[Korean literature in Japan which was brought from
Korea]. In Toksa yŏjŏk (1960): 32-40.
Korean.
                                           WH'68.
Bibliography.

04167 zeng   usa   b 0 n   1958
     Paige, Glenn D. A survey of Soviet
publications on Korea, 1950-1956. In Journal of
Asian Studies, 17 (Aug. 1958): 579-594.
English.
                                           WH'68.
Bibliography.   Korean studies in Soviet Union--
Bibliography.   Bibliography--1950-1956.

04168 zeng   sokor   b 0 n   1960
     Paige, Glenn D. Korea studies in the Soviet
Union. In Korean Research Center bulletin, 13
(1960): 47-57.
English.
                                           WH'68.
Bibliography.   Korean studies in Soviet Union--
Bibliography.

04169 zeng   sokor   b 0 n   1958
     Paige, Glenn D. The Korean collection of the
Division of Oriental Manuscripts, Institute of
Oriental Studies, Academy of Sciences of the USSR.
A bibliographical note. In Asiatic research
bulletin, 1, no.9 (September 1958): 2-3.
English. This article is a reprint without notes
of the original which appeared in HJAS, 19
(December 1956): 409-411.
                                           WH'68.
Bibliography--catalogs--U.S.S.R. Academy of
Sciences of the USSR, Institute of Oriental
Studies, Division of Oriental Manuscripts, Korean
Collection.

04170 xjap   japan   b 0 n   1949
     Chōsen no zasshi [Korean magazines]. In
Japan. Mombushō. Daigaku Gakujutsukyoku. Gakujutsu
chikuji kankōbutsu mokuroku. Tokyo, Monbushō,
1949: 1-12.
Japanese. DLC.
                                           LCF'50.
Bibliography--periodicals. 204.01 Catalogs,

Periodical. Bibliography--1910-1945.

"Lists 437 periodical titles published in Korea
with the names of issuing bodies, places of
publication [or addresses of publishers], and
frequency. All of these Japanese publications are
presumed to be no longer published in Korea."
LCF'50.

04182 zeng   kor   b 0 n   1903
       Catalog of the Landis Library. In
Transactions of the Korea Branch of the Royal
Asiatic Society, 3 (1904): 41-61.
English.
                                  Gompertz'63.
Bibliography--catalogs--Korea. Landis Library.

04183 zeng   japan   b 0 n   1928
       Layard, R. de B. Transactions of the Asiatic
Society of Japan index. First series, Vols. 1-50.
In Transactions of the Asiatic Society of Japan,
Second ser.5 (1928): 89-114.
English.
                                  Gompertz'63.
Bibliography--index.

04184 zeng   kor   b 0 n   1927
       Noble, Harold J. Transactions of Korea
Branch of the Royal Asiatic Society. Index to
transactions 1-16. In Transactions of the Korea
Branch of the Royal Asiatic Society, 17 (1927).
English.
                                  Gompertz'63.
Bibliography--index.

06021 xjap   japan   b 0 n   1953   1
       Nakamura, Eikō.   Chōsen-shi no henshū to
Chōsen shiryō no shūshū [The compilation of the
History of Korea and the collection of Korean
historical materials]. In Ko bunka no hozon to
kenkyū. February 1953.
Japanese.
                                  Okamoto'62.
History--Bibliography. 175.01   Method.

"Between Taishō 11 and Shōwa 12 (1922-1937) an
editorial committee, under the auspices of the
Government-General of Korea, compiled an
annalistic History of Korea in 35 books. Hand in
hand with the compilation went a large scale

gathering of Korean historical sources."
Okamoto'62.

06449 zjap   japan   b 0 n   1955
     Shimamoto, Hikojirō. Akiba Takashi Hakushi
no shōgai to gyōseki [Life and works of Dr. Akiba
Takashi]. In Chōsen gakuhō, 9 (Nov. 1955): 303-
322.
Japanese. CSt-H,CtY,MH-HY.
                                                  S.
Bibliography. Takashi, Akiba. 159.04   775.00
Biography. Shamanism. Community life. Social
groupings.

06761 zkor   sokor   b 0 n   1964
     Ch°oe, Chae-sŏk.   Sahoehak kwan'gye munhŏn
mongnok, 1945-1964 [Bibliography on sociology,
1945-1964]. In Han'guk sahoehak, 1 (Nov. 1964):
115-126.
Korean.
                                                  S.
Sociocultural pattern--Bibliography. 829.00
369.00 181.00 565.00 Sociology. Family. Rural
sociology. Urban sociology. Industrial
sociology. Population. Occupational sociology.
Sociology of law. Criminal sociology. Social
pathology. Social psychology. Ethnology.
Communications. Sociocultural change.
Bibliography--1945-1964.

06762 zkor   sokor   b 0 n   1966
     Ch°oe, Chae-sŏk.   Sahoehak kwan'gye munhŏn
mongnok, 1964. 9. 21--1965. 12. 31 [Bibliography
on sociology, Sept. 21, 1964-Dec. 31, 1965]. In
Han'guk sahoehak, 2 (Nov. 1966): 180-181.
Korean.
                                                  S.
Sociocultural pattern--Bibliography. 565.00
Sociology. Population. Family. Kinship. Rural
sociology. Religion. Sociocultural change.
Bibliography--1964-1965.

06763 feng   b 0 n   1967
     Yang, Key Paik. Present status of Korean
research tools. Kalamazoo, Michigan, 1967. [13]
p. 29 cm.
English. HRAF. Typewritten. Published as
"Present status of research on Korea". In Andrew
C. Nahm, ed. Studies in the developmental aspects
of Korea. Kalamazoo, Mich., School of Graduate

270

Studies and Institute of International and Area
Studies of Western Michigan University, 1969: 243-
253. Korean Studies series, 1. Proceedings of the
Conference on Korea held at Western Michigan
University, April 6-7, 1967.
S.
Bibliography--Bibliographies. Bibliographies.

06766 zeng   japan   b   0   n   1963
       Okamoto, Yoshiji.   Japanese studies on
Korean history since World War II. In Monumenta
Serica, 22, pt. 2 (1963): 470-532.
English. CtY.
S.
History--Biblicgraphy. Sociocultural pattern--
Bibliography. Polity--Bibliography. Economy--
Bibliography. Intercultural relations--
Bibliography. 113.02 217.00 814.00 815.00
565.00 Religicn. Arts.

07055 xkor   sokor   b   0   n   1966
       Ch°oe, Chae-sŏk.   Han'guk kajok kwan'ge
munhŏn mongnok 1900-1965 [Bibliography on Korean
family relations 1900-1965]. In Han'guk kajok
yŏn'gu. Seoul, 1966: 692-701.
Korean. HRAF.
S.
Family and kinship--Bibliography. 428.00 671.00
586.00 583.00 369.00 621.00 577.00 597.00
601.00 590.00 587.00 178.00 562.00 764.00
Surnames. Clans. Paekchŏng. Bibliography--1900-
1965.

07057 xeng   usa   b   1   m   1967
       A selected bibliography of materials on
Korean public administration. In Koh, Byung Chul,
ed. Aspects of administrative development in South
Korea. Kalamazoo, Mich., [1967]: 127-144.
English.
BAS'67.
Polity--Bibliography. 110.00 Public
administration.

07114 xrus   ussr   b   0   n   1900
       Bibliografiia Koreǐ. In Russia, Ministerstvo
finansov. Opisanie Koreǐ. III. 1900: 266-306.
Russian. MH-W. Most of the works referred to in
this bibliography are in Western languages.
MHW.
Bibliography.

09105   akor   sokor   b 0 n   1959
        Kungnip Tosŏgwan.   Ch'ulp'um tosŏ mongnok
(Book week exhibit). Oct. 20-26, 1959. Seoul,
Kungnip Tosŏgwan, [1959]. 35 p. 21 cm.
Korean. MH-HY.
                                       Yang'60.
Bibliography--catalogs--Korea. 110.00 Catalogs--
Book exhibitions. Bibliographical exhibitions.

"Contains a list of government periodical
publications of Republic of Korea." Yang'60.

10204   akor   sokor   b 0 ye187619101966
        Chŏn, Hae-jong. Han'guk kŭnse taeoe
kwan'gye munhŏn piyo (Manual of Korean foreign
relations, 1876-1910). By Chun Hae-jong. Seoul,
Sŏul Taehakkyo Mullikwa Taehak Tonga Munhwa
Yŏn'guso, 1966. 10, 304 p. illus. 26 cm.
(Kyujanggak tosŏ yŏn'gu ch'ongsŏ, 1)
Korean-English. DLC,MH-HY,WaU-FE.
                                       S,MHY.
Intercultural relations--Bibliography. 648.00
126.00 110.00 217.02 551.00 805.00 645.00
Yejo.

10205   akor   sokor   b 0 ye157019101966
        Han, U-gŭn, 1915-. Han'guk kyŏngje kwan'gye
munhŏn chipsŏng (Annotated bibliography of Korean
economic history, 1570-1910). By Han Woo-keun.
Seoul, Sŏul Taehakkyo Mullikwa Taehak Tonga Munhwa
Yŏn'guso, 1966. 22, [8] 223 p. 26 cm.
(Kyujanggak tosŏ yŏn'gu ch'ongsŏ, 2)
Korean. MH-HY,WaU-FE.
                                       S,MHY.
Economy--Biblicgraphy. 113.02 161.00 423.00
651.00 450.00 440.00 470.00 205.00 480.00
177.00 313.00 316.00 567.00 Pobusang.

10206   aeng   sokor   b 0 n   1966
        Pak, Tong-sŏ. Bibliography of Korean public
administration, September 1945-April 1966. By
Dong-suh Bark and Jai-poong Yoon.   [Seoul] 1966.
3, 174 p. 26 cm.
English. HRAF. Reproduced by United States
Operations Mission to Korea. This is a
translation into English by the authors, with the
assistance of Mr. Lee Chul Koo.
                                         S.
Law--Bibliography. Polity--Bibliography. 647.00

272

650.00   630.00   200.00   625.00   740.00   171.00
Public Administration.   Bibliography--1945-1966.

10207   feng   usa   b   0   yc190419101967
   Lew, Young Ick, comp.   Korea on the eve of
Japanese annexation; a classified bibliography for
the study of the late Yi dynasty Korean history in
relation to the Japanese intrusion, 1904-1910.
Boston, Harvard University, 1967.   195 l.
English.   HRAF.   Mimeographed.
                                                    S.
Sociocultural pattern--Bibliography.
Intercultural relations--Korea-Japan--
Bibliography.   Itō, Marquis.   110.00   204.00
   175.00   648.00   668.00   433.00   302.00   386.00
   671.00   648.00   640.00   630.00   668.00   669.00
   159.04   563.00   625.00   871.00   450.00   430.00
   470.00   440.00   423.00   241.00   316.00   489.00
   228.00   200.00   370.00   313.00   314.00   288.00
   317.00   427.00   270.00   656.00   243.00   Society.
Family.   Kinship.   Religion.   Philosophy.   Arts.
Polity.   Travelers' accounts.   Sociocultural
change.   Tōkanfu.   Chōsen Sōtokufu.   Overseas
Koreans.   Japanese in Korea.   Japanese military in
Korea.   Government-General of Korea.   Japanese
colonialism.   Japanese imperialism.   Japanese
nationalism.   Asianism.   Ajia-shugi.   Yi dynasty,
late.

10223   akor   sokor   b   0   n   1954
   Korea (Republic) Mun'gyobu.   Kŏm injŏng
kyokwayong illampʿyo [A catalog of authorized
textbooks].   Seoul, Mun'gyobu, 1954.   20 p.
Korean.
                                              Yang'60.
Bibliography.   Education.   110.00   871.00
Textbooks--catalogs.

"A list of textbooks inspected as of Dec. 1, 1953,
classified according to subjects."   Yang'60.

10269   akor   sokor   b   0   n   1966
   Kukhoe Tosŏgwan.   Seoul, Korea.   Sasŏguk.
Kaebyŏkchi chʿcngmokchʿa, 1920-1949
[Comprehensive table of contents of Kaebyŏk, 1920-
1949].   [Ed. by] Taehan Min'guk Kukhoe Tosŏgwan
Sasŏguk.   Seoul, 1966.   131 p.   18 cm.
Korean.   DLC,HRAF.
                                                    S.
Bibliography--index.   532.00   561.00   369.00

```
562.00  181.00  177.00  183.00  777.00  511.00
526.00  738.00  734.00  367.00  565.00  186.00
586.00  764.15  423.00  460.00  538.00  810.00
590.00  870.00  670.00  160.00  204.00  209.00
```
Arts. Folklore. Technology. Poetry. Economy.
Biography. Religion. Confucianism. Travelers'
accounts. Trade. Social conditions.
Independence Movement. Ch'ondo kyo. Overseas
Koreans. Pericdicals--Indexes. Indexes.
Bibliography--1920-1949.

10329 akor   sokor   b 0 n   1965
    Chŏng, Ch'ŏl, ed. Han'guk paksa-rok
[Korean scholars]. Seoul, Saebyŏk Ch'ulp'ansa,
1965. [697] p. ports. 21 cm.
Korean. DLC,MH-HY,WaU-FE. An earlier edition
appeared in 1962 (321 p.).
                                            MHY.
Bibliography--dissertations.

"This book lists recipients of doctoral degrees in
various parts cf Korea, in both natural and social
science."

10334 akor   sokor   t 0 n   1955
    Chŏng, In-bo. Tamwŏn kukhak san'go
[Tamwŏn's essays in Koreanology]. Seoul,
Mun'gyosa, 1955. 346 p. port., facsim. 21 cm.
Korean. CtY,CU-E,MH-HY,MiU,NN,WaU-FE.
Bibliography: p. 1-62.
                        S,MHY,KU'61,CUE.
Literature. Bibliography. Wang, Yang-ming.
538.00 113.02 814.05 764.15 173.00
Confucianism. Classics. Biography. Sirhak.
Bibliography--1725-1800.

"A compilation of essays on Korean classics
written by Chŏng In-bo, one of the leading
scholars in the field of Korean national
literature. These essays are in five chapters,
including an annotated bibliography of books and
manuscripts written by scholars of the Pragmatic
School of the late Yi Dynasty (1725-1800),
personal criticism on scholars in the field of
Korean national literature, an interpretation of
the teaching of Wang Yang-ming, etc." KU'61.

10560 aeng   japan   b 0 n   1967
    National Diet Library. Reference and
Bibliography Division, ed. Catalog of materials

on Korea in the National Diet Library, 2: Foreign
books. Tōkyō, 1967. 2, 1, 54 p. 25 cm.
English. HRAF. Introduction, in Japanese.
                                                    S.
Bibliography--catalogs--Japan. National Diet
Library. 110.00 204.00 648.00 457.00 480.00
369.00 870.00 815.00 524.00 530.00 190.00
175.00 130.00 102.00 670.00 Religion.
Christianity. Travelers' accounts. Polity.
Economy. Agriculture. Women. Independence
Movement. Korean War.

10570 ajap   japan   b 0 n   1966
     Kokuritsu Kokkai Toshokan, ed. Chōsen kankei
shiryō mokuroku [A list of data related to
Korea]. Tōkyō, 1966. 1 v.
Japanese. CU-E,MH-HY.
                                            CUE,MHY.
Bibliography. Catalogs, Book. Library catalogs.

10576 akor   sokor   b 0 n   195
     Kungnip Tosŏgwan. Kungnip Tosŏgwan
kwijungbon kosŏ mongnok [Bibliography of rare
books of the National Library]. Seoul, 195-?. 61
p. 26 cm.
Korean. CU-E. Cover title.
                                            CUE.
Bibliography--catalogs--Korea. National Central
Library. Kungnip Tosŏgwan. 110.00 Rare books.
Incunabula--Bibliography.

10582 akor   sokor   b 0 n   1964   1
     Sin, Sŏk-ho, 1904-. Han'guk saryo
haesŏlchip (Annotated bibliography on Korean
history). Seoul, Han'guksa Hakhoe, 1964. 2, 193
p. facsim., port. 22 cm.
Korean. CU-E,MH-HY.
                                            CUE,MHY.
History--Bibliography. 113.02 Historiography.

10592 akor   sokor   b 0 n   1967
     Kukhoe Tosŏgwan. Seoul, Korea. Sasŏguk.
Chʷamgo Sŏjikwa, ed. Hanmal Han'guk chapchi
mokchʼa chʼongnok 1896-1910 (Catalog of contents
of Korean periodicals published in the end of Yi
dynasty, 1896-1910). Seoul, Taehan Min'guk Kukhoe
Tosŏgwan, 1967. 6, 139 p. plate, table. 28 cm.
Korean. DLC.
                                            S,DLC.
Bibliography. 110.00 204.00 Indexes.
Periodicals--Indexes. Bibliography--1896-1910.

10754   akor   sokor   b   0   n   1964
        Yi, Sŏng-ŭi,   ed.   Na-Ryŏ yemunji--Silla,
Paekche, Koguryŏ [A bibliography of literature
and arts of the Three Kingdoms and Koryŏ]. [Ed.
by] Yi Sŏng-ŭi [and] Kim Yak-sil.   Seoul, Hongmun
Sŏgwan, 1964. 7, 346 p. facsims. 21 cm.
Korean. DLC,WaU-FE. Prefatory note also in
English. Limited issue: 250. Errata slip
inserted.
                                              WaU.
Literature--Bibliography. 110.00   530.00   538.00
Arts. Koryŏ. Silla. Koguryŏ. Paekche.

11177   aeng   usa   b   1   me195419641965
        Henthorn, William E. Korean views of America
1954-1964: an annotated bibliography. [Honolulu]
East-West Center, 1965. 66 l. 28 cm.
(Occasional Papers of Research Translations,
Institute of Advanced Projects, East-West Center,
Honolulu. Annotated bibliography series, no. 2)
English. DLC,HRAF. Survey of articles,
editorials, features, and translations found in
the periodicals Sasanggye (World of Thought),
Yŏwŏn (Women's Garden) and Hyŏndae Munhak (Modern
Literature).
                                          S,BAS'66.
Bibliography--index. 113.02   648.00   433.00
Values. Bibliography--1954-1964.

11241   ajap   kor   b   0   n   1912
        Chōsen geibunshi [Korean literary culture].
Seoul, Chōsen Sōtokufu, 1912. 122 p. 22 cm.
Japanese.
                                       Sakurai'41.
Bibliography--bibliographic essay. 217.03   217.04
110.00   213.00   212.09   182.03   532.00   212.00
814.00   813.00   816.00   538.00 Printing culture.
Sociology of knowledge. Ethnoscience.

11242   ajap   kor   b   0   n   1909
        Teishitsu tosho mokuroku [Catalog of the
imperial libraries]. Seoul, 1902. 387 p. 22 cm.
Japanese.
                                       Sakurai'41.
Bibliography--catalogs--Korea. Library catalogs.

11243   ajap   kor   b   0   n   1908
        Kanseki mokuroku kōhon [Provisional catalog

of Korean books]. Seoul, Tōkyō Gaikokugo
Gakkō/Kankoku Kōyūkai, 1908. 3, 57, 10 p. 22 cm.
Japanese. MH-HY. Supplement to Tōkyō Gaikokugo
Gakkō Kankoku Kōyūkai hō, no. 1.
                                        Sakurai'41.
Bibliography. Bibliography--Rare books. History-
-Sources--Bibliography. Bibliography--History--
Sources. Incunabula--Bibliography.

11290   akor   sokor   b O n   1966
        Sŏul Taehakkyo. Tosŏgwan. Sŏul Taehakkyo
kaegyo isipchunyŏn kinyŏm kwijung tosŏ chŏnsihoe
chŏnsi tosŏ mongnok 1966-nyŏn 10-wŏl 13-18-il   (A
bibliography of rare books, exhibited in
commemoration of the 20th anniversary of Seoul
National University, October 13-18, 1966). Seoul,
1966. [243] p. illus., plates. 21 cm.
Korean. DLC,MH-HY. Annotation in English also
added at end.
                                        MHY,DLC.
Bibliography--catalogs--Korea. Rare books.
Incunabula--Bibliography.

11291   akor   sokor   b O n   1967
        Yi, Hyŏn-jong, ed. Han'guksa yŏn'gu nonmun
ch'ong mongnok, 1900-1966 (Catalog of research
treatises on Korean history 1900-1966). [Ed. by]
Yi Hyŏn-jong [and] Yi Man-su. Seoul, Taehan
Min'guk Kukhoe Tosŏgwan, 1967. 191 p. 26 cm.
Korean-Japanese. HU-E,MH-HY.
                                        MHY,S.
Bibliography. 175.00   660.00   650.00   648.00
423.00   700.00   870.00   670.00   560.00   580.00
590.00   600.00   620.00   764.04   756.00   769.04
770.00   775.00   346.00   103.00   530.00   213.00
159.04   576.00   644.00   204.00   185.00   130.00
643.00   183.00   840.00   527.00   825.00   765.00
526.00   643.00   Women.   Confucianism.   Buddhism.
Christianity. Dolmen. Classics. Rare books.
Bullfight. Kwagŏ. Yangban. Hyangga. Paekchŏng.
Mudang. Mŏsŭm. Taejanggyŏng. Hallyang.
Han'gŭl. Ondol. Chuldarigi. Bibliography--1900-
1966.

11292   akor   sokor   b O ye184519101966
        Yi, Yong-hŭi, 1917-, ed. Kŭnse Han'guk
oegyo munsŏ ch'ongmok oegukp'yŏn (Catalog of
foreign diplomatic documents relating to Korea,
1845-1910). Ed. by Lee Yong-Hee. Seoul, Taehan

Min'guk Kukhoe Tosŏgwan, 1966. 19, 1,268 p. 26
cm.
Korean. MH-HY.
                                             MHY.
Bibliography. Intercultural relations--
Bibliography. 110.00

11293 akor   sokor   b O n   1966
       Sŏul Taehakkyo. Tosŏgwan. Ilsa Karam Mun'go
koso chŏja mongnok [An author catalog of rare
books of the Ilsa and Garam collections in Seoul
National University Library). Seoul, Sŏul
Taehakkyo Pusok Tosŏgwan, 1966. 344 p. 26 cm.
Korean. DLC,MH-HY.
                                             MHY.
Bibliography--catalogs--Korea. Ilsa and Garam
Collections. Seoul National University Library.
Pang, Chong-hyŏn. Yi, Pyŏng-gi. Ilsa and Garam
Collections. Seoul National University Library.
Sŏul Taehakkyo. 110.00 530.00 190.00 175.00
159.04 821.00 648.00 313.00 576.00 185.00
590.00 Rare bcoks. Classics. Religion.
Confucianism. Polity. Literature (Chinese)--
Bibliography.

11423 aeng   sokor   b O n   1967
       Chŏn, Munam. An index to English periodical
literature published in Korea, 1945-1966. Seoul,
Korean Research Center, 1967.
English.
                                          Yang'68.
Bibliography--index. Periodicals--Indexes.
Indexes. Bibliography--1945-1966.

11424 aeng   sokor   b O n   1967
       Murphey, Sunny. Koreana Collection (as of 1
April 1967). Seoul, Yongsan Special Services
Library, 1967. 77 p.
English. HRAF. Annotated bibliography of books
in English about Korea. Copies may be available
from the compiler, Librarian of the Yongsan
Special Services Library, 19th General Support
Group (USA Yongsan District) APD San Francisco,
96031.
                                Yang'68,BAS'67.
Bibliography--catalogs--Korea. Yongsan Special
Service Library. 291.00 576.00 205.00 647.00
204.00 214.00 159.04 457.02 183.00 538.00
190.00 815.00 241.00 252.00 530.00 161.00
113.02 217.00 870.00 Korean War.

11425   aeng   sokor   b   0   n   1967
         Steele, Marion.   Subject index to periodical
material on Korea in the Yongsan Special Services
Library.   Seoul, Yongsan Special Services Library,
1967. 68 p.
English.   HRAF. A subject index to articles in
English periodicals published in Korea, 1955-1966.
Copies may be available from the Yongsan Special
Services Library.
                                  Yang'68,BAS'67.
Bibliography--index.   Bibliography--catalogs--
Korea.   Yongsan Special Services Library.   700.00
726.00   450.00   159.06   842.00   640.00   162.00
530.00   217.01   190.00   423.00   439.00   369.00
457.00   722.00   590.00   527.00   290.00   252.00
251.00   524.00   377.00   547.00   228.00   186.04
824.00   464.00   743.00   485.01   390.00   426.00
204.00   580.00   702.00   551.00   736.01   344.01
812.00   625.00   660.00   650.00   160.00   200.00
496.00   643.00   526.00   455.00   346.00   764.00
484.00   871.00   546.00   110.00   554.06   Religion.
Education.   Law.   Economic conditions.   Blood
bank.   Business.   Ginseng.   Glass.   Dental
education.   Communism.   Bamboo.

11427   akor   sokor   b   0   n   1967
         Kukhoe Tosŏgwan.   Miguk esŏ suyŏdoen
Han'gugin paksarok   [List of doctorates received
in the U.S. by Koreans].   Seoul, 1967.
Korean.
                                  Yang'67.
Bibliography--dissertations.

11436   akor   sokor   h   0   n   1967
         Yi, Ki-baek, 1924-. Han'guksa sillon [New
discussion on Korean history].   Seoul, Ilchogak,
1967. 13, 465 p. illus., maps. 21 cm.
Korean.   MH-HY.   Bibliographical footnotes.
Bibliography: p. 407-439.   Revised and enlarged
ed. of the author's work under title: Kuksa
sillon.   Royal genealogical charts: p. 440-447.
                                  MHY.
History.   Sociocultural pattern--Bibliography.
Polity.   Economy.   Intercultural relations.
110.00   538.00   190.00   172.00   640.00   670.00
567.00   530.00   181.04   Conflict.   Patriarchy.
Buddhism.   Confucianism.   Slavery.   Agriculture.
Farmers.   Music.   Arts.   Alphabet.   Christianity--
Roman Catholicism.   Genealogy, royal.   Biography.

Social stratification. Sociocultural change.
Yangban. Hanmun.

11437 aeng   usa   b 0 n   1965
    Chung, Yong-Sun. Publications on Korea in
the era of political revolutions, 1959-1963; a
selected bibliography. Compiled with introduction
by Yong-Sun Chung. Kalamazoo, Mich., 1965. 10,
117 p. 27 cm. (Korea Research and Publication,
Inc. Monographic series on Korea, 2)
English. CtY,DLC,HU-E,MH-HY,MH-W. On mounted
label on t.p.: Distributed by the Cellar Book
Shop, Detroit, Michigan. On cover: Korea: a
selected bibliography, 1959-63. Issued also as
thesis (M.S. in Library Science)--Washington,
D.C., Catholic University of America. Thesis
title: a selected bibliography on Korea, 1959-
1963. A sequal to The Reference Guide to Korean
Materials, 1945-59, by K. P. Yang.
                                        S,CtY.
Sociocultural pattern--Bibliography. Polity.
Economy. Biography. Bibliography--1959-1963.

11440 ajap   kor   b 0 n   1911
    Tokio, Shunjo, comp. Chōsen kosho mokuroku
[A classified catalog of old Korean books].
Seoul, Chōsen Kosho Kankōkai, 1911. 30, 245 p.
23 cm.
Japanese. CtY,DLC,MH-HY. Introduction: p. 1-30,
contains analytical essays on old Korean books.
                            S,LCF'50,DLC.
Bibliography--bibliographic essay. Polity--
Bibliography. Law--Bibliography. Literature--
Bibliography. Religion and philosophy--
Bibliography. 175.00 130.00 110.00 533.00
765.00 190.00 144.00 577.00 821.00 870.00
Classics. Economy. Confucianism. Buddhism.
Taoism. Ethnoscience. Arts. Industry. Welfare.
Medicine. Military. Agriculture. Rare books.

"A catalog of old Korean books (i.e., Korean
imprints in Chinese-style bindings), classified
into classics, history and geography, government
and laws, philosophy, and literature. The
introduction, pp. 1-30, contains a brief
description of analytical essays on old Korean
books." LCF'50.

11441 akor   sokor   b 0 n   1965
    Kungnip Chungang Tosŏgwan. Seoul, Korea, ed.

Taehan Min'guk ch'ulp'anmul ch'ong mongnok, 1963-
1964 (Korean national bibliography, 1963-1964).
Seoul, Kungnip Chungang Tosŏgwan, 1965. 225 p.
26 cm.
Korean. HRAF,MH-HY. Preceded by Han'guk sŏmok,
1945-1962. Index; p. 129-225.
                                                    S.
Bibliography. Bibliography--1963-1964.

11442 akor   sokor   b 0 n   1966
       Kungnip Chungang Tosŏgwan. Seoul, Korea, ed.
Taehan Min'guk ch'ulp'anmul ch'ong mongnok, 1965
(Korean national bibliography, 1965). Seoul,
Kungnip Chungang Tosŏgwan, 1966. 119 p. 26 cm.
Korean. HRAF. Index, p. 77-119.
                                                    S.
Bibliography. 110.00 Bibliography--1965.

11443 aeng   usa   b 0 n   1955
       Eells, Walter Crosby, comp. The literature
of Japanese education, 1945-1954. Hamden,
Connecticut, The Shoe String Press, 1955.
English. CtY. Scattered references on Korea.
                                                    S.
Education--Bibliography. Japanese education.
Bibliography--1945-1954.

11445 feng   sokor   b 0 n   1967
       Kungnip Chungang Tosŏgwan. [Publication
list of the Central National Library, April 17,
1967]. Seoul, 1967. 19 p.
English-Korean. Short English explanations and
original titles (in parentheses) are given.
                                                    S.
Bibliography.

11446 xeng   usa   b 0 n   1966
       Yoo, Young Hyun. A selected bibliography of
materials on Korean economy. In Joseph Sang-hoon
Chung, ed. Korea: patterns of economic
development. Kalamazoo, Mich., 1966: 201-241.
English. DLC.
                                                    S.
Economy--Bibliography. 433.00 474.00 241.00
439.00 466.00 652.00 Economic history.
Economic geography. Bibliography. Economic
conditions--Bibliography. Economics--
Bibliography. Korea (D.P.R.K.) --Economic
conditions--Bibliography.

"This bibliography was compiled from the materials
available in the Korean Section of the Library of
Congress. The compiler attempted to include in
this bibliography all the available, important
research sources on North and South Korean
economy. No annotation is made, but, for an easy
reference, the materials are classified into the
following categories: I) Yearbooks and handbooks;
II) Statistics; III) Reports, collected works,
conference documents, etc.; IV) Periodicals; V)
Economic history; VI) Economic geography; VII)
Survey on Korean economic conditions; VIII)
Economic policy and reconstruction; IX)
Cooperatives; X) Agriculture; XI) Industry; XII)
Industrial management; XIII) Foreign trade; XIV)
Foreign aid; XV) Public finance, money and
banking; XVI) Labor relations. The call number of
The Library of Congress is given where it is
available." Yoo'66.

11447   ajap   japan   b 0 n   1961
        Nihon Minzokugaku Kyokai, ed.   Minzokugaku
kankei zasshi ronbun sōmokuroku, 1925-1959
[Bibliography of Japanese articles in ethnology,
1925-1959]. Tokyo, Seibundō Shinkōsha, 1961. 199
p.
Japanese. Korea: p. 177-178.
                                                S.
Religion and philosophy--Bibliography. 190.00
110.00 Recreation. Shamanism. Butchers.
Ethnology. Social groupings. Bibliography--1925-
1959.

11448   akor   sokor   b 0 n   1966
        Kukhoe Tosŏgwan. Seoul, Korea. Sasŏguk,   ed.
Han'guk sinmun chapchi ch'ongmongnok 1883-1945
[Catalog of Korean newspapers and periodicals,
1883-1945]. Seoul, Taehan Min'guk Kukhoe
Tosŏgwan, 1966. 8, 230 p. facsims. 22 cm.
Korean. DLC,MH-HY,WaU-FE. On verso of t.p.:
Catalog of Korean periodicals, 1883-1945. In
preface: comp. by Yang Ki-baek and Kim Kŭn-su.
        CONTENTS.- 1. Catalog of the
magazines in Korea.- 2. Catalog of magazines,
published outside of Korea.- 3. Catalog of the
newspapers.- 4. Chronology of the Korean
magazines. Supplement, 219-230.
                        MHY,WaU,S.
Bibliography--periodicals. 110.00 369.00 530.00
204.00 190.00 870.00 175.00 750.00 185.00

668.00 590.00 648.00 Periodicals. Polity.
Religion. Economy. Children. Ethnography.
Communism. Trade. Technology. Women.
Periodicals--Bibliography. Newspapers--
Bibliography. Bibliography--1883-1945. Yi
dynasty. Japanese Occupation.

11450 akor   sokor   b 0 n   1956
    Sŏul Taehakkyo. Ch'ulp'um tosŏ haesŏl (An
annotated list of rare books exhibited in
commemoration cf the tenth anniversary of Seoul
National University, October 13-17, 1956). Seoul,
1956. 95 p.
Korean-English. HRAF. Sŏul Taehakkyo kaegyo
sipchunyŏn kinyŏm ko tosŏ chŏnsihoe, siwŏl 13-17,
1956.
                                        S,SNU'56.
Bibliography. 648.00 History. Ethnography.
Intercultural relations. Travelers' accounts.
Religion. Archeology. Communications. Law.
Diaries. Administration. Literature.
Institutions. Marriage. Maps. Etiquette.

11451 akor   sokor   b 0 n   1966
    Pak, Tong-sŏ. Han'guk haengjŏng munhŏnjip,
1945-1966 (Bibliography of Korean public
administration, 1945-1966). [Ed. by] Bark Dong-suh
and Yoon Jai-pcong. Seoul, National University
Ch'ulp'anbu, 1966. 78 p.
Korean. HRAF.
                                                S.
Law--Bibliography. Polity--Bibliography . 177.00
173.00 655.00 652.00 647.00 625.00 648.00
369.00 624.00 870.00 620.00 630.00 175.00
489.00 744.00 666.00 Statistics.
Communications. Community development.
Government, Local. Administration, Local. Public
administration. Korean War. Kwagŏ.
Bibliography--1945-1966.

11452 aeng   usa   b 0 n   1962
    Harvard University. Library. Harvard-Yenching
Library. A classified catalog of Korean books in
the Harvard-Yenching Institute Library at Harvard
University. Cambridge, Massachusetts, 1962. 3,
194 l. 29 cm.
Korean-English. DLC,HRAF,HU-E,MH-HY,MH-W.
                                                S.
Bibliography--catalogs--U.S.A. Sociocultural
pattern--Bibliography. Harvard-Yenching Library.

779.00   812.00   172.00   159.04   175.00   130.00
433.00   670.00   871.00   190.00   538.00   204.00
Classics.   Sociology.   Polity.   Arts.

11453   aeng   usa   b   0   n   1966
        Harvard University. Library. Harvard-Yenching
Library.   A classified catalog of Korean books in
the Harvard-Yenching Library Harvard University.
V.2.   Cambridge, Massachusetts, 1966.   3, 225, 129
p.   28 cm.
Korean-English.   HRAF,MH-HY.   Author index p. A1-
A43 and title index p. A47-A129.
                                                        S.
Bibliography--catalogs--U.S.A.   Sociocultural
pattern--Biblicgraphy.   Harvard-Yenching Library.
779.00   812.00   172.00   159.04   175.00   130.00
433.00   670.00   871.00   190.00   538.00   204.00
Classics.   Sociology.   Polity.   Arts.

11558   feng   usa   b   0   n   1969
        Park, Yung-ja.   Korean publications in
series: a subject bibliography.   [Washington,
D.C.] [1969?].
English.   Thesis (Library Science) -- Catholic
University of America.
                                              Yang'68.
Bibliography.   110.00

11559   feng   usa   b   0   n   1969
        Row, Soon Myong Kim.   A checklist of Korean
periodicals, 1945-1966.   [Washington, D.C.]
[1969?].
English.   Thesis (Library Science) -- Catholic
University of America.
                                              Yang'68.
Bibliography.   110.00   Periodicals.   Bibliography-
-1945-1966.

11560   feng   usa   b   0   n   0000
        Yu, Hyŏn-suk.   Index to Korea, Japanese and
Chinese acquisitions reported in the Quarterly
Journal of the Library of Congress, 1943-1968.
[Washington, D.C.] [n.d.].
English.   Thesis (Library Science) -- Catholic
University of America.
                                              Yang'68.
Bibliography--index.   110.00   Bibliography--1943-
1968.

11566   akor   sokor   b   0   n   1962
        Tongguk Taehakkyo. Seoul, Korea. Tosogwan

Kosŏ mongnok chipsŏng [Catalog of Korean rare
books]. Seoul, Tongguk Taehakkyo/Tosŏgwan, 1962.
7, 338 p. 26 cm.
Korean. DLC,HU-E,MH-HY.
                                         DLC,Nunn'67.
Bibliography--catalogs--Korea. Tongguk Taehakkyo.
190.00 538.00 175.00 Rare books. Library
Catalogs--Bibliography.

11569 akor   sokor   b 0 n   1962
      Korea (Republic) Kongbobu. Kongboguk.
Chŏnggi kanhaengmul silt'ae illam   [Directory of
Korean periodicals and newspapers]. Seoul,
Kongbobu Kongboguk, [1962]. 31, 1,053 p. 26 cm.
Korean. DLC,HU-E,MH-HY.
                                    MHY,Nunn'67.
Bibliography--periodicals. 204.00

11572 ajap   kor   b 0 jc   1931
      Chōsen Keizai Kenkyūjo. Chōsen tōkei sōran
[An annotated bibliography of statistics and
statistical works concerning Korea]. [By] Shikata
Hiroshi, et al. Seoul, 1931. 747 (i.e. 749) p.
26 cm.
Japanese. NNC.
                              LCF'50,Nunn'67.
Bibliography. Economy--Bibliography. Statistics.
Administration. Statistics--Bibliography.
Economic conditions--Bibliography.

"This work is the basic index to the great volume
of statistical materials relating to Korea which
was published under Japanese auspices. The
introduction tc the volume is a bibliographical
discussion of these statistics, treating their
history and compilation. The main portion of the
work is a detailed classified index to statistical
tables recording all aspects of Korean economy and
administration." LCF'50.

11573 aeng   usa   b 0 mi   1964
      Blanchard, Carroll Henry, Jr. Korean War
bibliography and maps of Korea. [Albany] Korean
Conflict Research Foundation [1964]. 4, 181 p.
25 maps. 28 cm.
English. CtY,DLC,HU-E,MH-W.
                                    S,BAS'64,DLC.
Conflict--Bibliography. Intercultural relations--
Bibliography. 720.00 710.00 700.00 727.05
723.05 Maps. Korean War.

11590   aeng   usa   b 2 m   1964
     Kyriak, Theodore E., comp. and ed. North
Korea 1957-1961: a bibliography and guide to
contents of a collection of United States Joint
Publications Research Service translations on
microfilm. Annapolis, Research and Microfilm
Publications, [1964]. 1 v. 22 x 28 cm.
English. DLC,NUC,IaU. Index to the issues from
July 1962 on are continued in the compiler's Asian
developments.
                              BAS'64,Yang'67.
Bibliography. 113.02 Democratic People's
Republic of Korea. Eccnomic conditions--
Bibliography. Politics and government--
Bibliography. Social conditions--Bibliography.
Periodicals--Indexes. Indexes.

11654   akor   sokor   b 0 n   1967
     Kyŏngbuk Taehakkyo. Kyŏngbuk Taehakkyo sŏksa
nonmun palch'wejip (Kyŏngbuk University bulletin:
abstracts of master's theses). [Taegu], Kyŏngbuk
Taehakkyo/Taehagwŏn, 1967. 115, 21 p. 19 cm.
Korean-English. DLC,HRAF.
                              S,DLC.
Bibliography. 113.02 Dissertations, Academic--
Abstracts.

11656   aeng   usa   b 0 n   1967
     Nunn, Godfrey Raymond, 1918-. East Asia: a
bibliography of bibliographies. Honolulu, East-
West Center Library, University of Hawaii, 1967.
10, 92 l. 28 cm. (Occasional papers of East-West
Center Library, 7)
English. CtY,DLC,HRAF. Korea: p. 57-65, 78-79.
List of titles in Chinese, Japanese, and Korean
characters: p. 67-79. Index to authors and
titles.
                                             S.
Bibliography--Bibliographies. 113.02
Bibliographies.

11726   akor   sokor   b 0 n   1954
     Yi, Hong-jik, 1909-. Han'guk ko-munhwa
non'go (Studies on the ancient culture of Korea).
By Hong-jik Lee. Seoul, Ŭryu Munhwasa, 1954.
[10], 276 p. illus. 21 cm. (Han'guk munhwa
ch'ongsŏ, 14)
Korean. CtY,CU-E,DLC,MH-HY,MiU,WaU-FE. Table of

contents in English. List of old Korean
publications in Japanese libraries: p. 166-238.
Knez'68,CUE.
Archeology. Visual arts--painting. Kyŏngju.
172.00 110.00 764.05 532.00

"Deals with three topics: First, Koryo fresco
found in a tomb near Seoul; Second and third
topics are concerned on bibliographic studies of
Korean treasures and books which were brought to
Japan during the Hideyoshi invasion at the end of
the 16th century; and also libraries where the
Korean books were kept in Japan. This is an
important work in the study of Korean books."
Yang'60.

11760 zrus   ussr   b 0 n   1965
        Kontsevich, L. P. Pervyĭ pamiatnik koreĭskoĭ
pis'mennosti. In Narody Azii i Afriki, 4 (1965):
160-173.
Russian.
                                            BAS'65.
Bibliography. 110.00

11761 xeng   usa   b 0 me195019531965
        Lee, Chong-sik. Korea and the Korean War. In
Thomas T. Hammond, ed. Soviet foreign relations
and world communism: a selected, annotated
bibliography. Princeton, Princeton University
Press, 1965: 787-806.
English.
                                            BAS'65.
Conflict--Bibliography. 113.02 720.00 Korean
War.

11787 aeng   sokor   b 0 n   1962
        Han'guk Yŏn'gu Tosŏgwan. Seoul, Korea List
of the Korean Research Center Koreana collection:
in commemoration of sixth anniversary. [Ed. by
Chon Dong]. Seoul, Korean Research Center, 1962.
103 p.
English-Korean. DLC.
                                            BAS'62.
Bibliography--catalogs--Korea. Korean Research
Center. Koreana Collection. 110.00 Library
catalogs.

11788 arus   ussr   b 0 n   1963
        Petrova, Ql'ga Petrovna. Opisanie
pis'mennykh pamiatnikov koreĭskoĭ kultury v.2.

Moscow, Izd-vo vostochnoĭ lit-ry, 1963. 138 p.
10 facsims.
Russian. At head of title: Akademiia nauk SSSR.
Institut narodov Azii.
                                          BAS'63.
Bibliography--catalogs--U.S.S.R. Leningrad State
University. Oriental Institute. 110.00

11795 aeng   gtbr   b 0 me195019531960
      Great Britain. Imperial War Museum. Library.
The war in Korea, 1950-1953: a list of selected
references. [London, 1960?]. 9, 11 p.
English. Part I: British Commonwealth
publications; Part II: Foreign publications.
                                          BAS'62.
Conflict--Bibliography. 110.00 720.00 Korean
War.

11832 aeng   usa   b 0 n   1950
      Tewksbury, Donald G., comp. and ed. Source
materials on Korean politics and ideologies. New
York, Institute of Pacific Relations, 1950. 190
p. (Source books on Far Eastern political
ideologies, 2)
English.
                                      Ehrman'67.
Polity--Bibliography. Political ideology.

11834 aeng   usa   b 0 n   1967
      Ehrman, Edith. Preliminary bibliography on
East Asia for undergraduate libraries. By Edith
Ehrman and Ward Morehouse. New York, University
of the State of New York, State Education Dept.,
Center for International Programs and Services,
Foreign Area Materials Center, 1967. 10, 475 p.
English. HRAF. Korea: p. 224-239. Compiled
pursuant to a contract with the United States
Department of Health, Education, and Welfare,
Office of Education, under the provisions of Title
VI, Public Law 85-864, as amended, Section 602.
                                              S.
Bibliography.

11846 aeng   sokor   b 0 n   1967
      Incunabula exhibit: Korean movable type.
Seoul, Yongsan Special Services Library, 1967. 20
l.
English. HRAF.
                                              S.
Bibliography. 213.00 Rare books. Bibliography--
1420-1858.

11849   akor   sokor   b 0 n   1966
      Kukhoe Tosŏgwan. Seoul, Korea,   ed. Chŏngbu
kanhaengmul mongnok (Government publications in
Korea, 1948-1965). Seoul, Taehan Min'guk Kukhoe
Tosŏgwan [1966]. 58 p. 26 cm.
Korean. CU-E,DLC,MH-HY,WaU-FE.
                             MHY,DLC,CUE.
Bibliography. 110.00 214.00 Government
publications--Bibliography. Catalogs. Official
publications--Bibliography. Bibliography--1948-
1965.

11852   aeng   usa   b 0 n   1968
      Koh, Hesung Chun. Social science resources
on Korea: a preliminary computerized bibliography.
New Haven, Human Relations Area Files, 1968. 2 v.
(1) 146 p. (2) 4, 217 p.
English. HRAF. Contains approximately 2,000
entries, extensively indexed and annotated, on all
aspects of Korean culture.
                                              S.
Sociocultural pattern--Bibliography.   113.02
Sociocultural change.

11853   aeng   usa   b 0 n   1969
      Human Relations Area Files. HRAF source
bibliography. [Prepared by Joan Steffens and
Timothy J. O'Leary]. New Haven, Human Relations
Area Files, 1969. [543] p.
English. HRAF. Korea: p. 15-19. Lists the
sources analyzed for the HRAF Files. All are
English texts cr translations into English. 55
sources on Korea.
                                              S.
Sociocultural pattern--Bibliography.   110.00

11854   ajap   kor   b 0 n   1935
      Chōsen Sōtokufu Tosho-kan, ed. Chōsen kosho
shōkai [Biblicgraphy of old Korean books]. [n.p.]
1935.
Japanese.
                                       Paek'69.
Bibliography. Classics.

11855   ajap   kor   b 0 n   1935
      Chōsenshi Henshūkai, ed. Chōsen shiryō
shūshin oyobi kaisetsu   [Collection of Korean
historical materials and interpretation]. Seoul,

                        289

Chōsen Sōtokufu, 1935-1937. 9 facsims. 26 cm.
Korean-Japanese. DLC,MH-HY.
                                    Paek'68,MHY.
History--Bibliography.

11856 ajap   kor   b 0 n   1933
       Kusuda, Onosaburō. Chōsen Tenshukyō shi ni
kansuru omonaru sankō shoseki oyobi rombun
[Leading reference books and theses on Korean
Catholic church history]. Pusan, 1933.
Japanese.
                                    Paek'69.
Religion and philosophy--Bibliography. 797.00
Christianity--Roman Catholicism.

11857 ajap   kor   b 0 n   1934
       Kusuda, Onosaburō. Chōsen Tenshukyō shi ni
kansuru omonaru sankō chosho oyobi rombun
[Leading reference books and theses on Korean
Catholic church history]. Pusan, 1934.
Japanese.
                                    Paek'69.
Religion and philosophy--Bibliography. 797.00
Christianity--Roman Catholicism.

11858 ajap   japan   b 0 n   1928
       Ōta, Akira, 1884-. Kan-kan shiseki ni
arawaretaru Nik-Kan kōdaishi shiryō [Korean-
Japanese ancient historical materials which were
found in Chinese-Korean history sources]. Tokyo,
1924. 187 p. 21 cm.
Japanese. MH-HY.
                                    S,Paek'68.
History--Bibliography.

11859 ajap   b 0 n   1911
       Asami, Rintarō. Chōsen no geibun-shi
[Korean art and literature]. [n.p.] 1911. 1
facsims.
Japanese.
                                    Paek'68.
Literature--Bibliography. Arts.

11860 aeng   usa   r 0 ne 37219661969
       Seo, Kyung-bo. A study of Korean Zen
Buddhism approached through the Chodangjip.
Walnut Creek, California, Cho Ke Mountain Zendo,
[1969]. 421 p. 8 diagrs.
English. HRAF. Dissertation (Philosophy) --
Philadelphia, Temple University. Bibliography: p.

412-421 (mimeographed supplement).
                                              S.
Religion and philosophy, 171.00 177.00 795.00
159.04 110.00 Buddhism. Chodangjip. Zen.
Chogye. Silla. Koryŏ. Yi dynasty.

11885 akor   sokor   b 0 n   1964
    Yi, Pyŏng-mok. Han'guk ŭi taehak chŏnggi
kanhaengmul pu-kodŭng kyoyuk kigwan myonggam
[Bibliography of University periodicals of Korea,
1945-1964, with directory of institutions of
higher education]. Seoul, Yŏnse Taehakkyo
Tosogwanhak-kwa, 1964. 265 p. 26 cm.
Korean. CU-E. English abstract: p. 263-265.
English table of content.
                                            CUE.
Bibliography--periodicals. Education. 110.00
Bibliography--1945-1964.

11888 ajap   kor   b 0 n   0000
    Chōsen Sōtokufu Chōsenshi Henshū-kai.
Chōsen shiryō tenkan mokuroku [The exhibition
lists on Korean historical data]. Seoul, Chōsen
Sotokufu [n.d.].
Japanese. CU-E.
                                            CUE.
History--Bibliography. 110.00

11891 aeng   japan   b 0 n   1907
    Wenckstern, Friedrich von, comp.
Bibliography of the Japanese empire; being a
classified list of the literature in European
Languages relating to Dai Nihon (Great Japan)
published in Europe, America and in the East. V.2.
Comprising the literature from 1894 to the middle
of 1906 (27-39th year of Meiji) with additions and
corrections to the first volume and a Supplement
to Léon Pagès' Bibliographie japonaise. Added is a
list of the Swedish literature on Japan, by Miss
Valfrid Palmgren. Tokyo [etc.] Maruzen Kabushiki
kaisha (Z. P. Maruya and Co., Ltd.), 1907. [551]
p.
English. CU-E,DLC. Includes scattered references
on Korea.
                                          LCW'50.
Bibliography. 110.00 Bibliography--1894-1906.

11898 aeng   usa   b 0 nc150019001970
    Fang, Chao-ying. The Asami Library: a
descriptive catalog. Ed. by Elizabeth Huff.

Berkeley, University of California Press, 1970.
496 p. illus.
English. HRAF.
                                          S.
Bibliography--catalogs--U.S.A. History. Asami
Library. University of California (Berkeley).
113.02 814.01 159.04 Biography.

"The Asami Library of Korean literature, named for
the Japanese scholar who assembled it early in
this century and now a part of the East Asiatic
Library of the University of California, Berkeley,
includes approximately one thousand titles written
or printed in almost four thousand volumes between
the sixteenth and twentieth centuries. Most of the
works are in Chinese, which throughout the period
was the literary language of Korea, and some are
editions of Chinese classics. In addition to the
bibliographical data usually provided in such
catalogues, Mr. Fang's annotation includes
elaborate biographical and historical information
so wide ranging and precise that the work may be
described as a significant contribution to Korean
historiography." UC Press.

11899 akor   sokor   b 0 n   1963
      Kim, Kŭn-su.   Chosŏn tosŏ mongnok [A list
of Korean books]. Seoul, 1963.   326 p.
Korean.
                                        WH'68.
Bibliography--catalogs--Korea.

11900 akor   sokor   b 0 n   1961
      Kosŏ chŏnsi mongnok [A list of old books on
exhibition--Sungmyŏng Women's University]. Seoul,
Sungmyŏng Yŏja Taehakkyo, 1961.   34 p.
Korean.
                                        WH'68.
Bibliography--catalogs--Korea. Sungmyŏng Women's
University.

11901 akor   sokor   b 0 n   1957
      Chŏn'guk tosŏgwan illam [A nation-wide list
of libraries]. Seoul, Han'guk Tosŏgwan Hyŏphoe,
1957.
Korean.
                                        WH'68.
Bibliography--catalogs--Korea.

11902 akor   sokor   b 0 n   1967
      Sŏksa hagwi nonmun mongnok, 1956-1966   [A

list of M.A. theses, 1956-1966]. Seoul, Yŏnse
Taehakkyo, 1967. 48 p.
Korean.

WH'68.
Bibliography--dissertations. Bibliography--1954-
1966.

11903 akor   b 0 n   1840
     Kakto ch'aekp'an mongnok [A list of wood-
block printed books in each province]. [n.p.]
1840.
Korean.
                                       WH'68.
Bibliography--catalogs--Korea. 213.05

11904 akor   sokor b 0 n   1966
     Haengjŏnghak sŏksa hagwi nomun chemok   [A
list of the theses in administrative science for
the M.A. degree]. Seoul, Sŏul Taehakkyo, 1966.
26 p.
Korean.
                                       WH'68.
Bibliography--dissertations. Polity--
Bibliography.

11905 akor   sokor b 0 n   1966
     Sŏk Paksa hagwi nonmun chemok chip [A
catalog of M.A. theses and doctoral
dissertations]. Seoul, Sŏul Taehakkyo, 1966. 115
p.
Korean.
                                       WH'68.
Bibliography--dissertations.

11906 akor   sokor b 0 n   1966
     Chŏnsi tosŏ mongnok [A list of books on
exhibition--Secul National University]. Seoul,
Sŏul Taehakkyo, 1966. 146 p.
Korean. English translation included.
                                       WH'68.
Bibliography--catalogs--Korea.

11907 akor   sokor b 0 n   1956
     Ko-tosŏ chŏnsihoe ch'ulp'um tosŏ haesŏl [An
annotated bibliography of books put on exhibition
by the Old Book Exhibition Association]. Seoul,
Sŏul Taehakkyo Tosŏgwan, 1956. 95 p.
Korean.
                                       WH'68.
Bibliography--catalogs--Korea. 113.02

11913 ajap   japan   b 0 n   1958
      Naikaku Bunko Kanseki bunrui mokuroku [A
classified catalog of Korean books in the National
Diet Library]. Tokyo, 1958.
Japanese.
                                          WH'68.
Bibliography--catalogs--Japan. Naikaku Bunko.
National Diet Library.

11914 ajap   kor   b 0   1942
      Chōsen-nai hakkō shinbunshi ichiranhyō [A
catalog of newspapers published in Korea]. Seoul,
Chōsen Sōtokufu, Keimukyoku, 1942.
Japanese.
                                          WH'68.
Bibliography--periodicals. 204.01

11915 ajap   japan   b 0 n   1963
      Kichōsho maikurofirumu mokuroku [A list of
microfilm copies of valuable books]. Tokyo, 1963.
Japanese.
                                          WH'68.
Bibliography--catalogs--Japan. Seikadō Bunko.
Sonkeikaku Bunko.

11916 aeng   usa   b 0 n   1967
      Denney, Ruth N., tr. Selections from "The
holdings in Oriental Studies in the great
libraries of the Soviet Union. Articles and
notes". Honolulu, East-West Center, 1967. 155 p.
English.
                                          WH'68.
Bibliography--cat₋logs--U.S.S.R.

11917 xeng   ussr   b 0 n   1967
      Kim, G. F. Works of Soviet orientalists on
the history and economics of Korea. By G. F. Kim
and G. D. Tyagai. In Papers presented by the USSR
delegation, XXV International Congress of
Orientalists. Moscow, Oriental Literature
Publishing House, 1960: 18.
English.
                                          WH'68.
Economy--Biblicgraphy. History--Bibliography.
Korean Studies in U.S.S.R.--Bibliography.

11928 afren   fran   b 0 n   1902
      Courant, Maurice (Auguste Louis Marie), 1865-

1939. Catalogue des livres chinois, coréens, japonais. Paris, 1902-1912. 3 v.
French. Contains ca. 9,080 entries.
WH'68.
Bibliography--catalogs--France. Bibliothèque Nationale.

11933 aeng usa b 0 n 1904
Books in the Brooklyn Public Library on the Far East, China, Japan, Korea, Manchuria, Russia and Siberia. New York, 1904. 8 p.
English.
Gompertz'63.
Bibliography--catalogs--U.S.A. Brooklyn Public Library.

11935 aeng usa b 0 n 1926
Taylor, Louise Marion. Catalog of books on China in the Essex Institute, Salem, Mass., U.S.A. Salem, Massachusetts, 1926. 392 p.
English. Korea: p. 105-108, 233-234, 316.
Gompertz'63.
Bibliography--catalogs--U.S.A. Essex Institute. Salem, Mass.

11936 aeng japan b 0 n 1924
Catalog of the Asiatic library of Dr. G. E. Morrison (now a part of the Oriental Library, Tokyo, Japan). Tokyo, 1924. 2 v. 802, 551 p.
English.
Gompertz'63.
Bibliography--catalogs--Japan. Tōyō Bunkō.

11937 aeng kor b 0 n 1927
Catalog of the foreign books in the Government-General Library, Seoul, Korea. Seoul, 1927. 147 p.
English. Korea: p. 114-116.
Gompertz'63.
Bibliography--catalogs--Korea. Government-General Library.

11939 aeng gtbr b 0 n 1906
General index to the first twenty volumes of the Geographical Journal: 1893-1902. London, 1906. 629 p.
English. Korea: p. 343-344.
Gompertz'63.
Bibliography--index. Physical setting--geography.
Bibliography--1893-1902.

11940   aeng   gtbr   b 0 n   1925
         General index to the second twenty volumes of
the Geographical Journal 1903-1912. London, 1925.
25, 688 p.
English. Korea: p. 378-379.
                                      Gompertz'63.
Bibliography--index. Physical setting--geography.
Bibliography--1903-1912.

11943   aeng   usa   b 0 n   1904
         U.S. Library of Congress. Select list of
books (with reference to periodicals) relating to
the Far East. Compiled under the direction of
Appleton Prentiss Clark Griffin, Chief
Bibliographer. Washington, D.C., 1904. 74 p.
English.
                                      Gompertz'63.
Bibliography.

11945   aeng   gtbr   b 0 n   1963
         British Museum. London. [Department of
Oriental Printed Books and Manuscripts]. Title
index to the descriptive catalog of Chinese
manuscripts from Tunhuang in the British Museum.
By E. D. Grinstead. London, British Museum, 1963
[i.e. 1964]. 41 p.
English.
                                      Silberman'62.
Bibliography--catalogs--Great Britain. British
Museum. London. Department of Oriental Printed
Books and Manuscripts.

11946   aeng   usa   b 0 n   1960
         U.S. National Archives. Preliminary
inventory of the records of the Headquarters,
United Nations Command (Record Group). Compiled by
Paul Taborn and Andrew Putignano. Washington,
D.C., 1960. 5, 7 p. 27 cm. (Its Publication,
61-2. Preliminary inventories, 127)
English. DLC.
                                      Chŏng'66.
Bibliography--catalogs--U.S.A. U.S. National
Archives.

11948   fkor   kor   b 0 n   0000
         Sŏ, Myŏng-ŭng, 1716-1787, comp. Kyujang
ch´ongmok 4 kwŏn [Catalog of the Chinese
collection in the Royal Library, Kyujanggak].
[n.p.] [n.d.]. 3 v.

Korean. CU-E.
Fang'70.
Bibliography--catalogs--Korea. Kyujanggak.

11949 akor   kor   b 0 n   1911
Odaesan sago mongnok [List of manuscripts
and books stored in the Royal Archives at
Odaesan]. [n.d.] 1911. 1 v.
Korean. CU-E. Mimeographed.
Fang'70,YiHj'65.
Bibliography--catalogs--Korea. Odaesan sago.

11950 fkor   b 0 n   1912
Sŏ, Myŏng-ŭng, 1716-1787. Sŏsŏ sŏmok
ch'obon [Draft catalog of manuscripts and printed
books of Korea in the Royal Library]. [n.p.]
1912. 1 v.
Korean. CU-E. Manuscript.
Fang'70.
Bibliography--catalogs--Korea. Kyujanggak.

11962 akor   kor   b 0 n
Kyujanggak sŏmok [Catalog of the Royal
Library, Kyujanggak]. [n.p.] [n.d.]. 5 v.
Korean. KJK.
CTK'32,YiHj'65.
Bibliography--catalogs--Korea. Kyujanggak.

11976 aeng   usa   b 0 n   1970
Shulman, Frank J. Japan and Korea: an
annotated bibliography of doctoral dissertations
in Western languages, 1877-1969. Chicago,
American Library Association, 1970. 368 p.
English.
S.
Bibliography--dissertations. Intercultural
relations--Bibliography. 113.02 159.04
Bibliography--1877-1969.

"Comprehensive list of doctoral dissertations from
26 countries and written in fourteen western
languages. This annotated classified bibliography
notes the source of an abstract, if any, and lists
related published works, both books and articles,
by the dissertation author. Includes indexes by
author, degree-granting institution, and by
persons, for those dissertations primarily
biographical in nature." ALA.

11977   acze   czech   b 0 n   1956
    Prague. Národní a universitní knihovna.
Lidově demokratické zeme Asie: Korea, Vietnam,
Mongolsko; [výberový seznam literatury]. [Edited
by] M. Kaftan. Prague, 1956. 15 p. (Its Cteme a
studujeme, 1956, ses. 2)
Czech. MH-W.
                                                    MHW.
Bibliography.

11978   arus   ussr   b 0 m   1950
    **Moscow. Gosudarstvennaia biblioteka SSSR. im.
V. I. Lenina.** Za edinuiu nezavisi muiu
demokraticheskuiu Koreiu. Kratkiǐ rekomendatel'nyǐ
ukazatel' literatury. [By] N. I. Glagolevskiǐ
[and] L. P. Chernysheva. [Edited by] S. V.
Kazakov. Moscow, 1950. 26 p.
Russian. MH-W.
                                                    MHW.
Polity.

1 石 宙明　濟州島 關係 文獻集

10 國學研究論著總覽刊行會　國學
研究論著總覽

19 李 戴喆　韓國參考圖書解題 1910-1958

22 朝鮮總督府　朝鮮圖書解題

52 金 雲石　北韓傀集戰術 文獻集

53 朝鮮總督府圖書館　新書部 分類目錄

54 　　　　　　　朝鮮古書資料

57 國會圖書館 서울　　國內 刊行物記事
索引 1963年度

58 국립 중앙도서관　평양　서지학부
조선 서지학 개관

61 조선 민주주의 인민공화국 사회과학원 고전연구소
평양 문헌 연구실　조선고서 해제

62 櫻井義之　明治年間 朝鮮研究 文獻誌.

63 朝鮮關係史學 論文 目錄

65 原 三七　今西博士蒐集 朝鮮關係文獻
目錄

67 前間 恭作　古鮮 冊譜

68 京城府立圖書館　圖書目錄

69 서울 대학교 부속 도서관　서울 대학교 개교
십주년 기념 고도서 전시회 출품도서

70 延世大學校 商經大學 産業經營研究所
　　産業經濟 文獻 目錄 1945-1960

71 高 厚錫　　韓國圖書館 關係 文獻 目錄
　　1921-1961　　洪 淳泰 共編

72 崔 筍子　　韓國 雜誌 目錄 1896-1945

73 國立 中央 圖書館 서울　　韓國書目
　　1945-1962

75 國家 再建 最高 會議 圖書館　　藏書目錄--
　　東洋書 西洋書 分類 目錄　4294年 10月
　　15日 現在

76 서울 大學校 附屬圖書館　　奎章閣圖書
　　目錄-- 韓國

79 國立圖書館 서울　　藏書分類目錄--
　　解放以前 日書部

80 國立圖書館 서울　　古書部分類目錄

87 韓國研究院　　韓國 碩博士 學位 論文
　　目錄 1945-1960

88 東京外國語學校 韓國 校友會　　韓國
　　目錄 稿本

91 徐 居生　　東國通鑑

95 劉 聖鍾　　德信堂書目

100 錦繡江山　　금수강산

106 서울 大學校 文理科大學 東亞文化研究所
　　奎章閣圖書韓國本 總目錄

107 朝鮮總督府　　朝鮮總督府古圖書目錄

163　大阪府立 圖書館 韓本 目録

164　朝鮮總督府　　朝鮮に於ける 出版物概要

165　黒田 亮　　朝鮮舊書考

166　日朝協会　　朝鮮に関する 日本語版 図書
　　　目録

167　圖書總目録

168　李王職庶務課　　李王家藏書閣古圖書
　　　目録

169　櫻圃寺内文庫圖書目録

170　東洋文庫　　東洋文庫 朝鮮本分類目録
　　　附 安南本目録

171　東洋文庫　　朝鮮関係文献展示目録

172　東方学会　　東方学関係雑誌目録

175　京都大学文学部図書館　　今西文庫目録

176　廣瀬 敏　　日本叢書索引

177　末松 保和　　高麗文獻小録

178　東方学報 總目次

179　日朝協会 大阪連合会　　日本で出版された
　　　朝鮮に関する 図書目録

180　「勤労者」總目次

181　京城帝國大學 附屬圖書館　　京城帝國
　　　大學 附屬圖書館 和漢書名目録

182　京城帝國大學 附屬圖書館　　朝鮮古地圖
　　　展觀目録

183　須田 昭義　　朝鮮人 人類学に関する 文献

184 島 五郎　　朝鮮人 體質人類學に 關する
　　　文獻目錄

185 大村 益夫　　中國訳 朝鮮文学作品の 目録

186 朝鮮北半部の 農業問題に 関する 文献目録

187 中村 栄孝　　蓬左文庫 朝鮮展観書解説

189 東洋学文献センター連絡協議会　　　日本文・
　　　中国文・朝鮮文等 逐次刊行物 目録

191 日本 文部省 大學學術局　　　學術逐次
　　　刊行物目錄

192 朝鮮總督府　　　朝鮮總督府 圖書目錄

194 吉野 作造　　天道教研究 資料

197 人類學雜誌・總 索引

198 書香主要 記事 目錄

199 鮮滿關係 重要雜誌 記事目錄

300 大韓民國公報部　　　政府刊行物目錄

346 大韓民國公報部　　　定具月刊行物社會團體
　　　映畫業者및 公演者一覽表

389 関野 眞吉　　欧文 朝鮮関係 文献目錄 --
　　　1940年以後 刊行書目

390 池内 宏　　朝鮮関北の四地誌

393 末松 保和　　三峯集 縮刊芳

424 河内 良弘　　文献 紹介

1002 青丘學叢 論文著者別索引

1003 幣原 坦　　朝鮮史の 參考書目について

1004 櫻木 章　　朝鮮研究 の 栞

1005　桜井 義之　　宝迫 繁勝 の 朝鮮語学書に
　　　ついて 一附 朝鮮語学 書目

1006　史学会　　史学 文献 目録

1007　最近 朝鮮関係 雑誌・論文 目録

1008　朝鮮 科学院 寄贈 図書目録

1009　朝鮮 科学院 寄贈 雑誌 目録

1010　菅野 裕臣　　ソ連邦 発行 朝鮮関係 図書
　　　目録

1011　金澤 庄三郎　　朝鮮書籍目録

1012　満鐵 調査月報 總目録

1013　古谷 清　　徳川時代 に 於ける 朝鮮の書籍

1014　藤井 宗樹　　朝鮮佛教典籍展覧目録

1015　京城 天主公教會　　朝鮮 天主教史料 展覧
　　　目録

1016　三木 栄　　養安院蔵書中の 朝鮮医書

1017　小田 省吾　　朝鮮陶磁器に 關する 文献 に
　　　就いて

1018　奥田　　朝鮮國寶紹介

1019　小倉 進平　　欧米人の 朝鮮語研究の 資料と
　　　なった 和漢書

1020　三木 栄　　朝鮮医籍考

1022　小田 省吾　　朝鮮史籍解題講義

1023　森田 芳夫　　日本人の 朝鮮引揚に 関する
　　　文献 資料

1024　三木 栄　　朝鮮医書誌

1026 友邦協会 朝鮮資料研究会　朝鮮関係
　　　文献資料総目録　近藤剣一編

1027 徐有榘　鏤板考

1036 朝鮮文化史序説　金壽卿鷓譯

1039 朝鮮版古書目

1041 朝鮮古典目錄

1042 朝鮮總督府臨時土地調査局
　　　朝鮮地誌資料

1043 中央人民委員會諸文獻

1044 國立中央圖書館(臺北)　中國刊行韓國
　　　著述目錄

1046 遠藤元男　国史文献解説　下村富士夫編

1049 고려대학교　아시아문제연구소　서울
　　　한국근세사연구자료목록

1050 北鮮滿州樺太及び千島に於ける邦人の
　　　保護及び引揚に關する交渉關係文獻

1051 金澤庄三郎　亜細亜研究に関する文獻

1052 金根洙　韓國現代詩總覽

1053 金根洙　國語國文學古書集錄

1054 대한민국문교부　지정문화재목록

1057 教育資料目錄

1058 前間恭作　鮮册名題

1059 内藤雋輔　朝鮮史研究

1060 小田省吾　朝鮮陶磁史文獻考

1062 서울大學校圖書館　韓國書誌關係文獻目錄

1066　東國大學校　　高麗佛書展觀目錄

1067　東國大學校　　高麗寫經展觀目錄

1068　東國大學校　　李朝前期國譯佛書展觀
　　　目錄

1069　東國大學校佛教文化研究所　　李朝前期
　　　佛書展觀目錄

1072　이원식　　도설 고도서 고도화 해제

1073　朝鮮醫藥資料

1074　朝鮮關係歐文文獻目錄

1075　朝鮮關係歐文圖書解題

1076　朝鮮關係考古學文獻目錄

1078　福田德三　　韓國研究の文獻

1079　古川兼秀　　朝鮮の書籍

1080　韓國書誌·文獻一覽　1941-1942

1083　今西龍　　朝鮮佛教關係書籍解題

1084　金鐘旭　　韓國史關係研究論文目錄

1085　金元龍　　有刊記佛書目錄初稿

1086　共産主義問題研究文獻目錄

1088　久慈胖二郎　　地方文化の記錄：朝鮮の
　　　鄕土誌·地方史誌·

1092　民族文化關係文獻目錄

1093　名越那珂次郎　　朝鮮地誌·資料に就て

1094　小田省吾　　朝鮮古書の一瞥

1095　朝鮮書誌·序論　　小倉親雄飜譯

1096　朴性鳳　　韓國研究文獻目錄

1097 朴 性鳳　　韓國史研究 文獻 目錄：戰後
　　　日本學界

1099 櫻井 義之　　大正 年間 朝鮮關係 文獻 解題

1100 櫻井 義之　　朝鮮人口 勞働關係 文獻 資料

1101 多田 正知　　朝鮮文學 叢書

1103 李 兼岐　　朝鮮 文學 名著 解題

1104 柳 鐸一　　嶺南文獻 錄 （慶南篇）

1107 文獻 目錄：朝鮮

1108 朝鮮古書刊行會　　朝鮮古書目錄

1109 萩山 秀雄　　朝鮮史關係圖書解題

1112 연세대학교 국어국문학회

　　　　韓國古典文學研究 文獻 解題

1114 金 龍德　　國史關係著書 論文 目錄

1115 小山 富士夫　　朝鮮陶磁 文獻 目錄

1119 櫻井 義之　　朝鮮の 鄉土誌・地方史

1120 史學關係主要雜誌論文 目錄

1121 　　大學校 圖書館　　高麗文集目錄

1123 國立中央圖書館(臺北)　　臺灣公藏高麗本
　　　聯合目錄

1125 豐田 四郎　　朝鮮の 地圖について

1127 李 文永　　韓國經濟行政研究 爲
　　　資料考

1129 震壇學報 總・目次

1130 朝鮮總督府 官房文書課　　創刊以來の
　　　總・目次便覽

1131 邦文歷史學關係諸雜誌・東洋史論文 要目

1132 岩崎 繼生　朝鮮民俗學界への展望

1133 藤田 亮策先生 著作目錄

1134 高橋 亨先生 著作年表

1135 龜田 次郎　明治時代 日鮮兩語比較論
　　　論文表

1139 國立中央圖書館(臺北)　中國關於韓國
　　　著述目錄

1140・ 森田 岩村　ドクトル・リースの朝鮮に關する
　　　歐州近刊諸目錄

1141 三木 栄　朝鮮医学史及び疾病史の刊行に
　　　ついて

4073 朝鮮学会　朝鮮学報の第一輯から第五丁輯
　　　までの 総目次

4074 韓國書誌・文獻一覽 1937-1940

4075 韓國紙類文獻一覽 1905-1938

4076 白 麟齋　韓國書誌・關係文獻目錄

4077 白 麟　韓國書誌・關係文獻目錄

4078 서울 大學校 附屬圖書館 마이크로 필름
　　　目錄

4082 韓國反共聯盟　六・二五關係文獻概略

4083 金 良善　韓國古地圖研究

4084 朴 性鳳　韓國國史研究文獻目錄

4085 蘇 鎭轍　動亂史關係資料解題

4086 安 春根　韓國博譜書誌考

4087　李 秉岐　　韓國書誌· 研究

4090　韓國圖書館協會　　1967年度分選定圖書
　　　目錄

4092　張 基槿　　韓國文集　解題

4093　張 德順　　奎章閣 圖書朝鮮邑誌·所載
　　　說話分類

4094　成 大慶　　韓國書誌·의 書誌·

4095　國會圖書館 서울　　韓國關係文獻目錄:
　　　美 스탠포드 大學所藏

4096　國會圖書館 서울　　解放前 韓國關係文獻
　　　目錄: 本館 所藏本

4097　國會圖書館 서울　　解放前刊行 韓國雜誌·
　　　目錄: 本館 所藏

4098　李 謙魯　　朝鮮古地圖目錄

4100　國會圖書館 서울　　朝鮮總督府及所屬
　　　官署發行 圖書目錄

4111　國會圖書館 서울　　政治關係 文獻目錄

4115　古谷 清　　再び 德川時代に 於ける 朝鮮の
　　　書籍について

4116　林 泰輔　　朝鮮史籍考

4117　林 泰輔　　朝鮮の史籍

4118　今村 鞆　　人蔘文籍解題

4119　岸 謙　　朝鮮の 燈火關係 資料 など

4120　久慈 畔二郎　　朝鮮研究の 成果

4121　奧平 武彦　　朝鮮の 典籍

4122	奥田 真毅	高麗朝の典籍に就いて
4123	和田 清	朝鮮史料
4124	渡邊 彰	新羅時代の文藝史料
4125	李 在郁	朝鮮の小説
4127	麻生 武亀	李朝の法典
4128	圓 翁生	三國時代の典籍
4130	武者 練三	「朝鮮風俗集」所載の燈火關係文獻
4131	那珂 通世	臺灣・朝鮮・満洲史研究の技術
4132	西吉 麗鮮齊	韓國幣制關係文獻六種
4134	櫻井 義文	明治初期の朝鮮研究
4135	關野 眞吉	朝鮮近代圖書館史料
4136	三浦 周行	朝鮮最高の地理書について
4166	李 弘稙	渡日한 韓國의 文獻
4170		朝鮮の雑誌
6021	中村 栄孝	朝鮮史の編修と朝鮮史料の蒐集
6449	島本 彦三郎	秋葉隆博士の生涯と業績
6761	崔 在錫	社會學關係文獻目録 1945-1964
6762	崔 在錫	社會學關係文獻目録 1964, 9, 21 - 1965, 12, 31
7055	崔 在錫	韓國家族關係文獻目録 1900-1965

9105 國立圖書館 서울   出品圖書目錄

10204 全 海宗   韓國近世對外關係文獻 備要

10205 韓 佑劤   韓國經濟關係文獻集成

10223 大韓民國文教部   檢認定教科用一覽表

10269 國會圖書館 司書局 서울   開闢誌 總目次
       1920 – 1949

10329 鄭 喆   韓國博士錄

10334 鄭 寅普   薝園 國學散藁

10570 國立國會図書館 (東京)   朝鮮關係資料目錄

10576 國立圖書館 서울   國立圖書館 貴重本
       古書目錄

10582 申 奭鎬   韓國史料解說集

10592 國會圖書館 司書局 參考書誌課 서울
       韓末韓國雜誌 目次 總錄

10754 李 聖儀   羅麗藝文志 — 新羅 百濟
       高句麗   全 約瑟 共編

11241 朝鮮藝文志

11242 帝室圖書目錄

11243 韓籍目錄 稿本

11290 서울 大學校 圖書館   서울 大學校 開校
       二十周年記念 貴重圖書展示會展示圖書 目錄
       1966년 10월 13일 – 18일

11291 李 鉉淙   韓國史研究論文 總目錄
       1900 – 1966   李 萬烈 共編

11292 李 用熙   近世韓國外交文書總目 外國編

11293 서을大學校 圖書館   일사.가람 文庫古書
       著者目錄

11436 李 基白   韓國史新論

11440 釋尾 春仿   朝鮮古書目錄

11441 國立中央圖書館 서울
       대한민국 출판물 총목록

11442 國立中央圖書館 서울   大韓民國 出版物
       總目錄

11447 日本民族学協会   民族学關係 雜誌.論文
       總.目錄

11448 國會圖書館 司書局 서울   大韓新聞雜誌.
       總.目錄 1883 - 1945

11450 서울대학교 출품도서해설

11451 朴 東緒   韓國行政文獻集 1945-1966
       尹 左豊 共編

11566 東國大學校 圖書館   古書 目錄 集成

11569 公報部 公報局 서울   定期刊行物 實態
       一覽

11572 朝鮮 經濟硏究所   朝鮮 統計總覽
       四方 博等 編

11726 李 弘植   朝鮮古文化論攷

11849 國會圖書館 서울   政府刊行物目錄
       1948-1965

11854 朝鮮總.督行圖書館   朝鮮古書小解

11855 朝鮮史編修會   朝鮮史料集眞 及 解說

11856 楠田 丞三郎   朝鮮天主教に 關する 主なる
       參考書籍 及 論文

11857 楠田斧三郎　朝鮮天主教に關する主なる
　　　参考著書及論文

11858 太田亮　漢韓史籍に顯われたる日韓
　　　古代資料

11859 淺見倫太郎　朝鮮の藝文志.

11885 이병두　韓國　大學定期刊行物　附高等
　　　教育機關名鑑

11888 朝鮮總督府　朝鮮史編修會　朝鮮史料

11899 金根洙　朝鮮圖書目錄

11900 古書展示目錄

11901 全國圖書一覽

11902 석사학위 논문목록　1956～1966

11903 各道冊板目錄

11904 行政學碩士學位論文題目

11905 碩博士學位論文題目集

11906 展示圖書目錄

11907 古圖書展示會出品圖書解説

11913 内閣文庫　漢籍分類目錄

11914 朝鮮内發行新聞紙一覽表

11915 貴重書マイクロフィルム目錄

11930 朝鮮總督府　朝鮮總督府及所屬官署
　　　主要刊行圖書目錄　昭和9年6月末現在

11948 徐命膺　奎章總目　四卷

11949 五臺山史庫目錄

11950 徐命膺　西序書目草本

11962 奎章閣書目

SECTION IV
SERIAL PUBLICATIONS

American Geographical Society of New York. Current
geographical publications: additions to the
Research catalogue of the American Geographical
Society. v. 1- ; Jan. 1938- . New York, 1938.
v. monthly (except July and Aug.).
English. DLC. V. 1--reproduced from typewritten copy. See Section 2 and Photograph
Supplement under Asia-Korea. L.C. has microfilm,
27 reels, of the American Geographical Society
Research Catalogue covering publications before
1938. LCW'50.

10126

An, Hae-gyun, comp. Han'guk haengjŏng saegin
(Korean administrative index). 1961-. Seoul,
Sŏul Taehakkyo Haengjŏng Taehagwŏn.   v. 26
cm. irregular. Sŏul Taehakkyo. Seoul, Korea.
Haengjŏng Taehagwŏn. Chosa Charyo.
Korean. DLC,MH-HY. MHY.

01063

Annotated bibliography of economic geology. v.1-;
July 1929-. [Lancaster, Pa.] Economic Geology
Publication Co.   v. 24 cm.
English. DLC. Prepared under the auspices of
the National Research Council. Editor: July
1929- , J. M. Nickles. LCW'50.

"Several references to Korea are in almost every
volume. See Index under Korea." LCW'50.

00122

Bibliographie bouddhique. I-.; Jan. 1928/Mai 1929-
Mai 1934. Paris, P. Geuthner, 1930-1936.   v.
28 cm. irregular.
English. CtY,CU-E,DLC. Buddhist documents.
CUE,WH'68.

01047

Bibliographie géographique internationale. 25/29-;
1915/1919-. Paris, A. Colin, 1921.   v.
irregular.
French. DLC. Bibliographies for the years 1891
to 1913/14 were issued with Annales de géographie
(v. 1-23/24). V. 25/29 covers years 1915/19; v.
30/31 covers years 1920/21; beginning with v. 32
(1922) issued annually. 1945/46- (1947-)
published under the auspices of L'Union

Géographique Internationale. Title varies.
LCW'50.

"Articles and books pertaining to Korea are
listed from time to time in the index under
Corée." LCW'50.

00148

Bibliography of Asian Studies. v.1; Nov. 1956-. Ann
Arbor, Michigan [etc.] Association for Asian
Studies.   v. annual. Journal of Asian
Studies.
English. DLC. Published annually in September
as a fifth issue of The Journal of Asian Studies.
Originated as a separate publication, Bulletin of
Far Eastern Bibliography under the editorship of
Earl H. Pritchard (volumes 1-5, 1936-40); then
incorporated into The Far Eastern Quarterly from
1941 through 1955, as an annual compilation
beginning in 1949. Silberman'62.

"The section on Korea attempts to include all
scholarly books and articles written on Korea in
Western languages during the year. It is not
annotated but listings are by topic."
Silberman'62.

00162

Charyo mongnok [A list on materials]. no.1-; June
1964-. Seoul, Taehan Muyŏk Chinhŭng Kongsa,
1965.   v. 18 x 26 cm.
Korean. DLC,MH-HY. WH'68.

01038

Chosŏn chakp'um yŏn'gam [Yearbook of Korean
literary works]. 1939-. Seoul, Inmunsa.   v.
19 cm.
Korean. MH-HY. Comp.: Ch'oe Chae-sŏ. MHY.

00084

Chosŏn chŏnggi kanhaengmul mongnok (Catalog-
newspapers and periodicals from Korea). 1958-.
P'yŏngyang, Kukche Sŏjŏm.   v. annual.
Korean. DLC. Usually published once a year.
Appendix to Chosŏn sin'gan tosŏ or Chosŏn tosŏ.
Yang'60,DLC.

00098

Chosŏn munye yŏn'gam [Yearbook of Korean literature
and art]. 1939-. [Comp. by] Ch'oe Chae-sŏ.

Seoul, Inmunsa, 1939. Annual.
Korean. Yang'60.

"Contains a list of publications of the year
under subject arrangement." Yang'60.

09164

Chosŏn sin'gan tosŏ [Korean new books]. 1959-.
P'yŏngyang, Kukche Sŏjŏm.   v. 19 cm.
monthly.
Korean. DNAL,MH-HY. Published separately by
languages: edition in Korean; edition in Korean,
Chinese, Russian and English; edition in Korean
and Chinese (Ch'ao-hsien hsin k'an t'u shu);
edition in Korean and Russian (Koreiskie novye
knigi); edition in Russian. Chŏng'66,DLC.

00104

Chosŏn tosŏ mongnok (Korean books). no.1-; 19-.
P'yŏngyang, Chosŏn Ch'ulp'anmul Such'urip Sangsa.
monthly.
Korean. DLC,MH-HY. Former title: Chosŏn tosŏ,
published by Kukche Sŏjŏm. Text in Korean,
Russian, Chinese and English. MHY,DLC.

00099

Ch'ulp'an munhwa (The Korean books journal). no.1-
Feb. 1965-. Seoul, Taehan Ch'ulp'an Munhwa
Hyŏphoe.   v. illus. 26 cm. monthly.
Korean. DLC,MH-HY. MHY.

00105

Ch'ulp'an yŏn'gam [Korean books in print]. 1957-.
Seoul, Taehan Ch'ulp'an Yŏn'gamsa.   v. ports.
19 cm.
Korean. CU-E,DLC,MH-HY,NNC. 1957 issue has
subtitle: Taehan Min'guk kŏn'guk kujunyŏn
Chonghap t'ŭkchip. Editorial supervision: Kim
Ch'ang-jip. Editor: Yi Han-guk. This issue lists
about 5,000 titles published between 1950 and
August 1956. DLC.

09170

Ch'ulp'anmul nappon wŏlbo (Korean national
bibliography). no.101-; Jan. 1964-. Seoul,
Kungnip Chungang Tosŏgwan.   v. 26 cm.
monthly.
Korean. CU-E,DLC,MH-HY. Title varies: no. 1-14
(Jan. 1964- Apr. 1965) Han'guk sŏmok; no. 15-
(May 1965-) Ch'ulp'anmul nappon wŏlbo. CUE,DLC.

00074

315

Chungang Taehakkyo. Seoul, Korea. Mullikwa Taehak.
Kyoyuk Hakkwa. Han'guk kyoyuk mongnok (Korean
education index). v.1-; 1945/1959-. [Ed. by] Sŏ
Yŏng-ch´ae [et al.]. Seoul, Chungang Taehakkyo
Kyoyuk Hakpu Chulp´an'guk, 1960. v. 22 cm.
irregular.
Korean. CU-E,DLC,MiU,WaU-FE. Yang'67,WaU.
00060

Documents of international organizations; a selected
bibliography. v.1-; Nov. 1947-. Boston, World
Peace Foundation. v. quarterly.
English. DLC. LCW'50.

" 'Prepared by the staff of the World Peace
Foundation.' See especially United Nations--
General Assembly--Korea." LCW'50.
00149

Geological Society of America. Bibliography and
index of geology exclusive of North America. v.1-
; 1933-. [Washington, D.C.]. v. irregular.
English. DLC. Annual, 1933-1940; biennial,
1941/1942- . Editors: 1933-1944, J. M. Nickles
and others; 1945/1946, Marie Siegrist and Eleanor
Tatge. LCW'50.

"See Index to each volume under Korea.
Annotated." LCW'50.
00150

Haksul chapchi saegin (Korean periodical index).
v.1-2; 1960-1961/1962. Seoul, Han'guk Tosŏgwan
Hyŏphoe, 1963-1964. 2 v. 27 cm.
Korean. DLC,MH-HY,NNC. On verso of t.p.: Korean
periodicals index, comp. by Korean Library
Association. Superseded by Kungnae kanhaengmul
kisa saegin, 1963- pub. by
Taehan Min'guk Kukhoe Tosŏgwan (National Assembly
Library, Republic of Korea). Chŏng'66,MH-HY.
00055

Han'guk ch´ulp´an yŏn'gam (Books in print: Korea).
1963-. Seoul, Taehan Ch´ulp´an Munhwa Hyŏphoe.
v. illus. 20 cm. irregular.
Korean. CU-E,DLC. CUE,Chong'66.
00086

Han'guk Yŏn'guwŏn. Munhŏn sŏllok (Selected list
of the Korean Research Center Library
Collection). v.1-; 1959-. Seoul.   v. 26 cm.
annual.
Korean or English. DLC. Vols. for 1959-1961
issued under its earlier name: Han'guk Yŏn'gu
Tosŏgwan. WaU.
                                                        09003

Korea (Democratic People's Republic) Munhwa
Sŏnjŏnsŏng. Tosŏ Kwalliguk.   Kŭn'gan tosŏ
[Recent publications]. no.1-; 1955-. P'yŏngyang.
  v. monthly.
Korean. DLC. Yang'60.

An announcement of new publications of North
Korean government." Yang'60.
                                                        00102

Korea (Democratic People's Republic) Munhwa
Sŏnjŏnsŏng. Tosŏ Kwalliguk.   Sin'gan tosŏ [New
books]. no.1-; 1955-. P'yŏngyang.   v.
monthly.
Korean. DLC. Yang'60.

"An annotated catalogue of new publications of
North Korean government." Yang'60.
                                                        00103

Korea (Government-General of Chōsen, 1910-1945).
  Chōsen Sōtokufu oyobi shozoku kansho shuyō kankō
  tosho mokuroku   [List of publications by the
  Government-General of Korea and subordinate
  agencies, offices and bureaus]. Oct. 1930-.
  Seoul, Chōsen Sōtokufu. Irregular.
  Japanese. CSt-H,DLC,WaU-FE. LC has: 1930, 1932,
  1933, 1934, 1936, 1938. LCF'50.

"A classified catalog of the more important
official publications of the Government-General,
and its agencies and offices." LCF'50.
                                                        00190

Korea (Government-General of Chōsen, 1910-1945).
  Toshokan. Bunken hōkoku [Monthly bulletin].
  v.1-; Nov. 1935-. Seoul.   v.
  Japanese. DLC. LCF'50,DLC.

"This monthly bulletin contains articles on a
wide range of bibliographical subjects. It is

also a source of information on the libraries of
Korea and their development. It is especially
useful, however, in that at the end of its
monthly lists of accessions (new books, old
books, and Western books) it lists together newly
received works dealing with Korea, Manchuria,
Mongolia, and Siberia. It gives a very useful
monthly list of important periodical articles in
Japanese on Korea and Manchuria. It also lists
copies of all Korean publications in Japanese and
in Korean of which sample copies were submitted
to the Police Affairs Bureau. Since the police
control of Korean publication was very
comprehensive, this monthly list constitutes a
valuable record of Korean publication under
Japanese administration." LCF'50.

01001

Korean books in foreign languages. 1957-.
P'yŏngyang, Kukje Sŏjŏm, 1957.   v.   Biennial.
English. Chŏng'66.

09167

Koryŏ Taehakkyo. Seoul, Korea. Asea Munje Yŏnguso.
Asiatic research bulletin. v.1, no.1-; Dec. 1957-
. Seoul, Asiatic Research Center, Korea
University.   v. 27 cm. monthly.
English. DLC,MH-HY. Added cover title in
Chinese characters: . Holdings:-
DLC. v. 1, n. 1-to date; MHY. v. 1-6, 17.
Includes bibliographies and bibliographical
notes. MHY.

00299

Kungnae kanhaengmul kisa saegin (Korean periodical
index). v.1; 1963-. Seoul, Taehan Min'guk Kukhoe
Tosŏgwan, Ippŏp Chosaguk, 1964.   v.   26 cm.
annual.
Korean. CU-E. Supersedes the Haksul chapchi
saegin (Korean periodical index) 1960-1961/1962,
pub. by Han'guk Tosŏgwan Hyŏphoe (Korean Library
Association). CUE.

00043

Kungnip Chungang Tosŏgwan.   Tosŏgwan (Bulletin of
Central National Library). no.1-; Mar. 1946-.
Seoul.   v. 26 cm. monthly.
Korean. CUE,DLC,MH-HY. Title varies: no. 1-10,
Mar. 1946-Dec. 1946, Kungnip Tosŏgwan Kwanbo.-
No. 11-54, Jan. 1947-Jan 1956, Munwŏn.- No. 55-

100, July 1958-Dec. 1963, Kungnip Tosŏgwan po.-
No. 101- , Jan. 1966- , Tosŏgwan. No. 77, Jan.
1961, published uner title Munwŏn. DLC,MHY.
09043

Kyriak, Theodore E., comp. China and Asia:
bibliography--index to U.S. JPRS research
translations. no.1-; July/Sept. 1962-.
Annapolis, Research Microfilms.   v.   27 cm.
quarterly.
English. DLC. Formed by merging of two earlier
bibliographies China, and Asian developments with
the issue v. 3, no. 1, July 1964. DLC.
09171

London. University. School of Oriental and African
Studies. Library. Monthly list of periodical
articles on the Far East and South East Asia.
1956-. London.   v.   22 cm.
English. DLC. Silberman'62.

"A very useful bibliographical aid listing nearly
all articles published on Asia." Silberman'62.
00159

Monthly catalog of U.S. publications. Washington,
D.C., U.S. Government Printing Office.
English. WH'68.

"Lists many items dealing with Korea, e.g.,
'Political Reports on North Korea,' a series of
reports which includes translations, published by
the U.S. Joint Publications Research Service
during the period 1958-59. JPRS has also
translated several books concerning North Korea.
State Department publications chiefly concerning
South Korea and American-Korean relations are
also included." WH'68.
09173

National Geographic Magazine. Cumulative index to
the National Geographic Magazine. 1899-.
Washington, D.C., National Geographic Society,
1899.   v. irregular.
English. CtY. CtY.
09169

Nihon shuppan nenkan [Yearbook of Japanese
publications]. 1943-1947. Tōkyō, Nihon Shuppan
Kyōdō Kabushiki Kaisha.   2 v. 19 cm.

Japanese. CtY,DLC. Title varies: 1930-1941,
Shuppan nenkan, published by Tōkyōdō.-1942,
Shoseki nenkan, published by Kyōdō Shuppansha.-
1943-1947, Nihon Shuppan nenkan, published by
Nihon Shuppan Kyōdō Kabushiki Kaisha. Superceded
by Shuppan nenkan, published by Shuppan
Nyūshūsha, 1948- . UC'54.

"Lists Japanese publications on Korea from 1942
to 1945. Entries are arranged by author under a
detailed topical scheme and are unannotated.
There is a classified list of important
periodicals, with statements of their general
emphasis and content." UC'54.

00174

Reports of the Library of Congress. 1922-.
[Washington, D.C.].
English. Notes on Chinese, Korean and Japanese
accessions. Gompertz'63.

09168

Revue bibliographique de sinologie 1-; 1955-.
Paris, Mouton, 1957. v. 25 cm. annual.
French. CU-E,DLC. At head of title: Ecole
pratique des hautes études, 6 section. Editors;
1955- p. van Deloon. Abstracts of titles
listed: 1955- in English. CUE.

01118

Shoko v.1-. Dairen, Mantetsu Dairen Toshokan.
Japanese. MH-HY. MHY.

09112

Sōjihak. [Bibliographic studies]. 1968-. Seoul,
Han'guk Sōji Yōn'guhoe, 1968.
Korean. HU-E. HUE.

09172

Tōyōshi kenkyū bunken ruimoku (Bibliography of
oriental studies). 1934-. Kyōto, Kyōto Daigaku
Tōhō Bunka Kenkyūjo. v. 26 cm. annual.
Tōyōshi kenkyū.
Japanese. DLC,MH-HY. WH'68.

01102

Tōyōshi kenkyū bunken mokuroku [Bibliography on
Oriental history studies]. [n.p.], 1934. v.
26 cm. annual.
Japanese. Annually 1934-37; biennially

thereafter until 1945. WH'68.

01124

United Nations. Dag Hammarskjold Library. United
    Nations documents index; United Nations and
    specialized agencies documents and publications.
    v.1-; 1950-. Lake Success, N.Y., Documents Index
    Unit, Library, United Nations.   v. 27 cm.
    monthly. United Nations. [Document] ST/LIB/Ser.
    E.
    English. DLC. LCW'50.

    "Lists all documents and publications received by
    the Documents Index Unit from the United Nations
    and the Specialized Agencies, except restricted
    (confidential) materials and internal papers."
    LCW'50.

00114

U.S. Dept. of State. Office of Intelligence Research
    and Analysis. External research. ER list no.6:
    Korea. Pt.1-10; April 1953-April 1958. Compiled
    and distributed by External Research Staff.
    Washington, D.C., 1953.
    English. MH-P. Pt. 2-10 issued in no. 5/6: Far
    East and Asia General. Later issued by U.S.
    Dept. of State. External Research Division in its
    External research. ER list no. 2: Far East. MHP,
    S.

11944

1063 安 海均 韓國行政索引

1038 資料目錄

84 朝鮮作品年鑑

98 조선 정기 간행물 목록

9164 조선 문예 연감

104 조선 신간 도서

99 조선 도서목록

105 出版文化

9170 出版年鑑

74 출판물 납본 월보 (韓國書目)

60 中央大學校 文理科大學 敎育學科 編
　　韓國敎育目錄

55 學術雜誌 索引

86 韓國出版年鑑

9003 韓國硏究院　文獻選錄 (韓國硏
　　究圖書館)

102 조선 민주주의 인민공화국 문화 선전성 도서관리국
　　근간도서

103 조선 민주주의 인민공화국 문화 선전성 도서관리국
　　신간도서

190　朝鮮總督府　　朝鮮總督府 及び 所屬
　　　官署 主要 刊行圖書目錄

1001　朝鮮總督府 圖書館　　文獻報告

299　高麗大學校 亞細亞問題研究所
　　　亞細亞問題研究月報

43　大韓民國 國會圖書館 立法調査局
　　　國內刊行物記事索引

9043　國立中央圖書館　도서판 (국립도서관보)

174　日本出版年鑑

9112　書香 (滿鐵大連圖書館)

9172　書誌學　(서울 韓國書誌研究會)

1102　東洋史研究 文獻 類目　(京都大學東方
　　　文化研究所)

1124　東洋史研究 文獻目錄

APPENDIX: ADDITIONAL CITATIONS

ENGLISH

MONOGRAPHS

Korea for the Koreans; some facts worth knowing and
a reading list. 1943.   11942
Probsthain, Arthur. Encyclopedia of books on China,
Tibet, Korea, Indo-China, Siam and Formosa.
1927.   11938

JOURNAL ARTICLES

Books and articles on Oriental subjects published in
Japan. DLC,CtY.   01106

CHAPTERS IN BOOKS

Song, Sok-ha. The catalog of the book in foreign
language for the study of Korean folklore. In
Han'guk minsok ko. Seoul, Ilsinsa, 1960: 1-9
(2d group).   07118

OTHER

McCune, Shannan Boyd-Bailey. Books to read on
Korea. 1947.   11934

GERMAN

JOURNAL ARTICLES

Praesent, Hans, comp. Japan--bibliographie. In
Nippon: Zeitschrift für Japanologie, (1935-1944).
1949.   01098

CHAPTERS IN BOOKS

Lautensach, Hermann. Literaturübersicht. In Korea:
eine Landeskunde auf Grund eigener Reisen und der
Literatur. Leipzig, K. F. Koehler, 1945: 478-
520.   07115

JAPANESE

MONOGRAPHS

Chōsen Sōtokufu shuppanbutsu kaidai   1924.   11984

Korea (Government-General of Chōsen, 1910-1945)
Takushi-bu.   T˘akchibu insatsu-butsu mokuroku
Sakurai'41.   1910.   11932
Nihon Gakujutsu Kaigi, ed.   Bungaku, tetsugaku,
shigaku bunken mokuroku 13: Bunka jinruigaku
1962.   11931

JOURNAL ARTICLES

Chōsen kankeisho bassho mokuroku   In Dolmen, 2/4
(1933): 174.   CEACS'64.   04178
Inmin kyoyuk shi 1962 nen somokuji   In Chōsen kenkyū
geppō, 19 (1963): 35-43.   CEACS'64.   04179
Inoue, Hideo.   Bunken shokai In Chōsen kenkyū
nenpō, 1-5 (1959-1963).   CEACS'64.   04180
Sakurai, Yoshiyuki.   Meiji nenkan Chōsen kankei
bunken shōroku In Chōsen.   S.   04113
Sakurai, Yoshiyuki.   Chōsen kankei bunken shoroku
In Chōsen, 285, 286, 288-293 (1939).   CEACS'64.
                                                       04181

OTHER

Kōkogaku zasshi sakuin   CUE.   09068
Kokugakuin zasshi sōmokuji   CtY.   09117
Minzoku sōmokuji   NNC.   09115

KOREAN

MONOGRAPHS

An, Ch˘un-gŭn.   Han'guk sōjihak   1967.   11983
Chipkyŏngdang p˘osoe sōmok ch˘ongnok   CTK'32,
YiHj'65.   11957
Chipokje sōjŏk mongnok   CTK'32,KJK.   11958
Ch˘ulp˘an taegam   LCW'50.   00085
Ch˘unbang changsō ch˘ongmok   1905.   11959
Hongmun'gwan sōmok   1908.   11960
Imunwŏn pongan ch˘ongmok   CTK'32,YiHj'65.
                                                       11961
Kang, Sang-un, 1919-.   Han'guk kwan-gye oeguk nonmun
kisa ch˘ong mongnok   HUE.   11982
Kukhoe Tosōgwan. Sasōguk.   Chapchi Chokwang Ch˘ong
mokch˘a   1967.   11981
Kukhoe Tosōgwan, Seoul, Korea.   Changsō mongnok
1966.   11294
Kyŏngju kyowŏn sōch˘aengnok   Courant'01.   11974
Kyujanggak ch˘ongmok   Courant'01.   11952
Kyujanggak p˘osō mongnok   CTK'32,YiHj'65.
                                                       11963
Naegak pangsōrok   CTK'32,YiHj'65.   11964
Nŭngmullu sōmok   CTK'32,YiHj'65.   11965
Pomun'gak ch˘aek mongnok   CTK'32,YiHj'65.   11966

Pongmodang pongan ŏsŏ ch'ongmok   CTK'32,YiHj'65.
                                                         11967
P'yŏnjipkuk sŏch'aek mongnok   CTK'32.   11968
Samnam ch'aekp'an mongnok   CTK'32.   11969
Sŏhyanggak pongan ch'ongmok   CTK'32,KJK.   11970
Sŭnghwaru sŏmok   CTK'32,KJK.   11971
Taech'ukkwan sŏmok   CTK'32,YiHj'65.   11972
Tongguk munjŏk   Courant'01.   11955
Tongguk sŏmok   Courant'01.   11956
Yegak ch'aek torok   CTK'32,YiHj'65.   11973
Yi, Pyŏngmok, comp. Han'guk ŭi chŏnggi kanhaengmul
  1964.   11985
Yŏngnam kyowŏn sŏch'aek mongnok   CTK'32.   11975

JOURNAL ARTICLES

Kim, Chong-uk.   Han'guk kojŏn munhak kwan'gye
  yŏn'gu cheje ch'ongnam In Hyŏndae munhak, 13,
  no.2 (Feb. 1967): 312-316; 13, no.3 (Mar. 1967):
  319-324; 13, no.4 (Apr. 1967): 310-316; 13, no.5
  (May 1967): 299-302; 13, no.6 (June 1967): 321-
  327; 13, no.8 (Aug. 1967): 306-310. CUE,DLC.
                                                         01113

CHAPTERS IN BOOKS

Ch'oe, Ho-jin.   [Bibliography of Asian and Western
  sources and a list of Japanese and Korean
  publications on the socio-economic history of
  Korea after 1945]. In Kundae Han'guk kyongje-sa
  yon'gu: Yijo maryop e issoso ui saengsan-nyok
  yon'gu. Seoul, Tongguk Munhwasa, 1956: 169-210.
                                                         07119
Kim, Tu-jong.   [Bibliography of Korean medical
  works]. In Han'guk uihaksa. Seoul, Chongumsa,
  1955.   07117
Yi, Ch'un-nyong.   [Bibliography of classical works
  on Korean agriculture]. In Yi-jo nongop kisulsa.
  Seoul, Han'guk Yon'gu-won, 1964: 101-118. 07116

OTHER

Kyujanggak hyŏngjian   [1857?].   11953
Naegak changsŏ hwip'yŏn   Courant'01.   11954
Sŏ, Yu-gu, 1764-1845. Imwŏn simnyukchi inyong
  sŏmok   Fang'70.   11947
Tongsŏn p'umjŏl mongnok   Fang'70.   11951

327

11984　朝鮮總督府 出版物 解題

11932　朝鮮總督府 慶支部　　慶支部印刷物目錄

11931　日本学術会議　　文学 哲学 史学 文献
　　　　目錄 XIII : 文化人類学

4178　朝鮮關係書拔抄目錄

4179　[人民教育誌· 1962年總目次　　朝鮮
　　　　研究月報

4180　井上 秀雄　　文献 紹介　　朝鮮研究
　　　　年報

4113　櫻井 義之　　明治年間朝鮮關係文獻
　　　　抄錄　　朝鮮

4181　櫻井 義之　　朝鮮關係文獻 抄錄
　　　　朝鮮

9068　考古學雜誌· 索引　　日本考古學會

9117　國學院雜誌· 總目次　　國學院大學校出版

9115　民族總· 目次　　東京民族發行所

11983　安春根　韓國書誌學

11957　緝敬堂 曝曬書目 總錄 一冊

11958　集玉齋 書籍目錄 二冊

85　出版大鑑

11959　春坊藏書 總目 一冊

11960　弘文館書目 一冊

11961　摛文院奉安總目

11982　姜尚雲 編著　韓國關係外國論文記事
　　　　　總目錄

11981　國會圖書館 司書局　雜誌 朝光 總目次

11294　國會圖書館 司書司　藏書目錄 一 韓國
　　　　　語圖書篇

11974　慶州校院書冊錄

11952　奎章閣 總目

11963　奎章閣 曝書目錄

11964　內閣訪書錄

11965　隆文樓書目

11966　寬文閣冊目錄 一冊

11967　奉謨堂奉安御書摠目

11968　編輯局書冊目錄

11969　三南冊板目錄 一冊

11970　書香閣奉安 總目

11971 承華樓書目

11972 大畜觀書目

11955 東國文籍

11956 東國書目

11973 藝閣冊都錄

11983 李 炳穆　韓國　定期刊行物

11975 嶺南校院 書冊目錄

1113 金 鍾旭　韓國古典文學關係研究
題材總覽　　現代文學

7119 崔 虎鎮　近代韓國經濟史研究：
李朝末葉에 있어서의生産力研究

7117 金 斗鍾　韓國醫學史

7116 李 春寧　李朝農業技術史（韓國
研究院）

11953 奎章閣 形止安

11954 內閣藏書彙編

11947 徐 有榘　林園十六志 引用書目

11951 東選品節目錄

REFERENCES

California. University. Institute of East Asiatic
Studies. Korean studies guide. Comp. by B.H.
Hazard, Jr. et al. Ed. by Richard Marcus.
Berkeley, California, 1954.

00015

Chung, Yong-Sun. Publications on Korea in the era
of political revolutions, 1959-1963; a selected
bibliography. Compiled with introduction by Yong-
Sun Chung. Kalamazoo, Mich., 1965. 10, 117 p.
27 cm. Korea Research and Publication, Inc.
Monographic series on Korea, 2.

11437

Courant, Maurice [Auguste Louis Marie], 1865-1939.
Bibliographie coréenne: tableau littéraire de la
Corée, contenant la nomenclature des ouvrages
publiés dans ce pays jusqu'en 1890 ainsi que la
description et l'analyse détaillées des
principaux d'entre ces ouvrages. Paris, E.
Leroux, 1894-1896. 3 v. illus., 28 cm.
Publication de l'Ecole des langues orientales
vivantes, 3. ser., v. 18-20.

01032

Courant, Maurice [Auguste Louis Marie], 1865-1939.
Bibliographie coréenne. Supplement (jusqu'en
1899). Paris, Imprimerie rationale, E. Leroux,
1901. 10, 122 p. 28 cm. Publications de
l'Ecole des langues orientales vivantes, 3. ser.,
v. 21.

01033

Elrod, Jefferson McRee. An index to English
language periodical literature published in
Korea, 1890-1940. [Seoul] 1960.

00006

Fang, Chao-ying. The Asami Library: a descriptive
catalog. Ed. by Elizabeth Huff. Berkeley,
University of California Press, 1970.

11898

Gerow, Bert A. Publications in Japanese on Korean
anthropology: a bibliography of uncataloged
materials in the Kanaseki Collection, Stanford
University Library. [Stanford, Stanford

University, Department of Sociology and
Anthropology, 1952]. 4, 18 l. 28 cm.

00007

Gompertz, G. St.G. M. Bibliography of Western
literature on Korea from the earliest time until
1950. Seoul, Dong-a Publishing Co., 1963. 263
p. Transactions of the Korea Branch of the Royal
Asiatic Society, 40.

00117

Harvard University. Library. Harvard-Yenching
Library. A classified catalog of Korean books in
the Harvard-Yenching Institute Library at Harvard
University. Cambridge, Massachusetts, 1962.

11452

Harvard University. Library. Harvard-Yenching
Library. A classified catalog of Korean books in
the Harvard-Yenching Library Harvard University.
V.2. Cambridge, Massachusetts, 1966.

11453

Henthorn, William E., comp. A guide to reference
and research materials on Korean history: an
annotated bibliography. [Honolulu] Institute of
Advanced Projects, East-West Center, 1968. 3,
152 l. 28 cm. Occasional papers of Research
Publications and Translations, East-West Center,
Honolulu. Annotated bibliography series, 4.

01128

Knez, Eugene I. A selected and annotated
bibliography of Korean anthropology. By Eugene I.
Knez and Chang-su Swanson. Seoul, Taehan Min'guk
Kukhoe Tosŏgwan, 1968.

01138

Korea (Government-General of Chōsen, 1910-1945).
Chōsen tosho kaidai [Annotated bibliography of
Korean books]. Seoul, Chōsen Tsūshinsha, 1932.

00022

Korea: bibliography of Asian studies. In Journal of
Asian studies, every fifth issue.

06764

Koryŏ Taehakkyo. Asea Munje Yŏn'guso. Bibliography
of Korean studies: a bibliographical guide to
Korean publications on Korean studies appearing

from 1959 to 1962. [V.2]. Seoul, Asiatic
Research Center, Korea University, 1965.

00003

Nunn, Godfrey Raymond, 1918-. East Asia: a
bibliography of bibliographies. Honolulu, East-
West Center Library, University of Hawaii, 1967.
10, 92 l. 28 cm.

11656

Okamoto, Yoshiji. Japanese studies on Korean
history since World War II. In Monumenta Serica,
22, pt. 2 (1963): 470-532.

06766

Paek, In. Han'guk sŏji kwan'gye munhŏn mongnok
[A list of books related to Korean bibliography].
In Sŏjihak, 2 (1969): 62-76.

04076

Paek, In. Han'guk sŏji kwan'gye munhŏn mongnok
[A list of books related to Korean bibliography].
In Sŏjihak, 1 (1968): 34-54.

04077

Sakurai, Yoshiyuki, ed. Meiji nenkan Chōsen kenkyū
bunken shi [Annotated bibliography of Korean
studies in the Meiji era]. Seoul, Shomotsu
Dōkōkai, 1941.

00062

Silberman, Bernard S. Japan and Korea: a critical
bibliography. Tucson, University of Arizona,
1962.

00008

Sŏul Taehakkyo. Ch˘ulp˘um tosŏ haesŏl (An
annotated list of rare books exhibited in
commemoration of the tenth anniversary of Seoul
National University, October 13-17, 1956).
Seoul, 1956.

11450

Stucki, Curtis W. American doctoral dissertations
on Asia, 1933-1962, including master's theses at
Cornell University. Ithaca, Southeast Asia
Program, Department of Asian Studies, Cornell
University, 1963. 204 p. 28 cm. (Cornell
University. Southeast Asia Program. Data paper,
50.

00023

U.S. Library of Congress. Reference Department.
Korea: an annotated bibliography of publications
in Far Eastern languages. Compiled under the
direction of Edwin G. Beal, Jr., with the
assistance of Robin L. Winkler. Washington,
D.C., 1950.

00011

U.S. Library of Congress. Reference Department.
Korea: an annotated bibliography of publications
in Western languages. Compiled by Helen
Dudenbostel Jones and Robin L. Winkler.
Washington, D.C., 1950.

00025

Yang, Key Paik. Reference guide to Korean
materials, 1945-1959. [Washington, D.C.] 1960.
00020

Yang, Key Paik. Present status of Korean research
tools. Kalamazoo, Michigan, 1967.

06763

Yi, Hong-jik, 1909-. Kuksa taesajŏn [A dictionary
of Korean history]. Seoul, Chimun'gak, 1962-
1963.

11255

Yunesuko Higashi Ajia Bunka Kenkyū Senta, Tokyo.
Bibliography of bibliographies of East Asian
studies in Japan. Comp. by Centre for East Asian
Cultural Studies. [Tokyo] Centre for East Asian
Cultural Studies, 1964. 216 p. 21 cm. Centre
for East Asian Cultural Studies. Bibliography, 3.
01021